STECK-VAUGHN

CONNECTIONS

Basic Skills in Social Studies

REVIEWERS

Jim Barlow
Retired Vice-Principal
of Adult Education
Waterloo Region District
School Board
Educational Consultant
and Author
Kitchener, Ontario

William Burns
Instructor
San Mateo County
Office of Education
Palo Alto, California

Sherri Claiborne
Literacy Coordinator
Claiborne County
Adult Reading Experience
(CCARE)
Tazewell, Tennessee

Bill Freeland
Almonte Adult School
Almonte, California

Joanie Griffin-Rethlake
Adult Education Division
Harris County Department
of Education
Houston, Texas

Jim Scheil
Jersey City Adult Education Center
Jersey City, New Jersey

STECK-VAUGHN
COMPANY

A Division of Harcourt Brace & Company

www.steck-vaughn.com

Acknowledgments

Executive Editor: Ellen Northcutt

Project Editor: Julie Higgins

Design Manager: Jim Cauthron

Cover Design: Donna Neal

Cover Production: Donna Neal and Alan Klemp

Media Researchers: Claudette Landry, Christina Berry

Electronic Production: PC&F, Inc.

Photograph Credits: Cover and title page (flags) © Flag Folio, (globe, map) © MapArt; pp. 13, 16 © Superstock; p. 38 © D. Young-Wolff/PhotoEdit; p. 47 © Amy Sancetta/AP/Wide World; p. 73 © Scott Peterson/Liaison; p. 78 © D. Young-Wolff/PhotoEdit; p. 87 CORBIS/Bettmann; p. 103 The Granger Collection; pp. 108, 115 Brown Brothers; p. 130 Rick Williams; pp. 131a, 131b © PhotoDisc; p. 139 © Terry Farmer/Tony Stone Images, Inc.; p. 160 © Bob Grieser/AP/Wide World; p. 170 © M. Grecco/Stock Boston; p. 176 © Susan Van Etten/PhotoEdit; p. 179 © PhotoDisc; p. 194a © Christie's Images; p. 194b Photo courtesy of Sports Cards Magazine; p. 210 © Chuck Savage/The Stock Market; p. 216 CORBIS/Jacques M. Chenet; p. 223 International Museum of Photography, George Eastman House.

Illustration Credits: Maryland Cartographics, Inc. pages 1, 8, 22, 28, 33, 39, 41, 43, 90, 115b, 133, 135, 219

PC&F, Inc. pages 4, 6, 15, 21, 39, 44, 49, 51, 55, 62, 63, 82, 84, 96, 120, 126, 148, 155, 173, 182, 183, 187, 200, 206, 213, 217, 225, 227

Political Cartoons: p. 10 Ed Gamble © *Florida Times Union*, p. 69 Bob Dornfried © *Greenwich News*, p. 81 Ben Sargent © *Austin American-Statesman*, p. 142 Don Landgren © *The Landmark*, p. 166 David Horsey © *Seattle Post-Intelligencer*, p. 167 Steve Sack © *Minneapolis Star & Tribune*, p. 175 Steve Greenberg © *Seattle Post-Intelligencer*, p. 221 Gary Markstein © *Milwaukee Journal Sentinel*

ISBN 0-7398-0990-3

Contents

UNIT 4

UNIT 5

To the Student

How to Use This Book

This book allows you to build on what you already know to improve your social studies skills. You will increase your understanding of the five areas of social studies by reading interesting articles on many different topics. These topics are divided into the five units described below.

UNITS

Unit 1: Geography. This unit covers geography skills such as how to read rainfall, climate, and resource maps. You will use map keys and distance scales as you read maps and articles about the geography of the United States and other parts of the world.

Unit 2: World History. In this unit you will learn about important events in the world's history. You will learn about cultural and economic realities for various people.

Unit 3: American History. This unit covers such history skills as reading historical and political maps, understanding photos, and using timelines. The articles you read will increase your knowledge of major events in the history of the United States.

Unit 4: Government and Civics. In this unit you will learn about selected contents in political science. You will read diagrams, political ads, and political cartoons. You will also read about how laws are made and the roles of local, state, and federal governments.

Unit 5: Economics. This unit includes skills in economics. You will use graphic illustrations such as tables, line graphs, circle graphs, and bar graphs. You will gain an understanding of our economy by reading articles about supply and demand, world trade, and managing your money.

SETTING THE STAGE

Each section begins with an activity that helps you prepare to read the article. This is the activity that helps you *before reading*. First, determine what you already know about the subject of the article. Then, preview the article by reading and writing the headings of the article. Finally, write the questions that you expect the article will answer.

THE ARTICLE

The articles you will read are about interesting topics in social studies. As you read each article, you will see a feature called Applying Your Skills and Strategies. In these sections you learn a reading or social studies skill, and you do a short activity. After completing the activity, continue reading the article. Applying Your Skills and Strategies occurs twice in every article. These are the activities you do *during reading*.

THINKING ABOUT THE ARTICLE

These are the activities you do *after reading*. Here you answer fill-in-the-blank, short-answer, or multiple choice questions. Answering these questions will help you decide how well you understood what you just read. The final question in this section relates information from the article to your own real-life experiences.

SOCIAL STUDIES AT WORK

Social Studies at Work is a two-page feature in each unit. Each Social Studies at Work feature introduces a specific job and describes the skills the job requires. It also gives information about the other jobs in the same career area. This feature includes, as well, a writing activity related to the job that has been introduced.

CONNECTIONS

Connections is an interdisciplinary feature included in each unit that shows how social studies is related to another content area. It provides information about the relationship, an exercise to check comprehension, and an activity.

UNIT REVIEWS

All units include a Unit Review that lets you see how well you have learned the skills covered in the unit. Each Unit Review also includes a Social Studies Extension activity that provides an opportunity for further practice with the skills for the unit.

INVENTORY AND POSTTEST

The Inventory is a self-check to see which skills you already know. When you complete this book, you will take a Posttest.

ANSWERS AND EXPLANATIONS

Answers and Explanations to the exercises are listed at the back of this book on pages 229–252. Some exercise items have more than one possible right answer. In such cases, a sample answer is given.

Inventory

Use this Inventory before you begin Section 1. The Inventory will help you determine which content areas in social studies you understand well and which you must practice further. Read each article and study the graphics—map, timeline, graph, diagram, and cartoon. Then answer the questions on each page.

Check your answers on pages 229–230. Mark the number of correct answers you have in each content area on the chart on page 11. Use the chart to figure out which content area(s) to work on and where to find practice pages in this book.

The Elevation of the United States

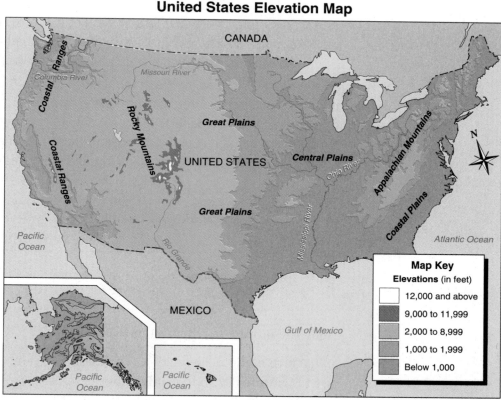

United States Elevation Map

Write the answer to each question.

1 What is the elevation of the Coastal Plains?

_____

2 Are the Central Plains or the Great Plains higher in elevation?

_____

Desert Regions

Every continent, except Europe and Antarctica, has at least one desert region. When people think of deserts, they often picture hot, dry, sandy, empty lands. Hot deserts are usually found at low latitudes and low elevations. The Sahara, a desert region in North Africa, is hot.

Indeed every desert is very dry with few or no plants at all. But not all deserts are hot. Some are cold. Cold deserts include the Gobi, a desert in northeastern Asia. Cold deserts are found at higher latitudes and higher elevations. The Gobi's elevations range from 3,000 to 5,000 feet above sea level.

Although many deserts have sand, most of them do not. Only five percent of the Gobi, for example, has sand.

Deserts are home to many different plants and animals. Desert plants and animals have adapted to the harsh environment. Desert plants have tough skins and few or thick leaves so they can keep any water they absorb. Some desert animals, like the mourning dove and the desert rat, are active at night when temperatures are cooler. Other animals need little water to survive. For example, kangaroo rats never actually drink water. Instead they get their water from the seeds they eat. Other desert animals, such as the camel, store water. It is able to go for long periods without water.

People have also found ways to live in the desert, just as they have in every other environment. Some people move from place to place with herds of camels, goats, or sheep. Other people farm in the desert. To do so, they must bring water to their fields from a distant underground spring or river. People have found oil and other natural resources in the desert. They often build cities in the desert, near the valuable resources.

Write the answer to each question.

3 Name one way all deserts are alike.

_____

4 Name one way some deserts are different.

_____

Circle the number of the best answer.

5 Which of the following is a conclusion that can be drawn from the article?
  (1) Animals can live only in hot deserts.
  (2) Living things have developed ways to survive in difficult environments.
  (3) Desert plants can go a long time without water.
  (4) Desert animals do not need much water to live.
  (5) People survive better in a hot desert than a cold desert.

Ancient Greek Culture

Jutting out into the Mediterranean Sea is a country called Greece. From about 750 to 336 B.C., the people there developed an advanced **culture.** This culture is famous for its religion, art, architecture, and customs, which influenced people throughout the Mediterranean region.

The Greek family of gods was an important influence on Greek culture. Unlike ancient Egyptians, who pictured their gods as animals, the Greeks believed their gods looked like humans. The Greeks also believed the gods lived on Mount Olympus in northeastern Greece.

The Greeks thought that each god controlled a part of nature. The chief Greek god was Zeus. The Greeks considered him Lord of the Sky, the Rain God, and the Cloud Gatherer. He was often described as throwing thunderbolts to Earth when he became angry. He was considered the most powerful god of all.

Poseidon was Zeus's brother and second in power. He was the Ruler of the Sea and Earth Shaker. The Greeks admired Poseidon because he gave them the first horse. He was often described as holding a three-pronged spear, which he would shake to disturb the sea or land.

Athena was Zeus's favorite child. She did not have a mother. The Greeks believed that she sprang full-grown from her father's head. She was the Goddess of the City. Athens, one of Greece's first cities, was named after her. She was noted for her wisdom and artistic talents.

The people wanted to keep the gods happy so that the gods would bring good fortune to them. For this reason, the Greeks built temples, sacrificed animals, and prayed to the gods. They also honored the gods through festivals. For the glory of Zeus, the Greeks organized the first Olympic Games in 776 B.C. From that date on, they had a series of athletic contests every four years.

Write the answers to each question.

6 What was the purpose of the first Olympic Games?

_____

Circle the number of the best answer for each question.

7 Which definition for *culture* is intended in this passage?
(1) expert training
(2) medium for growing bacteria
(3) to improve by study
(4) way of life
(5) taste in fine arts

The Korean War

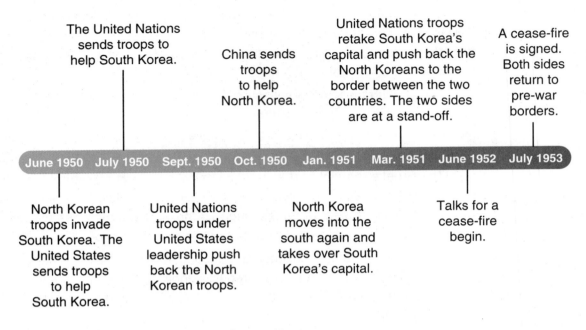

The United Nations sends troops to help South Korea.

China sends troops to help North Korea.

United Nations troops retake South Korea's capital and push back the North Koreans to the border between the two countries. The two sides are at a stand-off.

A cease-fire is signed. Both sides return to pre-war borders.

| June 1950 | July 1950 | Sept. 1950 | Oct. 1950 | Jan. 1951 | Mar. 1951 | June 1952 | July 1953 |

North Korean troops invade South Korea. The United States sends troops to help South Korea.

United Nations troops under United States leadership push back the North Korean troops.

North Korea moves into the south again and takes over South Korea's capital.

Talks for a cease-fire begin.

Write the answer to each question.

8 What event started the Korean War?

_____

9 Who fought on each side of the Korean War?

_____

_____

Circle the number of the best answer for each question.

10 Which event was probably a result of China's entry into the war?
  (1) North Korea gained control of South Korea's capital.
  (2) North and South Korea talked about a cease-fire.
  (3) United Nations' troops pushed back the North Koreans.
  (4) The United States sent troops to help South Korea.
  (5) The United Nations entered the war to help South Korea.

11 Based on the timeline, which of the following statements best summarizes the Korean War?
  (1) South Korea was winning the war at its start.
  (2) North Korea, with the help of Chinese troops, won the war.
  (3) The two sides were deadlocked for a year until truce talks began.
  (4) The two sides talked about a truce for more than one year.
  (5) Neither side gained territory from the war.

The American Revolution

The start of the American Revolution forced people in North America to take sides. Those who wanted to be free from Britain were called Patriots. Those who were loyal to Britain were called Loyalists. Most African Americans faced a hard choice. Many were enslaved. They chose the side that offered them their freedom.

Even before the revolution between the colonies and Britain began, African Americans were taking sides. African-American soldiers fought in all the early battles of the war. Then in November 1775, Patriot leaders said African Americans could no longer serve in the Patriot army. Those who had already joined were sent home. Slave owners did not want any African Americans to have guns. They were afraid African Americans would use the guns to fight against slavery.

Then the British promised to free any slave who joined their army. Many slaves accepted the offer. As a result Patriot leaders changed their minds. However, they decided to allow only free African Americans, not slaves, to join their army. In December 1777 George Washington took his army of about nine thousand men to Valley Forge, Pennsylvania. By the spring of 1778, Washington had fewer than six thousand soldiers. Many deserted, while others died of cold or hunger.

Washington desperately needed more soldiers. So the Patriot leaders finally decided to allow enslaved African Americans to enlist. By the end of the war, five thousand African Americans had taken part in the American Revolution. They came from every state and fought in every major battle. The efforts of African-American soldiers during the war helped convince people who lived in the northern states that slavery should not be allowed.

Write the answer to each question.

12 What is the difference between a Patriot and a Loyalist?

_____

13 Why were African Americans turned away from the Patriot army in 1775?

_____

14 What were the effects of the British decision to free any slave who joined their army?

_____

Circle the number of the best answer.

15 What event allowed enslaved African Americans to join the Patriots' army?
 (1) the start of the American Revolution
 (2) Britain's decision to free slaves who joined its army
 (3) the loss of so many soldiers at Valley Forge
 (4) African-American participation in earlier battles
 (5) the end of the American Revolution

Women's Right to Vote

Women's Suffrage in the United States

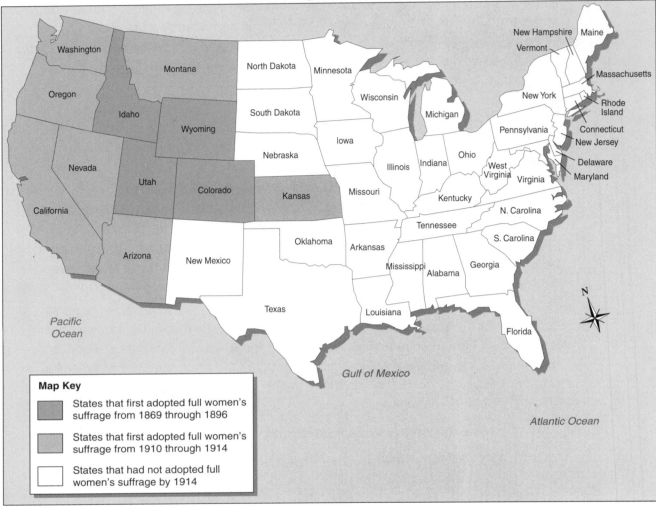

Source: *Mapping America's Past: A Historical Atlas*, 1996, p. 163

Write the answer to the question.

16 *Suffrage* means the right to vote. Which states first supported women voting in elections?

_____

Circle the number of the best answer.

17 Which statement is supported by the information in the map?
   (1) In 1900 men influenced American government more than women did.
   (2) Few women in eastern states wanted to vote.
   (3) Before 1914 fewer women lived in Colorado than in Pennsylvania.
   (4) By 1914 most states had given women the right to vote.
   (5) The Nineteenth Amendment gave women the right to vote in 1920.

   Go on to the next page.

Civil Rights

For many years after the Civil War, African Americans worked for equal rights. In the North and the South, they faced **discrimination.** White Americans did not treat them as if they had the same rights as whites did. In many states, schools were segregated. As a result, African American and white children could not attend the same school. African Americans were not allowed in many neighborhoods or to hold certain jobs. Some state laws even kept African Americans out of such places as restaurants, public swimming pools, movie theaters, and hotels.

In August 1963, nearly one hundred years after the Civil War ended, more than 250,000 Americans marched down the streets of Washington, D.C. They included white Americans and African Americans from every state and several foreign countries. They demanded that Congress finally pass a civil rights bill that would end discrimination in the United States.

Dr. Martin Luther King, Jr., was among the marchers. He was an African-American minister who was well known for his inspiring sermons. King captured the mood of the day. He said to the crowd, "I have a dream that one day this nation will rise up and live out the true meaning of its creed: 'We hold these truths to be self-evident; that all men are created equal.'"

President John F. Kennedy supported King's cause. He called on Congress to pass a strong civil rights bill. Kennedy did not live to see the bill become law. After Kennedy's death, Congress passed the Civil Rights Act of 1964. It protected the right of all citizens to vote. It outlawed discrimination in hiring and education. It also ended segregation in public places.

Write the answer to each question.

18 What do you think the word *segregated* means from the way it is used in the fourth sentence?

_____

_____

19 Why did Americans march in Washington, D.C., in 1963?

_____

Circle the number of the best answer.

20 Dr. King was calling on all Americans to
  (1) change the nation's values and beliefs.
  (2) live up to the nation's values and beliefs.
  (3) march down the streets of Washington, D.C.
  (4) pass a civil rights bill.
  (5) follow the leadership of President Kennedy.

Electing a President and Vice President

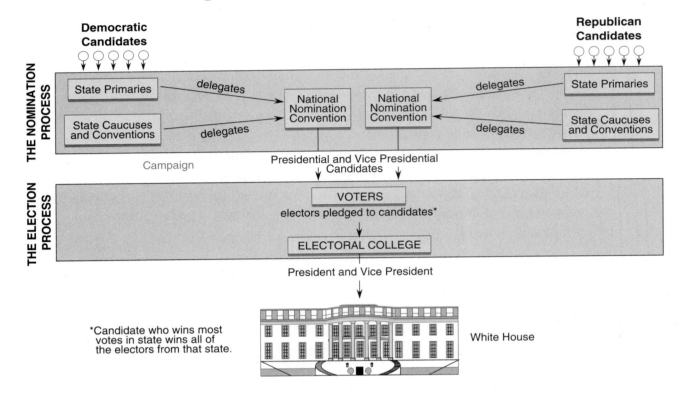

*Candidate who wins most votes in state wins all of the electors from that state.

Write the answer to the question.

21 From what two sources are delegates chosen to represent both the Democratic and Republican parties at their nominating conventions?

_____

_____

Circle the number of the best answer.

22 Based on the information provided in the diagram, which group directly elects the president and vice president?

(1) the voters for the national candidates
(2) party delegates from the national conventions
(3) electors of the Electoral College
(4) party caucus of each political party
(5) state primaries of each political party

Taxes

The government of the United States provides many goods and services to its citizens. To pay for these, it collects taxes from individuals and businesses. Taxes are generally collected on income, sales, and property. Taxes collected in the United States usually follow one of two basic tax principles.

One is the benefit principle. This says that those who benefit the most should be the ones taxed. It also says that they should pay in proportion to the amount of benefit they receive. Gasoline taxes are an example of benefit taxes. Those people who use the most gasoline pay the most gasoline taxes. People who do not own a car do not pay any gasoline tax.

The second tax principle is the ability-to-pay principle. This says that those who make the most income should pay a higher rate of taxes than those who make less money. Most income taxes are based on this principle. The federal government, state governments, and sometimes city governments charge income taxes using this principle. This idea comes from the belief that people with higher incomes can afford to pay higher taxes. So Americans pay different percentages based on their income. A single person in 1999 who made $25,000 of taxable income paid 15 percent, or $3,750, in federal income taxes. A person who made $50,000 of taxable income paid 15 percent on $25,750 and 28 percent of the rest for a total of $10,652.50 in federal income tax. And a single person who made $283,150 of taxable income in 1999 paid $90,200.50, or almost one-third of his or her income, in federal income tax.

Many Americans object to the ability-to-pay principle. They argue that everyone should pay the same percentage of his or her income in federal tax. Such a tax is called a flat tax.

Write the answer to each question.

㉓ What is the difference between a benefit tax and an ability-to-pay tax?

_____

_____

㉔ If the government switched to a flat tax of 20 percent, whose taxes would go up—those who make $25,000 a year or those who make $50,000 a year?

_____

Circle the number of the best answer.

㉕ What American ideal is reflected by the principle the federal government currently uses to determine income tax.
   (1) loyalty
   (2) equality
   (3) punishment
   (4) fairness
   (5) freedom

The Global Economy

Write the answer to each question.

26 Who does the man hanging from the limb represent?

_____

27 How does the cartoonist show that the United States economy is strong although in danger?

_____

Circle the number of the best answer.

28 What message is the cartoonist trying to communicate?
   (1) Asia is saving the United States economy.
   (2) A ball and chain can pull a man off a cliff.
   (3) Global economies succeed or fail together.
   (4) Business confidence is at an all-time high.
   (5) The American and Asian economies are not related.

Inventory Correlation Chart

The chart below will help you determine your strengths and weaknesses in the five content areas of social studies.

Content Areas	Items	Total Correct	Practice Pages
Geography (Pages 12–45)	1, 2, 3, 4, 5	_____ out of 5	Pages 14–19 Pages 20–25
World History (Pages 46–85)	6, 7, 8, 9, 10, 11	_____ out of 6	Pages 48–53 Pages 72–77
American History (Pages 86–137)	12, 13, 14, 15, 16, 17	_____ out of 6	Pages 94–99 Pages 106–111
Government and Civics (Pages 138–171)	18, 19, 20, 21, 22	_____ out of 5	Pages 152–157 Pages 158–163
Economics (Pages 172–217)	23, 24, 25, 26, 27, 28	_____ out of 6	Pages 186–191 Pages 204–209

TOTAL CORRECT FOR INVENTORY _____ out of 28

Directions

In the Items column, circle the number of each item that you answered correctly on the Inventory. Count the number of items you answered correctly in each content area. Write the amount in the Total Correct blank in each row. (For example, in the Geography row, write the number correct in the blank before *out of 5*). Complete this process for the remaining rows. Then add the five totals to get your Total Correct for the whole 28-item Inventory.

If you answered fewer than 25 items correctly, look more closely at the five content areas of social studies listed above. In which areas do you need more practice? Each content area makes up a part of this book. Look for the page numbers of that section in the chart's right-hand column. Then complete that part of the book for further practice.

Geography

Have you ever wondered why people choose to live in a certain place? You probably could list several reasons why people live where they do. Perhaps their families have always lived there. Some people may go to a place looking for jobs. Or perhaps people simply choose a place because they like it. It may have year-round warm weather, or maybe it's near the ocean or mountains.

Geographers study the many places on Earth and the people who live there. They study a place's physical features, such as weather, land, animals, plants, and minerals. Geographers also study the place's cultural features—the people's customs and the ways they make their living.

◐ What do you know about the rain forest? How do you think it differs from your area?

◐ How do you think people in the Arctic, the area near the North Pole, make a living? Do you think many jobs they do differ from the jobs people in your area hold?

SECTIONS

① **People and Regions**

② **Climatic Regions**

③ **Rescuing an Environment**

④ **A Matter of Resources**

1 People and Regions

Setting the Stage

In 1993 Canada gave the Inuit people their own territory in the Canadian Arctic. The Inuit are the native people of north central Canada. They now own and control the land and mineral wealth of Nunavut—their new territory. Nunavut is a large territory, covering 20 percent of Canada.

PREVIEW THE ARTICLE

You will get a better understanding of what you read if you look over an article before reading it. Look at the title of this article and the headings, or subtitles. Also look at the title of the map. What are some things you can expect to learn about in this article?

_____

_____

_____

RELATE TO THE TOPIC

This article is about the Arctic and a group of Native Americans who live there.

In what part of the world do you live? In what part of your state do you live? What makes your neighborhood different from a neighborhood nearby? Write your answers on the lines below.

_____

_____

_____

VOCABULARY

region	**vegetation**	**tree line**
climate	**tundra**	

Check your answers on page 230.

The Arctic

Located around the North Pole, the Arctic is one of Earth's unique regions. A **region** is an area that differs in one or more ways from the places around it. Physical features, such as mountains or plants, may set the region apart. The culture of the people or the way they make their living also may set a region apart. Few regions have real borders that mark where one region ends and another begins.

Vegetation and Climate

Vegetation can define a region. **Vegetation** is the plants that grow naturally in an area. The Arctic region, however, is often defined by the plants that cannot grow there. It is the land north of the tree line. The **tree line** marks where temperatures become too cold for trees to grow. Generally, the warmest temperature of the year in the Arctic is 50°F (10°C).

The vegetation of a region depends on its climate. **Climate** is the general weather of a region over a long time. The climate of the Arctic includes short summers and long, very cold winters.

Permanent snow and ice cover the North Pole and the land along the Arctic Ocean. Algae and other plants that thrive on rocks may grow in this part of the Arctic. The rest of the region is **tundra.** This treeless stretch of land has only a thin layer of soil above the frozen earth. Herbs, vines, mosses, wildflowers, and small shrubs grow on the tundra during the Arctic summer.

The Arctic Region

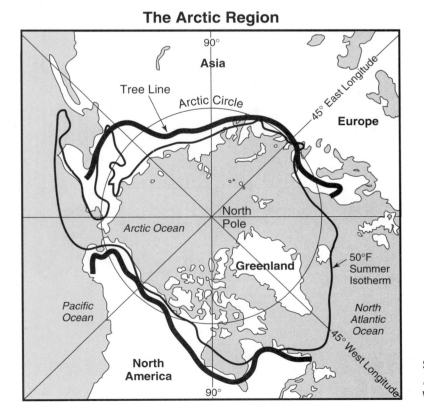

Source: *The World Book Encyclopedia,* © 1991, World Book, Inc., p. 637.

Reading a Map Key   Maps use symbols to tell about places. Symbols can be lines, dots, colors, or pictures. The map key explains what each symbol means. Find the map key on page 15. Then study the map. In what two continents is the tree line closest to the North Pole?

    a.   Europe and North America

    b.   Europe and Asia

The Early Inuit

The Arctic region spans North America, Europe, and Asia. In North America, the Arctic region lies in northern and western Alaska and northernmost Canada. Native Americans who live in the Arctic region are called the Inuit, a word that means "the real people."

The Inuit were once called Eskimos. They are descended from Asian whale hunters who came to Alaska. They moved east to Canada and Greenland in about A.D. 1000.

The Arctic climate is too harsh for farming. So, the Inuit relied on fishing and hunting for food. Most settled along the coastlines, where they hunted seals, walrus, and whales. Others traveled in small groups made up of several families and lived in camps. In the spring, they fished, hunted caribou, and gathered berries. In the winter, they hunted whales and seals and trapped birds. They traveled on foot during the short summer and by boat or dog team during the rest of the year.

The Inuit depended on animals for other needs, too. They used animal hides and bones to build shelters, boats, and sleds. They also dressed in layers of seal skins and caribou hides. The layers trapped warm air near the body. The outer layer generally had fur for greater warmth.

Native people in Canada's Arctic region today combine modern ways with traditional ones.

Check your answer on page 230.

The Inuit had a very rich culture. The people generally chose their best hunter as their leader. However, they made decisions through group discussion. And they used storytelling and singing, rather than writing, as their main ways of communicating.

Over time, part of the Arctic came under Canadian control. From the 1950s through the 1970s, Inuit children attended Canadian schools during the fall and winter. They learned their lessons in English and French. The children forgot not only their Inuit language but also the Inuit way of life.

The Canadian Inuit Today

Today the Inuit number about 100,000. Half live in Alaska and Canada. The other half live in Greenland. The Inuit in Canada still hunt and fish, but most of them also earn wages. They need cash to buy tools, rifles, and snowmobiles. So many Inuit work at mining camps or on oil rigs. They also make cash by selling furs or native arts and crafts.

The Inuit have struggled to keep their traditions. Inuit leaders have looked at the schools their children attend and have suggested changes to the government. Today the schools teach native languages and customs to Inuit students.

In 1987 the Inuit of Alaska, Canada, and Greenland joined forces to protect the Inuit way of life. Their leaders organized an annual Inuit conference. They discussed wildlife rights and land claims. They agreed that the Arctic region in their nations should be "used for peace and environmentally safe purposes." This cooperation gives the Inuit political power to help hold on to their way of life.

Most of the 25,000 Canadian Inuit live in the eastern Northwest Territories. Their families have lived and hunted there for nearly a thousand years. Until recently, however, the Inuit did not own the land. So Canada's Inuit began demanding control of their hunting grounds. In 1993 the Inuit and the Canadian government agreed to form a new territory that the Inuit began governing in April 1999. The Inuit named the territory Nunavut, which means "our land." They own the mineral rights in some parts of the land and also earn a share of the profits from oil and mineral development in other parts.

Finding the Main Idea   One way to make sure you understand what you read is to find the main idea of each paragraph. A paragraph is a group of sentences about one main idea or topic. The main idea usually is stated in one sentence, called a **topic sentence.** The topic sentence makes a general statement that sums up all the details in the other sentences of the paragraph. Reread the paragraph that begins "In 1987." Note that the first sentence is the topic sentence and states the main idea of the paragraph.

What is the topic sentence of the first paragraph under "The Canadian Inuit Today"? Circle the letter of the correct answer.

a.   The Inuit in Canada still hunt and fish, but most of them also earn wages.

b.   They also make money by selling furs or native arts and crafts.

Thinking About the Article

Practice Vocabulary

The terms below are in the passage in bold type. Study the way each term is used. Then complete each sentence by writing the correct term in the blank.

region	vegetation	tree line
climate	tundra	

1 The _____ is land on which few plants grow.

2 Bitter cold temperatures and very short summers make up the Arctic _____ .

3 _____ that grows in warm and wet places differs greatly from what grows in warm and dry places.

4 In North America trees grow in the area south of the _____ .

5 A _____ may be defined by its natural features, climate, plant and animal life, or people.

Understand the Article

Write the answer to the following.

6 Describe the climate and vegetation of the Arctic region.

_____

_____

7 Describe the early Inuit way of life. How did they get food? What were their clothes like? How did they get from place to place?

_____

_____

_____

8 List three ways the Inuit worked together to save their way of life.

_____

_____

_____

Check your answers on page 230.

Apply Your Skills

Circle the number of the best answer for each question.

9 Look at the map on page 15. According to the map key, which of the following statements describes the Arctic region?
   (1) More of the Arctic region is tundra than ocean and permanent ice cap.
   (2) The tundra in Alaska covers less land area than the tundra in Greenland.
   (3) The tundra in Europe is flatter than the tundra in North America.
   (4) The tundra in North America covers less land area than the tundra in either Asia or Europe.
   (5) Greenland's land area is mostly frozen ice.

10 Read the paragraph on page 16 that begins "The Arctic climate." What is the main idea of this paragraph?
   (1) The Inuit met their needs by fishing and hunting.
   (2) The Inuit traveled from place to place.
   (3) The Inuit did not farm.
   (4) The Inuit lived in a cold climate.
   (5) The Inuit ate berries.

Connect with the Article

Write your answer to each question.

11 What do you think was the most valuable thing the Inuit gained by working together? Why?

_____

_____

_____

12 A few decades ago, Inuit children went to school far from their homes. Imagine that children in your family or children you know had to go to a school in another country for six months of the year. What changes might you expect to see in their behavior when they returned? Think about language, dress, and sense of closeness to you and your family.

_____

_____

_____

_____

Climatic Regions

Setting the Stage

From your window, the day looks sunny. So, you step outside without a hat or an umbrella. Before you walk two blocks, rain starts pouring down. Has something like this ever happened to you? Weather certainly can change in just minutes. A region's climate, on the other hand, changes more slowly. Different factors, such as sun, rain, and wind, determine a region's climate.

PREVIEW THE ARTICLE

Begin to think about what you will be reading. Look at the title of the article, the headings (subtitles) within the article, and the title of the map. What are some things you can expect to learn about climate from this article?

_____

_____

_____

RELATE TO THE TOPIC

This section is about climate and the factors that determine it. If you could live in any part of the world, where would you choose? What is the climate like there? Was the climate something you thought about when making your choice?

_____

_____

_____

VOCABULARY

equator	latitude	current
longitude	precipitation	elevation

Check your answers on page 230.

Factors Determining Climate

Earth has many different climates. One factor that influences a region's climate is its location on Earth, especially its distance from the equator. The **equator** is an imaginary line that circles Earth exactly halfway between the North Pole and the South Pole. Nearby mountain ranges or large bodies of water also affect climate. The kinds of winds that blow across the region make a difference, too.

The Equator and Climate

All year round, places along the equator receive direct rays from the sun. Direct sunlight is very strong. As a result, temperatures near the equator are usually warm. Places away from the equator, on the other hand, receive slanted rays from the sun. In other words, the sun's rays strike Earth at an angle. This indirect sunlight is weaker than direct sunlight. As a result, temperatures far from the equator are generally cooler than those near the equator.

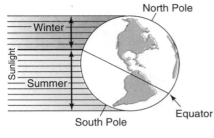

This diagram shows winter north of the equator. Notice that the Sun's rays hit Earth at more of an angle in the Northern Hemisphere.

The amount of sunlight a place gets depends on its distance from the equator. This distance is measured with lines of **latitude.** Lines of latitude run east and west like the equator.

The lines of latitude farthest from the equator lie near the North Pole or South Pole. Places along these lines get less sunlight than other places on Earth. They get no sunlight for part of the year and slanting rays for the rest of the year. As a result, the polar regions are cold all year and have short summers.

Earth is tilted slightly. The tilt of the Earth affects how sunlight strikes the Earth. The northernmost line of latitude that receives almost direct rays from the sun is called the Tropic of Cancer. The southernmost line of latitude that receives almost direct rays from the sun is called the Tropic of Capricorn. The region between these two lines of latitude is called the *tropics.* Most places in the tropics have warm temperatures year-round.

Between the tropics and the two polar regions are the middle latitudes. These two regions have temperate climates. Temperatures there are cooler than those in the tropics but warmer than those at the poles. Temperatures in the middle latitudes vary from place to place and from season to season.

Identifying Details   A paragraph is a group of sentences about one main idea. **Details,** or small pieces of information, explain or support the main idea. The main idea in the first paragraph under the heading "The Equator and Climate" is "The location of a place determines the amount of sunlight it receives."

Reread the first paragraph under the heading "The Equator and Climate." Which of the following details from the paragraph supports its main idea?
   a.   Lines of latitude run east and west.
   b.   Places along the equator receive direct rays from the sun all year round.

Check your answer on page 231.

Water and Wind

Latitude explains why Alaska is colder than Florida. However, latitude does not explain why winters in southern Alaska are often warmer than winters in Montana. What is the reason? Southern Alaska borders the Pacific Ocean, and Montana lies inland.

Oceans and large lakes help keep temperatures mild. These large bodies of water do not gain or lose heat as quickly as land areas do. In summer, ocean water stays cold long after the land has grown warm. Large bodies of water also hold the summer's heat as the land cools in fall. The temperature of water affects the air above it. After winds blow over the water, they cool the land in summer and warm the land in winter. As a result, places near an ocean or a large lake often have milder temperatures than places not near large bodies of water.

Another reason helps explain why the climate in southern Alaska is mild. A warm ocean current flows along Alaska's coast. A **current** is like a river in the ocean. Some ocean currents carry warm water, while others are very cold. Without the warm current, the ocean along the coast of southern Alaska would be frozen all winter.

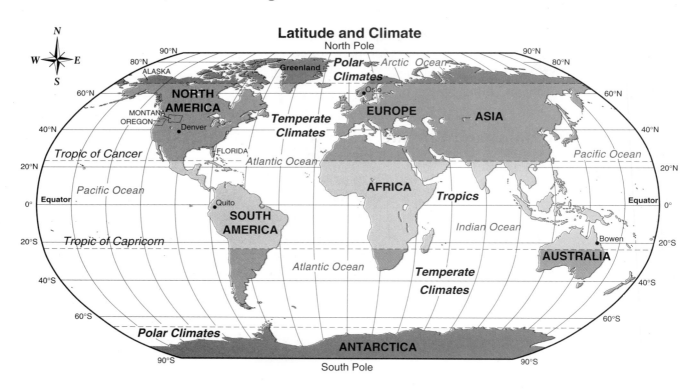

Using Latitude   Many maps have two sets of lines. These lines cross each other to form a grid. You can use this grid to locate places on a map of Earth. Lines of latitude, called **parallels,** measure distances from the equator in degrees. The equator lies at 0° latitude. All other parallels lie either north or south of the equator, and are labeled *N* or *S.* Lines of **longitude,** or **meridians,** reach from pole to pole. These lines measure distances from the Prime Meridian in degrees. The Prime Meridian lies at 0° longitude. All other meridians lie east or west of the Prime Meridian and are labeled *E* or *W.*

Look at the map on page 22 to answer the following questions.

❶   Which city lies closest to 40° N latitude?
   a.   Denver   b.   Oslo

❷   Which city shown on the map is outside the tropics?
   a.   Bowen   b.   Quito   c.   Oslo

Montana and other places surrounded by land and far from large bodies of water have a continental climate. Places with continental climates have cold winters and hot summers. Even the amount of **precipitation**—rain or snow—follows a pattern. Cities such as Des Moines, Iowa, have a continental climate. They get more snow than New York City and other places on the northeastern coast.

Mountains and Climate

Mountains also affect climate. The most important factor in a mountain climate is elevation. **Elevation** is the height of the land, and it affects both temperature and precipitation. This is because air cools as it rises. Temperatures at the top of a mountain are much colder than at the bottom of the mountain. As a result, some mountains along the equator are snowcapped all year long.

Mountains affect temperatures in other places, too. For example, mountains in the western United States block mild winds from the Pacific Ocean. So the moist, mild ocean air never reaches Montana and other places that lie east of the mountains. These places have colder winters and hotter summers than places along the Pacific coast.

Mountains also influence precipitation. In Oregon, for example, mountains line the coast. Moist winds from the Pacific Ocean rise up the western slopes of the mountains. As the air rises, it cools. Cold air cannot hold as much moisture as warm air. So clouds form and rain falls on the western side of the mountains. When the air reaches the eastern side of the mountains, it has dropped all its moisture and is dry. So this side of Oregon's mountains gets very little rain.

Many factors—latitude, winds, elevation, and nearness to mountains and large bodies of water—determine the climate of a place. Climate determines how people live. It influences their choice of food, housing, and clothing.

Thinking About the Article

Practice Vocabulary

The terms below are in the passage in bold type. Study the way each term is used. Then complete each sentence by writing the correct term in the blank.

equator   **latitude**   **current**

longitude   **precipitation**   **elevation**

1. The sun's rays shine directly on places along the

    _____ year-round.

2. A warm ocean _____ can give places located along a northern coastline a fairly mild climate.

3. _____ may fall to Earth as rain or snow.

4. The factor that determines the climate of polar regions is

    _____.

5. A mountaintop is colder than the foot of the mountain because of

    _____.

6. The Prime Meridian is the starting point on a map for measuring

    _____.

Understand the Article

Write the answer to each question.

7. What are three factors that affect the climate of a place?

    _____

8. How would you describe the climate in the tropics? Middle-latitude areas? Polar regions?

    _____

9. How do oceans keep land temperatures mild in both summer and winter?

    _____

    _____

Check your answers on page 231.

Apply Your Skills

Circle the number of the best answer for each question.

10 Which of the following details supports the main idea that latitude affects climate in the tropics?
  (1) The tropics lie close to the poles.
  (2) Winds from the ocean bring moist air to places in the tropics.
  (3) Rain usually falls on the windy side of a mountain.
  (4) Warm ocean currents keep water from freezing in winter.
  (5) The tropics receive almost direct rays from the sun.

11 Look at the map on page 22 to determine which of these lines of latitude lies in the tropics.
  (1) 90° S latitude
  (2) 60° N latitude
  (3) 40° S latitude
  (4) 10° N latitude
  (5) 60° S latitude

12 Which two continents does the equator pass through?
  (1) North America and Europe
  (2) South America and Africa
  (3) Australia and Asia
  (4) Africa and Asia
  (5) South America and Australia

Connect with the Article

Write your answer to each question.

13 The Rocky Mountains cover the western third of Montana. Do you think the western or the eastern part of the state gets more precipitation each year? Explain your answer.

_____

_____

_____

14 On the map on page 22, find the approximate location of your home state. Use climate words from this article to write a sentence that describes the climate in your area.

_____

_____

Rescuing an Environment

Setting the Stage

March 24, 1989, was the date of the worst oil spill in North America. Along the southeastern coast of Alaska, a huge oil tanker ran off course and struck a reef. The tanker's bottom tore open. Almost 11 million gallons of oil spilled into the sea. Many people rushed to clean up the oil spill and save the wildlife along Alaska's coast.

PREVIEW THE ARTICLE

One way to get a quick idea of what an article is all about is to read the introduction to the article. The introduction is usually the first few paragraphs at the beginning of the article.

Read the first two paragraphs on page 27. What can you expect to learn from this article?

_____

_____

_____

RELATE TO THE TOPIC

This article is about how people rescued Alaska's southern coast from an oil spill. Smaller but similar problems with pollution can affect everyone's surroundings. What could you do to improve a garbage-strewn park in your neighborhood?

_____

_____

_____

VOCABULARY

sound   environment   glacier

iceberg   crude oil

    Check your answers on page 231.

Oil Spill in Alaska

The oil spill took place in Prince William Sound. A **sound** is a narrow body of water. Prince William Sound, which is between the Gulf of Alaska and the Alaskan coastline, has a marine, or sea, environment. An **environment** is all of the living and nonliving things that make up a place's surroundings. People, fish, seaweed, and other animals and plants are the living parts of that place's environment. The nonliving parts are soil, rocks, water, and glaciers that line the coast. A **glacier** is an enormous mass of ice that moves slowly over land.

Every part of an environment is closely tied to all its other parts. Sea otters, for example, depend on fish and birds for food. Seal meat and fish are important to Native Alaskans' diet. Many people of the Prince William Sound area fish for a living. Others work in the tourist business. Thousands of tourists visit parks, forests, and wildlife refuges near the sound.

Some people who live along the sound work in the oil industry. They store and ship oil. The Alaskan pipeline carries oil from Alaska's Arctic region to Valdez. This is a small port on Prince William Sound. Oil tankers come to Valdez each month to carry Alaskan oil to other parts of the United States.

Using the Glossary or Dictionary   When you read the sections in this book, you will come across words in **bold type.** Circle these words. You can find their meanings in the glossary at the back of this book. You may also come across other words that you do not understand. Circle these words, too. Look in a dictionary to find the meaning of each word. Then, on the lines below, write the definition that best fits the use of the word in the article.

_____

_____

_____

_____

Disaster in Prince William Sound

On Thursday evening, March 23, 1989, an oil tanker called the *Exxon Valdez* left port and headed for California. Shortly after midnight, the tanker turned sharply to avoid a dangerous iceberg. An **iceberg** is a huge block of floating ice that has broken off from a glacier.

The tanker missed the iceberg but ran over a reef. The smell of untreated oil, called **crude oil**, filled the air. The ship was leaking. By dawn on March 24, a thick oily film called an *oil slick*, covered six square miles of Prince William Sound. By early evening, about ten million gallons of oil had spilled. The oil slick stretched more than 18 square miles.

The slick continued to spread. Wind and water carried the oil farther into the sound. Then a storm hit just four days after the spill, carrying the oil into tiny inlets and coves along the shore. After the storm, the oil slick covered 500 square miles. The oil spill traveled southwest with the ocean currents, polluting more than 1,200 miles of Alaskan coastline.

The spill claimed the lives of 1,000 sea otters. It also killed 100,000 birds, including about 150 bald eagles. People who fished for a living wondered if the oil would harm the salmon, herring, and other fish they depended on.

The Cleanup

No one had ever cleaned up an oil spill as large as the one in Prince William Sound. So no one knew exactly what to do. The Exxon Corporation sent about 11,000 workers to help. It owned the *Exxon Valdez.* The company that managed the Alaskan pipeline also took some responsibility for the cleanup. The state of Alaska, the U.S. Coast Guard, and several U.S. government agencies helped, too. But it was not always clear who was in charge.

The cleanup crews tried many ways to remove the spilled oil. Some tried to skim the oil from the water. They transferred it to other ships. The workers needed special equipment, but it was slow to arrive.

Some experts wanted to spray the sound with chemicals. These chemicals act much like a detergent. But the company did not have enough chemicals to treat the whole spill. Besides, state and federal officials were slow to permit the spraying. By the time everybody was ready to act, it was too late. In the end, cleanup crews recovered less than ten percent of the oil in the sound.

Exxon Valdez Oil Spill

Map Key

■ Areas affected by the oil spill

○ Parks or wildlife refuges

0   150 MILES

0   150 KILOMETERS

ALASKA

Anchorage

Valdez

Kenai Peninsula

Bering Sea

Peninsula

Prince William Sound

Alaska

Kodiak

N

Kodiak Island

Gulf of Alaska

Meanwhile, workers attacked the spill on the beaches. Some crews tried to blast the oil from rocks. Others sprayed the beaches with hot water and fertilizer. The fertilizer encouraged the growth of bacteria that eat oil.

Some of the cleanup methods worked, while others did more damage than the oil. The hot water killed some wildlife. It also sent oil deep into the gravel beaches, where it was unreachable, but still harmful to the environment. The bacteria ate up the oil on some beaches. But the fertilizer killed seaweed, a plant important to the Prince William Sound environment. Workers rescued some of the many fish, birds, and animals. They also protected some fish hatcheries. But later on, some wildlife died after eating fish or animals that were poisoned by the spill.

Drawing Conclusions Recall the last time you listened to someone talk about a problem. Did you make judgments about how the problem started? Or get ideas about how to fix the problem? Or guess how people might react to it? If you did any of these things, you were drawing a **conclusion**. You based your conclusion on the facts as you understood them.

Reread the paragraphs on pages 28–29 that are under the heading titled "The Cleanup." From the information presented, what conclusion can you draw about why the oil spill was difficult to clean up? Write your conclusion on the lines below.

_____

_____

The Effects of the Oil Spill

Just after the oil spill, many people believed that wildlife would never return to Prince William Sound. Yet less than a year later, the air and water were clear again. Fish and whales that had survived the spill returned to the sound in the spring as they always had. Plants began to grow again.

The environment had changed, however. By spring of 1991, many groups of sea birds had not recovered from the spill. Scientists said it would take from 20 to 70 years for the birds to build up their numbers to the population levels before the spill. Injuries to other wildlife were just beginning to show up. Studies showed that oil still at the bottom of the sound continued to harm the sea life.

In 1994 a federal court jury ordered the Exxon Corporation to pay $5 billion to Alaskans who earned their living fishing. Native American companies and Alaskan cities also shared this award. In a separate settlement, the United States and Alaskan governments won millions of dollars to set up the *Exxon Valdez* Oil Spill Trustee Council. This group used the money to restore the natural resources and human services that the spill damaged. In March 1999—ten years after the oil spill—the council held a public meeting in Anchorage, Alaska. Speakers at the meeting discussed the achievements of the council's recovery efforts. They also summed up lessons learned about cleaning up oil and preventing spills.

Check your answer on page 231.

Thinking About the Article

Practice Vocabulary

The terms below are in the passage in bold type. Study the way each term is used. Then complete each sentence by writing the correct term in the blank.

sound	environment	glacier
iceberg	crude oil	

1 A(n) _____ is often located between a coastline and a larger body of water.

2 A nearby body of water has a strong influence on the surroundings in a marine _____ .

3 A(n) _____ is formed when snow and ice accumulate on land over a long period of time.

4 Tar and gasoline are two products that come from

_____ .

5 A(n) _____ poses dangers to ocean liners and other ships traveling in northern waters.

Understand the Article

Write the answer to each question.

6 Describe how the accident in Prince William Sound occurred.

_____

_____

7 What caused the oil spill to travel so far from the accident site?

_____

_____

8 What happened to the environment around Prince William Sound as a result of the oil spill?

_____

_____

Check your answers on page 231.

Apply Your Skills

Circle the number of the best answer for each question.

9 Which of the following dictionary definitions for *sound* gives the meaning used in the article?
(1) Anything that can be heard
(2) A long narrow channel connecting large bodies of water
(3) A long inlet of the ocean that runs along the coast
(4) Energy in the form of pressure waves
(5) An air-filled bladder in a fish's body

10 The spring after the oil spill, plants sprouted, whales returned, and salmon catches were high. Based on this information and what you read in the article, which conclusion might you draw about the cleanup?
(1) Every part of the cleanup was a success.
(2) The cleanup harmed more living things than it helped.
(3) The water in the sound could no longer support life.
(4) The cleanup removed all the oil in Prince William Sound.
(5) The cleanup helped some living things in the environment.

Connect with the Article

Write your answer to each question.

11 Locate the wildlife refuges on the map on page 28. What problems might workers at hotels near these refuges have faced during the rest of 1989? Explain your answer.

_____

_____

_____

12 The year after the oil spill, Congress created an oil-spill cleanup fund as a result of the *Exxon Valdez* accident. The money for the fund comes from taxes on crude oil. Do you think this tax affects the price you pay for oil products, such as gasoline? Explain your answer.

_____

_____

_____

_____

4 A Matter of Resources

Setting the Stage

Millionaires are common in many countries in the Middle East. Their millions come from oil and natural gas that they discovered there. These discoveries have turned the Middle East into one of the richest regions in the world. Yet, in the daily lives of Middle Easterners, water is much more important than oil.

PREVIEW THE ARTICLE

You will get a better understanding of what you read if you look over an article before reading it. Look at the title of an article and its headings, or subtitles. Read the title and the headings on pages 33–35. What are two things you expect to learn from reading this article?

_____

_____

RELATE TO THE TOPIC

This article is about the Middle East and why oil and water are so important to the people who live there. Think back over the past 24 hours. How many times did you use water? How often did you rely on gasoline or motor oil? How important would you say that water and oil are in your daily life?

_____

_____

_____

VOCABULARY

resource   nonrenewable resource   desert

oasis   irrigation   desalination

Check your answers on page 232.

The Middle East

The Middle East is the land between the Mediterranean and Arabian seas. It connects Africa, Asia, and Europe. For thousands of years, people had known there was oil in the Middle East. In some parts of the Middle East, a sticky, black liquid—crude oil—would seep through underground rocks to the land's surface. But no one paid much attention to it until the early 1900s. Then thousands of recently manufactured automobiles needed fuel, and suddenly oil became valuable.

"Black Gold," the Valuable Resource

Oil is one of the world's most valuable natural resources. A **resource** is anything that people can use to satisfy their needs. Some resources, like oil and water, come from nature. Others, such as knowledge or tools, come from humans. Like other minerals, oil is a **nonrenewable resource.** In other words, Earth's oil supplies will someday run out.

Today oil is more useful than gold. It fuels airplanes and tractors, runs machines, and heats buildings. Oil supplies much of the world's energy needs. Yet, it is more than a fuel. Oil goes into hundreds of important products, including plastic, asphalt, paint, fertilizers, and even lipstick.

The Middle East has about 65 percent of the world's known oil reserves. This oil is found mainly in countries along the Persian Gulf. Saudi Arabia has 25 percent of the world's reserves. Iraq, the United Arab Emirates, Iran, and Kuwait each has 10 percent or nearly 10 percent. Because oil is a valuable and limited resource, the countries of the Middle East jealously guard their oil supplies.

Mineral Resources of the Middle East

Updated and verified: National Geographic Satellite Map, May 1988, p. 651, *Rand McNally Picture Atlas of the World* © 1991, pp. 56–57, 69

Reading a Resource Map   **Resource maps** use symbols to show you where resources are found. The map key tells the meaning of each symbol. Study the resource map on page 33. It shows that oil is the main mineral resource of the Middle East. Use the map to answer the questions below. Write your answers on the lines provided.

❶   Which country has the greatest number of oil sites? _____

❷   Which country has the most natural gas sites? _____

Water, the Scarce Resource

Water is in very limited supply in the Middle East. Most of the region receives very little rain. In fact, some areas are **desert.** This kind of land receives so little rain that few plants can grow there.

With so little rain, most people in the Middle East live in river valleys and along coastlines. For example, more than 90 percent of all Egyptians live in the Nile River valley. Most people in Syria and Iraq live between the Tigris and Euphrates rivers.

Very few people live in the desert. Those who do live near oases. An **oasis** is a desert area with an underground spring called an **aquifer.** Desert dwellers dig wells to reach the water in aquifers.

Many farmers in the Middle East dig canals or build pipelines to carry water from rivers and aquifers to their fields. This method of getting and using water is called **irrigation.** More than 85 percent of the water taken from Middle Eastern rivers and aquifers is used for farming.

Middle Easterners also dam their rivers. This way they can store water for use in the driest season. The largest of these dams is the Aswan High Dam in Egypt. Before the dam was built, the Nile River flooded every summer. During the following fall, Egyptian farmers would plant their crops. The land was too dry for farming during the rest of the year. Now the dam stops the Nile River from overflowing. The dam traps the water in a reservoir so farmers have water whenever they need it.

Dams have created problems as well as solved them. For example, rivers once carried nutrients into the Persian Gulf. These nutrients help fish in the gulf to multiply. But dams block river-water nutrients that once flowed into the gulf. Without these nutrients, fewer fish in the gulf survive. As a result, people who earn their living fishing in the Persian Gulf have fewer fish to catch.

Some places in the Middle East do not have any bodies of fresh water. These countries build desalination plants. **Desalination** is the process of removing salt from salt water. Special machines, which are very costly, at desalination plants remove the salt from seawater. Then the water can be used for drinking and watering crops. However, countries in the Middle East, especially those rich with oil, willingly pay the cost.

Check your answers on page 232.

Sharing Borders and Resources

Resources cross national borders in the Middle East. The people of Kuwait and Iraq drill oil from the same field. The people of Israel and Jordan draw water from the same river. Because of the region's scarce water and valuable oil, resources are at the center of many conflicts in the region.

Some people in Turkey have suggested a "peace pipeline." This pipeline would pump water from rivers in northern Turkey to dry lands in Syria, Iraq, and the United Arab Emirates. This idea sounds helpful, but it would take water from Syria and Iraq. Their water comes from the Tigris and Euphrates rivers, and a pipeline might interrupt the rivers' natural flow.

The Middle East has used its control of oil supplies to gain political and economic power in the world. Recent discoveries of large natural gas reserves have given the countries yet another reason to fight. In fact, efforts to control oil and natural gas reserves led to the Iran-Iraq War, which was fought from 1980 to 1988.

With oil in great demand, some Middle Eastern rulers consider the money from oil as a way to improve life for their people. Others see the power they have in controlling oil supplies as a way to become world leaders. Rich as they are, many of these countries cannot afford to make enemies because they need their neighbors' goodwill.

Some oil-rich countries have small populations. So the governments hire workers from outside their borders. Other countries in the Middle East have so little water that they cannot grow food. So most of their food comes from other countries. Depending on outside workers and food encourages these countries to cooperate with other nations.

Despite all the reasons to get along, conflicts continue to erupt in the Middle East. Many world leaders urge Middle Easterners to stop fighting over water, oil, and natural gas. They believe the countries must work together—as a region—to manage these important resources.

Getting Meaning from Context   As you read, you may come across an unfamiliar word. Often you can figure out its meaning from the **context,** or the rest of the words in the sentence. Use context to figure out the meaning of the words *reserves* and *nutrients* in this article. Then circle the letter of the definition that fits the way each word is used.

1   The word *reserves* in the fourth paragraph on page 33 means
    a.   caution in one's words and actions.
    b.   resources available for future use.

2   The word *nutrients* in the sixth paragraph on page 34 means
    a.   food necessary for health and growth.
    b.   pure, salt-free water.

Thinking About the Article

Practice Vocabulary

The terms below are in the passage in bold type. Study the way each term is used. Then complete each sentence by writing the correct term in the blank.

resource	**nonrenewable resource**	**desert**
oasis	**irrigation**	**desalination**

1 Some Middle East countries use _____ to obtain more water for drinking.

2 Most of the water taken from rivers and aquifers in the Middle East is used for _____.

3 A(n) _____ that is abundant in Turkey is coal.

4 A(n) _____ provides water to people who live in desert areas.

5 A(n) _____ is in limited supply, and once used up, it is gone.

6 The driest kind of area in the Middle East is a(n)

_____.

Understand the Article

Write the answer to each question.

7 Why was oil not considered valuable until the early 1900s?

_____

_____

8 Why is water so scarce in the Middle East?

_____

_____

9 What are some ways people in the Middle East could cooperate in using water resources?

_____

_____

_____

Check your answers on page 232.

Apply Your Skills

Circle the number of the best answer for each question.

10 Look at the map on page 33. Which of the following statements describes the location of oil fields in the Middle East?
  (1) Iran has more oil fields than it has natural gas fields.
  (2) Most Middle Eastern oil fields are in Iran.
  (3) Egypt, Syria, and Jordan have no major oil fields.
  (4) Most oil fields are located near bodies of water.
  (5) The eastern parts of Oman, Iran, Iraq, and Saudi Arabia are called the oil zones.

11 Read the fifth paragraph under the heading "Water, the Scarce Resource" on page 34. Which other words in that paragraph help you understand the meaning of the word *reservoir*?
  (1) dam, river
  (2) flowing, gulf
  (3) river water blocked, fewer fish
  (4) flooded, summer
  (5) traps water, whenever they need it

Connect with the Article

Write your answer in the space provided.

12 Explain why millionaires are common in the Middle East and why many Middle Eastern countries are among the richest in the world.

_____

_____

_____

13 Oil-producing nations in the Middle East have sometimes cut the amount of oil they ship as a way of protesting a political situation they did not like. Such a stoppage of shipments is called an embargo. If there were an oil embargo today, what changes might you predict would occur at your local gas station?

_____

_____

_____

Geography at Work

Transportation: Ticket Agent

Some Careers in Transportation

Transportation Ticket Agent
makes reservations, sells tickets, and answers customers' questions

Station Agent
assists travelers with special needs

Travel Clerk
plans routes, calculates mileage, and answers questions

Passenger Rate Clerk
sells tickets, plans special or chartered trips, works with customers

An agent sells a ticket to a customer.

Many people love to travel and to see new places or visit old favorites. Other people travel for business or personal reasons. Whether it's travel to a local or faraway spot, ticket agents help travelers get to their destinations on trains, subways or elevated rail cars. Ticket agents work for railroads or public transit systems. Because they have contact with customers, they should enjoy working with people.

Ticket agents help customers plan departure and arrival times, determine how long a trip will take, book reservations, and buy their tickets. Agents need to have good geography skills. They need to read maps, use tables and charts, and work with fare schedules. They must have a good understanding of directions and know where places are. Because they help customers set travel schedules, ticket agents must have good time measurement and arithmetic skills.

Look at the chart showing some of the careers in transportation.

- Do any of the careers interest you? If so, which ones?

- What information would you need to find out more about those careers? On a separate piece of paper, write some questions that you would like answered. You can find out more information about those careers in the *Occupational Outlook Handbook* at your local library.

Rail ticket agents help customers plan their trips and make reservations. **Use the timetable and map below to fill in the spaces in the conversation that follows.**

Train	Washington, D.C.	Baltimore	Philadelphia	New York
	Departure Time	Arrival/Departure Times		
18	5:30 A.M.	6:15 A.M./6:20 A.M.	7:34 A.M./7:39 A.M.	8:59 A.M.
126	6:15 A.M.	7:00 A.M./7:05 A.M.	8:19 A.M./8:24 A.M.	9:44 A.M.
150	9:00 A.M.	9:45 A.M./9:50 A.M.	11:04 A.M./11:09 A.M.	12:29 P.M.
200	1:56 P.M.	3:41 P.M./3:46 P.M.	4:50 P.M./4:55 P.M.	6:15 P.M.

Eastern Rail Line Timetable—Route: Washington, D.C., to New York, NY

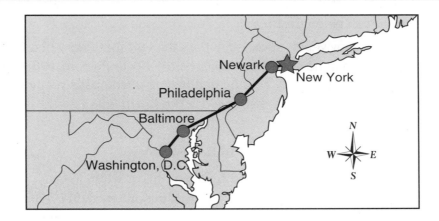

RAIL AGENT: "Good morning. This is the Eastern Rail Line. May I help you?"

CUSTOMER: "Yes. Do you have any trains leaving from the Washington, D.C., area that will get me into New York City by 12:30 p.m.?"

RAIL AGENT: "We have _____ trains that arrive before 12:30 p.m. The train numbers are: _____ ; _____ ; and _____ ."

CUSTOMER: "I have an appointment at 12:45 p.m. in New York. Which train should I take?"

RAIL AGENT: "There is a train that arrives at _____ , but that will only leave you 16 minutes to get to your meeting. I recommend you take train number 126. It arrives in New York at _____ . It will give you plenty of time to get to your meeting."

CUSTOMER: "What is your first stop north of Washington, D.C.?"

RAIL AGENT: "_____ is the first stop north of Washington, D.C."

CUSTOMER: "That stop is closer to my house; I will catch the train there. Thank you. I'd like to buy my ticket now."

RAIL AGENT: "I will be happy to help you."

Robert E. Peary Reaches the North Pole

Explorer Robert E. Peary led many trips to the Arctic. The first was in 1891 when Peary explored northern Greenland and proved that it is an island. In 1898 he set out to find the North Pole. On that trip, Peary came within 390 miles of the pole, but hardships forced him to turn back.

In 1902 and from 1905 to 1906, Peary tried twice more to reach the pole. On the 1905–1906 trip, he came within 200 miles. This time, ice storms forced him to go home. However, Peary refused to give up. In 1908 he organized a fourth expedition, which included his assistant Matthew Henson and four Inuit. Finally, Peary succeeded. On April 6, 1909, his group reached the North Pole. They had traveled as far north as anyone can go on Earth.

For many years, some scientists thought that Peary had figured his location incorrectly and had not really reached the North Pole. In 1989 a group of explorers carefully studied Peary's notes and his log of compass readings. These proved Peary and his group were the first to reach the North Pole.

Circle the number of the best answer.

1 What is the main idea of this article?
(1) Robert E. Peary was the only person ever to reach the North Pole.
(2) Peary was the first person to prove that Greenland is an island.
(3) Peary and his group were the first people to reach the North Pole.
(4) Peary tried to reach the North Pole over almost a dozen years.
(5) Some people doubted that Peary had reached the North Pole.

2 Study the map on page 41 and reread the article. Based on the map and passage, which of the following conclusions might you draw about why Peary succeeded in 1909?
(1) Peary followed the same route each time and eventually made it.
(2) Peary followed a northerly route from the land that lay closest to the pole.
(3) In 1909 Peary started in Canada rather than in Greenland.
(4) Peary figured he could double his 1906 distance in 1909.
(5) Peary followed a northerly route along the 70° W line of longitude.

    Check your answers on page 232.

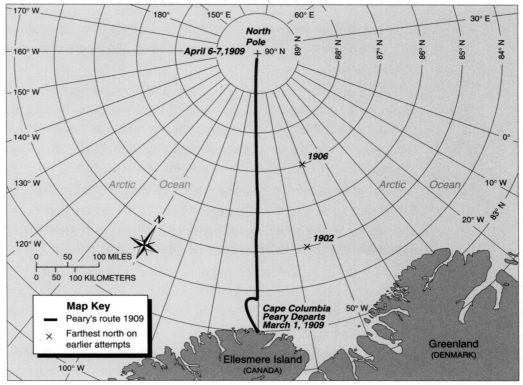

Robert E. Peary Reaches the North Pole

Write or circle the answer to each question.

3 Where did the ocean-going part of Robert E. Peary's final trip to the North Pole begin?

_____

4 What latitude did Peary reach on his trip in 1902? _____

5 What latitude did Peary reach on his trip in 1906? _____

6 Which of the following was the <u>most</u> important of Peary's activities in locating the North Pole?
(1) checking the depth of the Arctic Ocean
(2) figuring the latitude of his current location
(3) recording weather conditions
(4) calculating his distance from Greenland
(5) tracking his speed of travel

The Geographic Regions of Texas

Texas is so large that geographers divide it into four regions. Each region has different resources. Those resources help make Texas one of the richest states in the country.

One region of Texas is called the Gulf Coastal Plain. It covers eastern and southern Texas. The climate in this region is warm and wet. Long ago forests covered the Gulf Coastal Plain. Today, much of the land has been cleared for farming and ranching. Farmers grow cotton, vegetables, rice, and fruit. Oil and natural gas are among the important natural resources of this region.

Another region of Texas is the North Central Plains. Here the climate is drier. Grasslands make up a large part of the North Central Plains. Ranchers graze cattle and sheep on the grasslands. Farmers in this region grow cotton. The North Central Plains are rich in resources such as coal, oil, and natural gas.

The Great Plains region is colder and drier than the other three regions. Farmers must irrigate their wheat fields. Irrigation also helps supply water to the ranchers of this region. Some of the richest oil fields in Texas lie beneath the Great Plains.

The Basin and Range region is the mountainous area in western Texas. Miners have found resources such as gold, copper, and silver in these mountains. Like the Great Plains, the climate is dry. Ranching and farming are possible only through the use of irrigation.

Circle the number of the best answer.

7 The farmers and ranchers of Texas use irrigation
- (1) as a way to find rich oil fields.
- (2) to help them find gold and silver.
- (3) as a way to find natural gas deposits.
- (4) to get water for their crops and animals.
- (5) to get water from other regions.

8 Which of the following explains why Texas is divided into four regions?
- (1) Texas is one of the richest states.
- (2) Rainfall in Texas varies from place to place.
- (3) Texas has many resources.
- (4) Texas is large with varied landforms.
- (5) Farms and ranches lie throughout Texas.

Check your answers on page 233.

Top Ten Cattle-Raising and Oil-Producing States

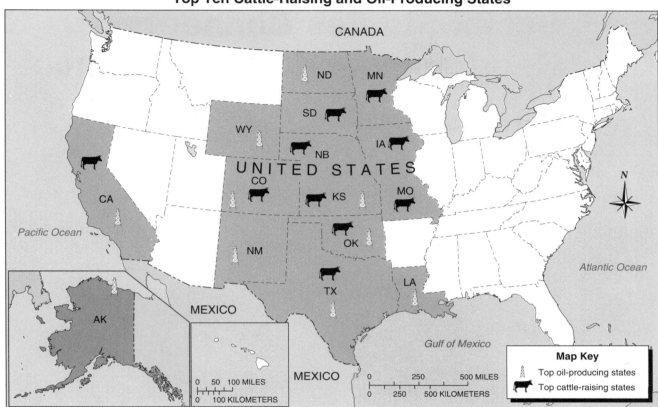

Source: U.S. Department of Agriculture; U.S. Energy Information Administration

Write or circle the answer to each question.

9 Which map symbol is used to show the top oil-producing states?

_____

10 Which symbol on the map is used to show the top cattle-raising states?

_____

11 Which of the following <u>cannot</u> be determined from the map?
(1) how many southern states are top oil producers
(2) how many western states are top cattle raisers
(3) how much oil is produced in the top oil-producing states
(4) how many states are the top producers of both oil and cattle
(5) where the top cattle-raising states are located

Borrow a videotape about the Arctic from your local library. As you watch the video, list the features that make the Arctic region special. Write down at least one new fact about the region that you learn from the video.

Social Studies Connection: Geography and Earth Science

Hurricane Mitch

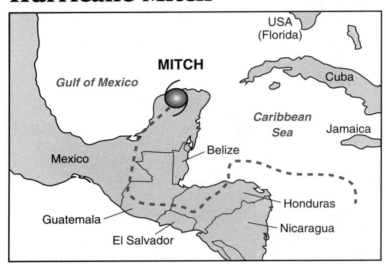

Hurricane Mitch's destructive path

They're fast. They're powerful. They're a wonder of nature but a disaster for mankind. Depending on where you live, you call them cyclones, typhoons, or hurricanes. They are fierce storms that cause incredible damage. In the Western Hemisphere, we call them hurricanes.

One of recent history's worst hurricanes hit Central America in late October and early November of 1998. Hurricane Mitch was notable not only for its strength but also for the tremendous amount of death and destruction it caused. Some have called it the deadliest Atlantic hurricane since 1780. Hurricane Mitch killed over 10,000 people in Costa Rica, Nicaragua, Honduras, El Salvador, and Guatemala.

Hurricane Mitch was noteworthy for another reason. Instead of weakening after it hit land, it gained strength! After passing over Mexico as a tropical depression, it strengthened to a tropical storm, moving east over the Gulf of Mexico and Florida.

Earth Science: Categories of Hurricanes

Hurricanes begin as tropical disturbances over warm tropical or subtropical seas. The storms gather strength and begin to spiral in a counter-clockwise direction. Almost all storms peak as a hurricane and then lose strength after they hit land. They end as a tropical storm or depression.

Four conditions must be present for a hurricane to develop:

• Ocean or sea temperatures must be greater than 79° Fahrenheit or 26° Celsius.
• The air above the water must have a high relative humidity.
• The atmosphere above the water must be unstable.
• The weather system must be within 4 to 5 degrees above or below the Equator.

Use the information on the previous page and the chart to answer the questions below.

Categories of Tropical Weather Systems				
Type of System	Category	Damage	Pressure (mb)	Wind Speed (in mph)
Tropical Depression	TD		——	<39
Tropical Storm	TS		——	39–73
Hurricane	1	Minimal	>980	74–95
Hurricane	2	Moderate	965–980	96–110
Hurricane	3	Extensive	945–965	111–130
Hurricane	4	Extreme	920–945	131–155
Hurricane	5	Catastrophic	<920	>155

1 According to the map, Hurricane Mitch passed directly over
- (1) Jamaica.
- (2) Belize.
- (3) Honduras.
- (4) Nicaragua.
- (5) Cuba.

2 Hurricane Mitch had winds that registered over 155 miles per hour. Based on the chart above, which category of hurricane was it?
- (1) Minimal
- (2) Moderate
- (3) Extensive
- (4) Extreme
- (5) Catastrophic

3 Which condition could not be a factor in a developing hurricane?
- (1) Water temperature of 28°Celsius in the Gulf of Mexico
- (2) Cool, dry air above the Caribbean Sea
- (3) A tropical storm off the coast of Belize
- (4) Warm, moist air above the Caribbean Sea
- (5) Water temperature of 81°Fahrenheit in the Gulf of Mexico

4 Tropical storms are given names even before they turn into hurricanes. Complete the chart below by categorizing each weather event according to the information used by scientists at the top of the page. The first entry has been done for you.

Name	Type of System	Category	Pressure (mb)	Wind Speed (in mph)
Alex	*Tropical storm*	TS	1,000	45
Georges			938	130
Ivan			975	80
Nicole			985	75

World History

Lately you cannot pick up the newspaper or watch the nightly news without hearing about disasters in other countries. They may be hurricanes in the Caribbean or downturns in Asian markets. Or a terrorist group makes a life-threatening attack in a city halfway across the world. Do these events really affect your life? Such events can have a strong impact on Americans.

More than ever before, Americans should know about other countries. Knowing about a nation's natural resources and its type of government are just a start. Instant information and transportation technology make us neighbors with all nations and peoples. Because Americans are such a mix of many cultures, we can benefit from learning how people in other countries handle conflicts and manage to cooperate.

◯ What international stories appear on television news shows?

◯ What has caused conflict among countries throughout history? Why have countries depended on one another throughout history?

SECTIONS

5 The Age of Empires

6 A Time of Enlightenment

7 The Rise of Nations

8 Democracy and Independence

9 Global Interdependence

The Age of Empires

Setting the Stage

Long ago, China was made up of many kingdoms. The ruler of Qin (pronounced Chin), one of the largest kingdoms, set out to conquer his neighbors. By 221 B.C. he united all of China's kingdoms and took the name of Qin Shi Huangdi, which means the "First Emperor of China." People who lived north of China invaded Shi Huangdi's newly conquered lands because they thought these kingdoms were without leaders. In response, Shi Huangdi sent his leading general and 300,000 troops to drive out the invaders. Shi Huangdi also ordered his army to build a wall to keep out enemies. This was the beginning of the Great Wall of China.

PREVIEW THE ARTICLE

Begin to think about what you will read. Look at the title of the article, the headings (subtitles) within the article, the title of the map, and the caption with the picture. What will you learn about the history of China from the article?

_____

_____

RELATE TO THE TOPIC

This article is about the Great Wall of China. It describes the wall's development during different periods in Chinese history. Imagine Shi Huangdi as the head of a large company. Why do you think emperors and business leaders prefer large kingdoms and companies to smaller ones?

_____

_____

VOCABULARY

empire   civilization   barbarian

peasants   dynasty

The Great Wall of China

The Great Wall of China runs from the western city of Jiayuguan to the Yellow Sea. Between these points, the wall zigzags across 2,150 miles. It is so long that astronauts can make radar images of the wall from space. Building this marvel took 1,800 years and millions of laborers.

Beginning the Great Wall

As early as 500 B.C., local Chinese rulers had walls erected to mark their borders and to keep out invaders. This piecemeal wall building went on for about 300 years. Then Shi Huangdi established his empire. An **empire** is a group of countries or territories governed by one ruler. These early Chinese kingdoms were independent states. But their people shared similar ways and values, such as love for learning. In other words, they had a common **civilization.**

Huns and other groups who wandered Mongolia—the land north of China—followed a different way of life. They valued strength in battle and skill with horses. The Chinese considered them barbarians. A **barbarian** is someone whom others regard as inferior and ignorant.

Shi Huangdi decided to keep barbarians out of China and to mark his empire's northern border with a great wall. He had his army and half a million **peasants**—poor, uneducated farmers—create this wall from the many earlier walls. Most of the early walls were crude structures, so the workers rebuilt them as well as building the connecting sections. The wall followed the land. It snaked along rivers rather than across them and up hills rather than around them. By the end of Shi Huangdi's fifteen-year rule, about 1,200 miles of wall had been completed.

The Great Wall of China

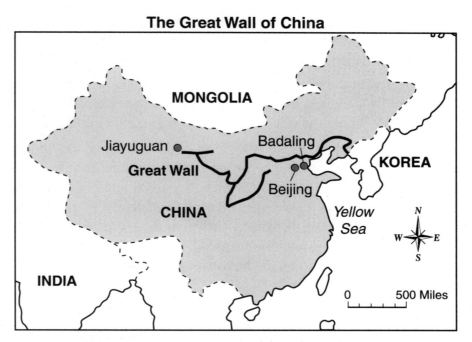

Source: Hawkes, Nigel, *Structures: The Way Things Are Built,* Macmillan. New York, 1993, p. 128.

Shi Huangdi's workers put up a closed, wooden framework along the planned route of the wall. Then they packed the space inside the frame with three to four inches of dirt. They pounded each layer of dirt before adding the next layer. Eventually the wall rose more than twenty feet.

Shi Huangdi's wall was only the beginning. In A.D. 446 another emperor drafted 300,000 people to work on the wall. About one hundred years later, another emperor forced 1.8 million peasants to continue building the wall. The last work on the Great Wall for several centuries was finished by A.D. 618 under the Sui dynasty. A **dynasty** is a ruling family whose members govern over a long time.

Mongol Rule in China

After the Sui dynasty, the Tang and the next dynasties built up the army rather than the Great Wall. Meanwhile, the tribes of Mongolia united under Genghis Khan and conquered lands from Korea to Russia and into India. In 1279 Mongols led by Kublai Khan, the grandson of Genghis, crossed the crumbling wall. They defeated the Chinese army and added China to their empire.

Kublai Khan established the Yuan dynasty, which ruled China for about one hundred years. The Mongols put themselves and foreigners, such as Italian Marco Polo, into high positions. The Chinese resented the way their Mongol rulers tolerated people who did not follow age-old Chinese beliefs.

In the mid 1300s, famine and flooding in China sparked uprisings. A peasant leader and his followers drove the Mongols out and founded the Ming dynasty. To keep the Mongols out, Ming rulers chose to rebuild the wall rather than the army.

Revisiting the Ming Dynasty

Much of the Great Wall that remains today dates back to the Ming dynasty. To build new sections of wall, workers laid foundations of stone. Other workers set up ovens called kilns to make bricks and tiles and to burn lime for mortar.

With the bricks, workers built facing walls. They filled the space between the walls with dirt, stones, and rubble. Finally bricklayers topped the sections of wall with brick walks. Where the wall rose at steep angles, the workers laid steps.

Comparing and Contrasting   To **compare** ideas is to figure out how they are alike. To **contrast** ideas is to figure out how they are different. Compare and contrast the method that builders used during Shi Huangdi's rule with the one that builders used during the Ming dynasty. Write *s* in the space before the Ming building method that is similar to one used during the Sui dynasty. Write *d* in the space before the Ming building method that differed from those used during the Qin dynasty.

_____   a.   They filled the space between the walls with dirt.

_____   b.   Workers topped the sections of wall with brick walks.

Check your answers on page 233.

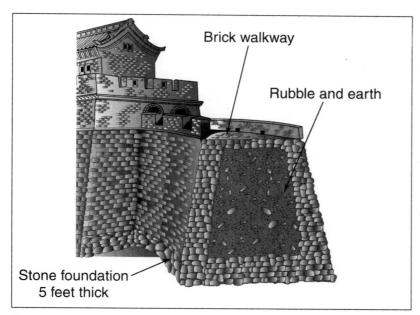

Cross-section of the Great Wall built during the Ming dynasty
Source: Hawkes, Nigel, *Structures: The Way Things Are Built*, Macmillan; New York, 1993, p. 131.

Brick walkway

Rubble and earth

Stone foundation 5 feet thick

The wall served as a pathway as well as a barrier. Every 200 yards the builders erected a stairway on the Chinese side of the wall. Soldiers climbed the stairway to the top of the wall, where they could march ten abreast. In this way, they could rush to any part of the wall under attack.

The builders also included about 25,000 watchtowers in the wall. Each tower housed thirty to fifty soldiers. In peacetime, the soldiers kept the wall repaired and oversaw the traders who entered through the wall's gates. During wartime, the soldiers drove off invaders with cannons atop the towers.

The Great Wall proved a good defense for almost three hundred years. But in 1644, a Chinese traitor opened a gate in the wall to let in Manchu warriors. They were wanderers like the Mongols and came from the land northeast of China. The Manchus defeated the Ming army and set up the Qing (ching) dynasty, which ruled China until 1911.

The best-preserved part of the Great Wall is probably the Badaling section built during the Ming dynasty. From its top, you can still see the mounds where soldiers built fires for sending smoke signals. These signals warned troops miles away of approaching invaders.

Other sections of the wall have not fared as well as Badaling. The government of China has allowed many parts out of tourists' reach to decay. Even so, historians today consider the Great Wall a wonder of the world. It affirms, for all to see, a people's ingenuity.

Applying an Idea to a New Context Ideas, such as the Great Wall of China, are often presented in one particular situation, or **context.** But the early Chinese were only one people who built a wall along their border. Today immigration officials in the United States have suggested putting up a high fence along the Mexican border. Do you think the United States would be building the fence for the same reasons that the early Chinese built the wall? Circle the letter of each reason they seem to share.

    a.   to keep out foreigners

    b.   to mark the border

    c.   to provide a pathway for troops

Check your answers on page 233.

Thinking About the Article

Practice Vocabulary

The terms below are in the passage in bold type. Study the way each term is used. Then complete each sentence by writing the correct term in the blank.

empire   **civilization**   **barbarian**

peasants   **dynasty**

1 Sui emperors considered a Mongol a(n) _____.

2 The emperor of China depended on the _____ for food and labor.

3 The last _____ in China was the Qing.

4 Warriors and riders held honored places in Mongol

_____.

5 In 1279 Kublai Khan made China part of the Mongol

_____.

Understand the Article

Write the answer to each question.

6 Why did Shi Huangdi have the Great Wall built?

_____

_____

7 How did emperors immediately following the Sui dynasty try to stop invaders?

_____

_____

_____

8 Why did the Chinese resent their Mongol rulers?

_____

_____

9 Why do you think sections of the Great Wall that builders repaired during the Ming dynasty are still standing?

_____

_____

Check your answers on page 233.

Apply Your Skills

Circle the number of the best answer for each question.

10 Contrast the Mongols with the Chinese they conquered. How did
they differ?
(1) The Mongols were Christians.
(2) The Mongols relied on the strength of their army.
(3) The Chinese had built a vast empire.
(4) The Mongols resented Europeans.
(5) The Chinese valued learning over physical strength.

11 Compare the following dynasties. Which were the most alike?
(1) Yuan and Ming
(2) Sui and Ming
(3) Tang and Sui
(4) Ming and Tang
(5) Mongol and Yuan

12 The United States government spends much of its defense budget on the
military and counterattack weapons. Which dynasty applied this same
idea for defense in early China?
(1) Qin
(2) Sui
(3) Tang
(4) Mongol
(5) Ming

Connect with the Article

Write your answer to each question.

13 The Great Wall can no longer keep invaders out of China. How do you
think aircraft helped make the wall an ineffective defense in wartime?

_____

_____

_____

14 Do you consider any structures in the United States as awe-inspiring as
the Great Wall of China? Explain your answer.

_____

_____

_____

_____

A Time of Enlightenment

Setting the Stage

The 1700s in Western Europe and North America were an exciting time. Historians call this period the Enlightenment. During the Enlightenment, thoughtful people began questioning the right of their rulers to govern. They also took a fresh look at nature and the arts. The biggest influence on the thinkers of the Enlightenment was modern science. The new scientific method held that knowledge came not from following tradition but from observing and experimenting. One result of all this observation and experimentation was a flood of inventions.

PREVIEW THE ARTICLE

Begin to think about what you will read. Look at the title of the article, the headings (subtitles) within the article, and the timeline. What kinds of inventions will you read about in this article?

_____

_____

RELATE TO THE TOPIC

This article is about inventions from the 1700s. It describes advances made in music, timekeeping, and medicine. List three ways your life might be different without musical instruments, watches, and up-to-date medical care.

_____

_____

_____

VOCABULARY

century   orchestra   chronometer

smallpox   vaccination   immune

       Check your answers on page 234.

The Age of Inventions

The eighteenth **century,** or 1700s, was a fruitful time for inventors. They produced advances in many fields—music, timekeeping, and medicine, to name just a few. The fruit they bore amounted to more than inventions. They made possible richer music, a keener sense of time, and longer lives.

Inventions of the 1700s

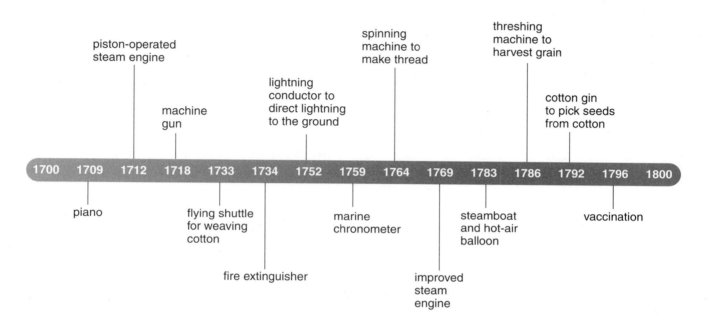

Source: Reid, Struan. *The Usborne Illustrated Handbook of Invention & Discovery.* London: Usborne, 1986, pp. 105–107.

Reinventing Music

Since the early 1400s, musicians had been making do with a keyboard instrument called a harpsichord. When a player pressed one of the keys, a pick inside the harpsichord popped up and plucked a tight metal string. The string vibrated and made a sound. How lightly or firmly the player touched the key made little difference in tone. All sounds that the harpsichord made were equally loud. Any musician who wanted to play softly or build to a loud finish was disappointed.

In 1709 Italian Bartolomeo Cristofori replaced the picks in a harpsichord with hammers. Instead of plucking the strings, the hammers hit them with the same force that the fingers struck the keys. Now players could control how softly or loudly a note sounded. Cristofori named the new instrument "harpsichord with softness and loudness." In Italian the last part was said *piano e forte.* Over the years, English-speaking people shortened the instrument's name to *pianoforte* or *piano.*

The piano was only one of several new or improved instruments that came out in the eighteenth century. Many instruments achieved a greater range of sound. For example, between 1775 and 1780, French violin maker François Tourte developed the modern shape of the violin bow. Rubbing the bow on an instrument's strings makes sound. Tourte's bow allowed the same violin to make powerful or delicate music.

Great eighteenth-century **composers**—Franz Joseph Haydn, Wolfgang Amadeus Mozart, and Ludwig van Beethoven—embraced the variety of sounds. A piece of music they wrote might require pianos, violins, drums, and flutes. To play this kind of music, the orchestra emerged.

Once, the word *orchestra* meant only "the space in front of a stage." During the early 1700s, **orchestra** also came to mean "a group of musicians performing music together." By the mid 1700s, the modern orchestra's four sections—woodwinds, brass, percussion, and strings—were already in place. Music had blossomed into a rich and complex art.

Reading a Timeline   A **timeline** shows when a series of events took place. It also shows the order in which these events happened. It can be used to find the amount of time between events. Look at the timeline on page 55. Then match each pair of inventions below with the correct number of years that passed between the appearance of the first invention and the second one.

_____ piano/piston-operated steam engine   a.   fourteen years

_____ machine gun/fire extinguisher   b.   three years

_____ flying shuttle/spinning machine   c.   six years

_____ threshing machine/cotton gin   d.   sixteen years

_____ improved steam engine/steamboat   e.   thirty-one years

Taking Clocks to Sea

In early times, ships sometimes lost their way going long distances at sea. During the 1700s, however, the oceans became the main channels of trade. By 1700 a **navigator**—the person who charts the position and course of a ship—already knew how to figure out latitude. He also knew that the earth turned 15 degrees of longitude each hour. But the only way he could figure out a ship's longitude was by observing the moon. Often a navigator lacked the skill or the clear weather to determine how far east or west the ship was.

But if a navigator had a **chronometer,** or very accurate clock, he could easily find the ship's longitude. How? The clock would be set at London time. When the sun shone directly overhead, the time aboard ship was noon. If the clock said that the time in London was 2:00 P.M., then the navigator would know that the ship was 30 degrees west of London.

In 1700 most clocks were run with pendulums. A **pendulum** is a weight that swings back and forth at regular intervals, ticking away the minutes. On a rolling ship, a pendulum clock could not stay accurate because movement would disturb its regularity. A mistake of one minute would mean being 450 miles off course.

The British government offered a prize for the invention of a seagoing chronometer. English carpenter John Harrison wanted the prize. He observed clocks in which springs did the work of pendulums. In clocks that Harrison made, he added a second spring that kept the first spring moving. In 1762, after 34 years of experimenting, Harrison had a small clock that kept accurate time despite heat, cold, or the motion of a ship on a 156-day voyage. He won the prize. His chronometer also gave the world a model for portable and accurate clocks that people called *watches*. Now people could carry the time and always be aware of it.

Preventing Disease

At one time, people feared **smallpox** more than the black plague or yellow fever. Smallpox spread by way of sneezes, coughs, or items handled by someone with the disease. Smallpox symptoms included a rash that filled with pus. Four out of ten people who came down with the disease died. Those who survived had deep pits in their skin where the rash had been. Some survivors were left blind.

English doctor Edward Jenner observed many milkmaids—women who milked cows for a living—with cowpox. This was a mild form of smallpox passed from cows to humans. Jenner noted that milkmaids who had had cowpox never caught smallpox.

In 1796 Jenner tried an experiment. He injected the pus from a cowpox sore into a healthy boy, who then developed cowpox. Afterward Jenner injected the same boy with pus from a smallpox sore. The disease failed to develop.

Jenner had invented the first practical smallpox **vaccination,** which got its name from the *vaccinia* virus that produces cowpox. He encouraged other doctors to vaccinate against smallpox. The practice became widespread.

In 1979 the World Health Organization declared smallpox a disease of the past. Meanwhile researchers had developed vaccines for other diseases, such as measles, mumps, and polio. So vaccination came to mean "injecting a substance that would make a person **immune,** or safe, from a disease that spreads."

Summarizing   When you **summarize** something, you reduce a large amount of information to a few sentences. These sentences restate only the major points of the information. For example, the sentence that defines vaccination in the last paragraph summarizes Jenner's process. Reread the information under "Preventing Disease." Then summarize it by completing the sentences below.

a.   Dr. Edward Jenner observed that _____

b.   He experimented by _____

c.   The results of the experiment were _____

Thinking About the Article

Practice Vocabulary

The terms below are in the passage in bold type. Study the way each term is used. Then complete each sentence by writing the correct term in the blank.

century	orchestra	chronometer
smallpox	vaccination	immune

1 One of the worst diseases of the 1700s was _____ .

2 Violins and French horns are instruments in a(n)

_____ .

3 A(n) _____ helps prevent disease, not cure it.

4 A navigator uses a(n) _____ to figure out the exact position of a ship at sea.

5 A vaccine for polio was developed in the twentieth

_____ .

6 Jenner injected a boy with the cowpox virus to make him

_____ from a worse disease.

Understand the Article

Write the answer to each question.

7 How do a harpsichord and piano differ?

_____

8 Why was a pendulum clock useless at sea?

_____

_____

9 Why were watches not practical until John Harrison invented his chronometer?

_____

_____

10 How did Edward Jenner get the idea he could prevent smallpox?

_____

_____

                                   Check your answers on page 234.

Apply Your Skills

Circle the number of the best answer for each question.

11 You have read that accurate watches were developed from the chronometer. What other inventions on the timeline on page 55 were probably linked in a similar way?

(1) fire extinguisher and lightning conductor

(2) steam engine and steamboat

(3) machine gun and threshing machine

(4) spinning machine and cotton gin

(5) steamboat and hot-air balloon

12 What time span does the timeline on page 55 cover?

(1) the 17th century

(2) 15 years

(3) 10 years

(4) 100 years

(5) from 1700 to the present

13 Which of the following sentences best summarizes the last paragraph under "Taking Clocks to Sea"?

(1) John Harrison's chronometer kept accurate time during a 156-day voyage.

(2) Harrison adapted and improved a spring-driven clock.

(3) Harrison's clock was simply a pendulum clock without a pendulum.

(4) To win a prize, John Harrison spent thirty-four years inventing a seagoing chronometer.

(5) All clocks were pendulum-driven until Harrison's chronometer.

Connect with the Article

Write your answer to each question.

14 Think of a musical instrument you play or like to hear. How is sound produced?

_____

_____

15 Name two diseases today for which you would like researchers to find a vaccine and governments to require widespread vaccinations. Explain why you chose these diseases.

_____

_____

_____

The Rise of Nations

Setting the Stage

In 1521 the land that is now Mexico became a part of Spain's large empire in the Americas. Mexico stayed under Spain's rule for 300 years, until a revolution gained it independence in 1821. Then one leader after another used force to gain control of the young nation's government. Mexico's unstable politics kept its economy undeveloped. Meanwhile other countries were using new inventions to industrialize. Fifty-five years after independence, Porfirio Díaz took control of Mexico. He modernized its economy on the eve of the twentieth century.

PREVIEW THE ARTICLE

Begin to think about what you will read. Look at the title of the article, the headings (subtitles) within the article, and the titles of the table and graphs. What can you expect to learn about from this article?

_____

_____

RELATE TO THE TOPIC

This article is about how Porfirio Díaz modernized Mexico's economy between 1876 and 1911. His improvements, however, came at a high price for most Mexicans. Recall a situation when someone in authority told you what to do "for your own good." List the feelings you had about the order and about the person who gave it.

_____

_____

VOCABULARY

conservatives	**liberals**	**diplomat**
democracy	**duties**	**capital**

Check your answers on page 234.

Modernizing Mexico

After Mexico became independent, different groups fought for control of the government. In its first fifty-five years, Mexico had seventy-five leaders. These leaders were either conservatives or liberals. **Conservatives** wanted little change. They were wealthy landowners whose ancestors came from Spain. They wanted a government with a strong army to enforce laws. Most Mexicans, however, were of Indian or mixed ancestry. Many were poor farmers. They wanted a government that cared about them. They were called **liberals.**

A Backward Nation

Porfirio Díaz was part Indian and part Spanish. He had fought with the liberals in a civil war against the conservatives. Many Mexicans considered Díaz a hero and thought he should lead Mexico. After liberal President Benito Juárez died, Díaz and his soldiers drove out the president who followed Juárez.

Díaz took over the Mexican government in 1876. At the time, Mexico's economy was in shambles. One reason was that Mexico had spent more money on the goods it bought than it received for the goods it sold. Also, wealthy Mexicans and foreign investors would not risk their money in a nation without leadership. So Mexico had little of the advanced technology seen elsewhere in the world.

Díaz realized that Mexico had a low standing among nations. Few diplomats lived there. A **diplomat** is a person whom a nation's leader chooses to handle relations with another nation. Díaz invited diplomats from the United States, Europe, and Asia to Mexico. He wanted to show them that Mexico had a firm leader in charge. Perhaps then their countries would invest in Mexico's economy.

Identifying Faulty Logic   A statement with faulty logic may seem reasonable at first. However, when you think about it, the statement makes little sense. Often such statements contain a hasty generalization. A **hasty generalization** is based on little or no evidence. Words such as *all, none, never,* and *always* may signal hasty generalizations. Review the article above. Then select the statement with faulty logic from the following sentences.

  a.   After independence Mexicans spent all their time on politics and none on their economy.

  b.   Liberal Mexicans outnumbered conservatives, so the liberals sometimes took control of the government from the wealthy.

Díaz Modernizes

Díaz's motto was "Order, Then Progress." His advisors told him to improve the economy first and to put democracy on hold. **Democracy** is a system of government that gives the people the power to make choices.

Díaz sent soldiers to all parts of the country. He added more *rurales* (rural police) to rid the countryside of bandits. He had the police shoot criminals who tried to escape. Mexico also needed the money from **duties,** or taxes collected on goods entering the nation. But smugglers paid no duties. If caught, they suffered heavy penalties.

Next Díaz worked on progress. Land belonging to Indians was put up for sale. When some Indian peoples protested, Díaz's troops enslaved them and made them work for wealthy landowners.

Investors began spending on Mexico's economy. Foreign **capital**—money spent for production or investment—was put to good use. It bought modern equipment for textile, paper, and steel mills. It also paid for developing Mexico's natural resources. An American investor bought land and explored for oil. As a result, Mexico became one of the world's largest oil suppliers by the early 1900s.

Figures below show the growth in Mexico's gross national product. The **gross national product** is the total value of everything a nation produces. A country's gross national product indicates the growth and health of its economy.

MEXICO'S ECONOMIC GROWTH INDICATORS

Gross National Product*							
Year	Mining	Agriculture	Manufacturing	Oil	Transportation	Other Activities	Total
1895	431	2,107	806	none	204	5,315	8,863
1900	541	1,991	1,232	none	237	5,890	9,891
1905	848	2,543	1,475	1	299	7,294	12,460
1910	1,022	2,692	1,663	19	295	7,833	13,524

in millions of pesos at 1950 prices

Foreign Capital in Mining and Industry 1896–1907

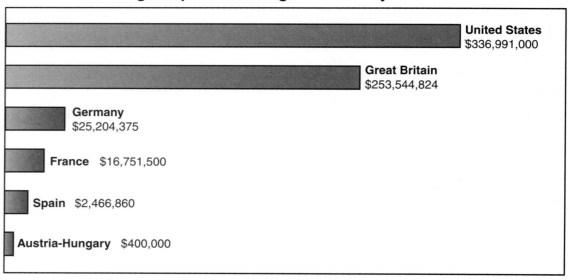

United States $336,991,000

Great Britain $253,544,824

Germany $25,204,375

France $16,751,500

Spain $2,466,860

Austria-Hungary $400,000

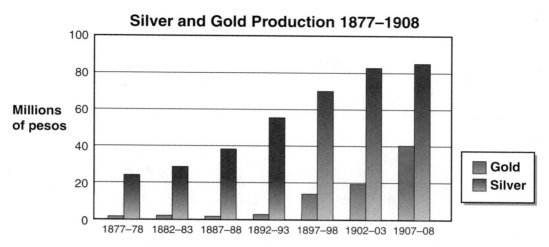

Silver and Gold Production 1877–1908

Millions of pesos

Gold
Silver

1877–78 1882–83 1887–88 1892–93 1897–98 1902–03 1907–08

Source: Meyer & Sherman, *Course of Mexican History* © 1995 Oxford University Press.

Drawing Conclusions from Tables and Graphs To draw a **conclusion**, you must identify what facts are important. Then you decide what they tell you about the topic. One way of presenting facts is a **graph**, a special kind of drawing that is used to compare information. A **table** is a kind of list with information organized in columns and rows. Look at the table and graphs on pages 62 and 63. They show facts about Mexico's economic growth under Díaz's leadership. Based on the facts in the table and graphs, which of the following conclusions can you draw?

a.   The value of agricultural products outstripped the value of mining products because of foreign investments.

b.   Foreign capital and modern equipment helped Mexico uncover its gold and silver.

The Toll on Mexicans

Mexico's economic boom did not help most Mexicans. They worked at difficult and dangerous jobs. Factories stayed open fifteen hours a day. Workers, including children, worked the entire time with only two short breaks for meals. Mines were very unsafe. One reported 500 deaths in five years.

Díaz made sure that workers had little power. He made **strikes** illegal. In some industrial towns, joining a **union** was a crime. Without labor unions, workers had no protection against their bosses' abuse.

Mexico's population went from 8.7 million in 1876 to more than 15 million in 1911. With such growth, proper housing was a major problem. Many people lived in rundown shacks. Several families often lived together in very small quarters. These conditions led to increased illnesses and deaths. Between 1895 and 1911, more people died in Mexico City alone than in the entire United States.

By 1910 Díaz had achieved his peaceful and united nation, but Mexicans were far from happy. Most had longed for democracy. Instead they experienced violence and growing poverty. The Mexican people would have to face another revolution before they achieved democracy.

Check your answer on page 234.

Thinking About the Article

Practice Vocabulary

The terms below are in the passage in bold type. Study the way each term is used. Then complete each sentence by writing the correct term in the blank.

conservatives	**liberals**	**diplomat**
democracy	**duties**	**capital**

1 The _____ invested in Mexico by business people from other countries helped Porfirio Díaz modernize Mexico.

2 The majority of Mexicans were _____ who wanted a democratic government.

3 _____ collected on goods at the American border helped Mexico build up its treasury.

4 Wealthy Mexicans who wanted the strong protection of the military behind the government were called _____.

5 A _____ from Japan was one of the first from Asia to visit Mexico.

6 Mexicans would go through a second revolution before they achieved _____.

Understand the Article

Write the answer to each question.

7 How did Porfirio Díaz create order in Mexico?

_____

_____

_____

8 Why did Díaz invite diplomats to Mexico?

_____

_____

_____

9 Why did so many people die in Mexico City between 1895 and 1910?

_____

_____

Apply Your Skills

Circle the number of the best answer for each question.

10 Which statement about Mexico under Díaz is a hasty generalization?
  (1) Soldiers tried to collect duties on imports at the borders.
  (2) Capital from industrial countries was used to boost industry.
  (3) Díaz kept order by increasing the number of police.
  (4) All foreign diplomats to Mexico approved of its government.
  (5) Díaz decided to delay democracy.

11 Look at the table on page 62. Which of the following conclusions is supported by the economic facts?
  (1) Mining production decreased during Díaz's presidency.
  (2) Manufacturing doubled while Díaz was in office.
  (3) The gross national product tripled under Díaz's leadership.
  (4) Mexico had a growing oil industry in the 1800s.
  (5) Agricultural production remained the same between 1895 and 1910.

12 Based on the graph from page 62, which conclusion can you draw about investors in Mexico?
  (1) Americans invested more money than the combined investment from Europeans.
  (2) Germany invested more in Mexico than any other European country.
  (3) Spain invested the least money of all the countries shown.
  (4) Great Britain's investment equaled the combined money from Germany, France, Spain, and Austria-Hungary.
  (5) Foreigners invested more than one billion pesos in Mexico between 1896 and 1907.

Connect with the Article

Write your answer to each question.

13 Another popular slogan during Díaz's time in office was *pan e palo*, or "bread and the stick." What do you think this slogan meant to Mexican workers?

_____

_____

14 Would you give up your rights and freedom for a well-paying job? Explain why or why not.

_____

_____

Democracy and Independence

Setting the Stage

Black South Africans will long remember 1994. That year they voted for their leaders for the first time. For decades, laws had stripped them of any political rights and freedoms and separated them from white South Africans. But years of oppression and protest were over. Now blacks and whites needed to work together to build harmony in their new government.

PREVIEW THE ARTICLE

Begin to think about what you will read. Look at the title of the article, the headings (subtitles) within the article, and the political cartoon. Based on these clues, what do you think were the sources of conflict in South Africa's past?

_____

_____

RELATE TO THE TOPIC

This article is about South Africa's long-standing policy of separating whites and blacks. Hatred between groups exists in many parts of the world. In recent years in the United States, some states have passed laws that give stiffer punishments to criminals guilty of hate crimes. Do you think our court system should handle these types of crimes differently from other crimes? Explain your answer.

_____

_____

_____

VOCABULARY

republic	**suffrage**	**civil rights**	**parliament**
apartheid	**racist**	**sanctions**	

          Check your answers on page 235.

Against Apartheid

For nearly six hundred years, native black Africans and descendants of white Europeans have lived in South Africa. During most of this time, the whites ruled and mistreated the blacks. However, in the 1990s, black South Africans gained political power in their homeland.

The Fight over Land

Thousands of years ago, hunters and food-gatherers called the San made what is now South Africa their home. Their descendants, the Khoikhoi (KOY koy), raised sheep, goats, and cattle. Other black African groups who spoke the Bantu language migrated from the north to the area. They farmed the fertile soil and developed tools that helped improve their harvests. They fashioned some tools from iron.

In the 1400s and 1500s, Europeans searched for trade routes to Asia. One route went around the Cape of Good Hope at the southern tip of Africa. Portuguese sailors stopped on their way to Asia. They traded goods with the Khoikhoi. Later Dutch traders built a **colony** at the cape where sailors could rest on their long voyages. These Dutch were the first Europeans to settle in southern Africa.

During the 1600s, the mountains and rich valleys on the Cape of Good Hope attracted settlers from other European countries. All the Europeans called themselves Boers, the Dutch word for "farmers." The Boers stole Khoikhoi land and livestock to start farms of their own.

At first, the black Africans viewed the Europeans as mere visitors. The black Africans welcomed the trade, especially when they received iron in return for animal hides. But when they saw the Europeans planned to stay, some Khoikhoi rebelled. In 1659 they attacked the Boers, hoping to gain back herds they had lost. The attempt failed.

The Khoikhoi could not win against the Boers' firearms. In 1713 smallpox, a disease brought from Europe, killed many Boers and nearly all the Khoikhoi. The population decline brought a decline in the Khoikhoi's way of life and culture. Many Khoikhoi became servants of the Boers.

Recognizing Values   A people's culture influences the values that they hold. **Values** are what people feel are important, right, and good. People may indicate their values by what they say. Yet people's actions often reveal more about their values than words do. Reread the third and fourth paragraphs under "The Fight Over Land." Then match each beginning and ending below to form statements about the values of the European settlers and the native Africans.

❶ The Boers stole from the Khoikhoi because _____

❷ The black Africans welcomed European trade because _____
    a.   they valued land.
    b.   they valued iron for tools.

The White Minority and the Black Majority

European domination of South Africa only began with the Boers. During the 1800s, the British built an empire in Africa. They saw the riches of South Africa much as the Boers had. The Boers, however, refused to share the land that they considered theirs. By 1854 they had carved out two republics, the Transvaal and the Orange Free State. A **republic** is a self-governing territory. The British started colonies in a place called Natal and on the Cape of Good Hope.

British rule angered the Boers who lived on the cape. Some decided to leave. As Boer settlers moved north and east from the cape, they met Bantu-speaking groups, such as the Xhosa (KOH suh), Sotho, and Zulu. The Boers captured black Africans and enslaved them. The European Africans believed that owning slaves was their right even though blacks outnumbered the whites.

Discoveries of gold and diamonds in present-day South Africa led to war between the British and the Boers. The British eventually won the Boer War, which lasted from 1899 to 1902. As a result, the Boer republics became British colonies. In exchange, the British guaranteed positions of power to the white residents, who now called themselves *Afrikaners*. The British also refused to grant the black majority **suffrage,** or the right to vote.

In 1910 the four South African provinces united under one constitution. Black Africans still could not vote. So they organized a political group devoted to gaining their civil rights. **Civil rights** are peoples' freedoms, including the right to be treated equally with other people. This political group would later be known as the African National Congress (ANC).

Soon after the union, the South African **parliament,** or law-making body, passed laws that caused hardships for black Africans. For example, a law in 1911 reserved high-paying jobs for whites. The law forced even skilled blacks into the lowest-paying jobs. A 1913 land act set aside just ten percent of the country's land for blacks—although blacks made up nearly eighty percent of South Africa's population.

In 1948 the white government passed a formal policy that separated whites from blacks. Called **apartheid,** which means "apartness," the policy described who was "black," who was "white," and who was "colored"—a person of mixed race. Blacks and coloreds had to carry cards showing their race. In the 1950s, black Africans also had to carry small books with their fingerprints, racial background, and other details of their lives. Police demanded to see this book whenever a black African was in a city or in a whites-only area. If the person was not carrying the book, the police could put him or her in jail.

Apartheid caused much pain among black South African families. Most were very poor. Families broke apart when fathers went to jail. The government-run schools paid low salaries to the poorly trained teachers of black students. Officials decided what was taught, and they discouraged important subjects, such as mathematics. When the ANC decided to start its own schools, the government outlawed private schools.

The Long Road to Democracy

The ANC knew it needed to take stronger action against apartheid policies. They joined with other groups to encourage protest among black Africans. During the early 1950s, the police arrested nearly nine thousand blacks for purposefully disobeying apartheid laws. By the 1960s, the ANC promoted even stronger opposition. New young leaders, such as Nelson Mandela, spoke of a government with equality for all Africans. ANC members also began training for an armed uprising. In 1962, when word of ANC plans reached the government, it arrested Mandela and seventeen other leaders.

Other nations became keenly aware that South Africa's government was **racist,** or favored one race over another. News stories began to cover the protests and riots between the police and black South Africans. The Olympic organizers even banned South Africa from the 1968 and 1972 games. In 1976 thousands of black children in Soweto, near Johannesburg, marched to protest their poor schooling. As they sang freedom songs, police used tear gas. When the children threw rocks, the police opened fire and killed 176 people. To show disapproval of South African policies, many nations started sanctions. **Sanctions** are economic or military measures that nations use to pressure another nation to stop violating some international law or human right.

During the 1980s, white South Africans began to feel the pressure from their own anti-apartheid political parties and the world community. Global economic sanctions had harmed the South African economy. Cries to release Nelson Mandela, who had been in prison for more than twenty years, grew louder. So the government freed Mandela in 1990, and the ANC dropped its plans for an armed uprising. The white government dropped its apartheid policy and began to work toward equal rights for blacks and coloreds.

However, distrust between whites and blacks made peace difficult. Violence continued as some groups refused to cooperate with their enemies. In April 1994, 22 million South Africans went to the polls. Seventeen million were blacks who were voting for the first time. They elected Mandela to be president of a government that would give power to all South Africans, regardless of color.

Reading a Political Cartoon   A **political cartoon** expresses an opinion on an issue. The artist uses symbols and exaggerated drawings to express his or her views. Labels often provide important clues to what the cartoonist is trying to say. Study the cartoon above. What does the boat represent?

    a.   the government of South Africa

    b.   peace between the people of South Africa

Thinking About the Article

Practice Vocabulary

The terms below are in the passage in bold type. Study the way each term is used. Then complete each sentence by writing the correct term in the blank.

republic   suffrage   civil rights   parliament

apartheid   racist   sanctions

1 The South African _____ began making anti-black laws in the early 1900s.

2 In 1948 the government's abuse of black South Africans' rights became a policy called _____.

3 Black South Africans wanted the same _____ that white South Africans had.

4 _____ practices in South Africa date back to the Boers who enslaved the black Africans they defeated in battle.

5 South Africa was a colony in the British empire, but in 1961 the colony became a(n) _____.

6 One way a government shows its disapproval of another government's actions is through _____.

7 Black South Africans practiced their newly won _____ in 1994 when they voted for Nelson Mandela to lead their government.

Understand the Article

Write the answer to each question.

8 Why did the Boers resist British control in South Africa?

_____

9 List three ways that apartheid violated the basic freedoms of black South Africans.

_____

_____

10 How did the African National Congress try to fight apartheid?

_____

Check your answers on page 235.

Apply Your Skills

Circle the number of the best answer for each question.

11 Which of the following actions of the ANC is evidence that they value learning?
 (1) They planned to fight the government, if necessary.
 (2) They devoted time to working for civil rights.
 (3) They joined other groups to encourage resistance among black Africans.
 (4) They sent their leaders to universities in Europe.
 (5) They tried to open nongovernment schools for black children.

12 Look again at the cartoon on page 69. What is the cartoonist trying to show about the men who refuse to bail out their boat?
 (1) They are lazy.
 (2) They are proud.
 (3) They are afraid.
 (4) They are sleepy.
 (5) They don't care.

13 In the cartoon, what is used to symbolize problems that were destroying peace in South Africa?
 (1) the buckets
 (2) the boat
 (3) the water
 (4) white clothing
 (5) black clothing

Connect with the Article

Write your answer to each question.

14 Why did sanctions against South Africa discourage apartheid?

_____

_____

15 Nelson Mandela became the leader of South Africa after the 1994 election. If you had been elected president of South Africa instead of Mandela, what would your first actions as the head of its government have been?

_____

_____

_____

_____

Global Interdependence

Setting the Stage

The year was 1944, and World War II was still raging. Even so, Great Britain, the United States, and China were looking ahead to peacetime. Their delegates met at Dumbarton Oaks, a mansion in Washington, D.C. They drew up a plan for a world organization called the United Nations. Its purpose was to stand up to national leaders who bullied their neighbors, or even their own people, as Germany and Japan had done at the start of the war.

PREVIEW THE ARTICLE

Begin to think about what you will read. Look at the title of the article, the headings (subtitles) within the article, and the caption under the photo. What are some areas of the world that have faced conflicts since World War II?

_____

_____

_____

RELATE TO THE TOPIC

This article is about United Nations peacekeeping forces. It describes who they are and what they do in the trouble spots they protect. Recall a recent newspaper or television report about fighting in some far-off region of the world. Where was the fighting, and what was it about?

_____

_____

_____

VOCABULARY

charter	**neutral**	**cease-fire**	**mediators**
deadlocked	**provinces**	**civilians**	

    Check your answers on page 235.

UN Peacekeeping Forces

By the end of World War II, most leaders had realized that they needed the combined strength of several nations to stand up to powerful enemies. So in 1945, fifty countries joined the United Nations (UN). Their representatives approved its **charter,** or plan, at a meeting in San Francisco.

The UN Charter created a Security Council. The Security Council is responsible for maintaining peace in the world. The United States, Great Britain, Russia, China, and France are permanent members of the Security Council. The General Assembly—delegates from the 185 countries who now belong to the United Nations—elects ten temporary members.

Peacekeepers to the Rescue

The members of the Security Council decide how to handle trouble-making governments, warring countries, or warring groups within a country. The council's actions can range from public scolding to sending troops. Troops under UN command are known as peacekeeping forces. The secretary-general, the chief officer of the UN, appoints their commander.

Peacekeeper forces must be **neutral.** In other words, they cannot take sides. So the soldiers come from countries that are not directly involved with the conflict at hand. The soldiers fall into two groups—observers and peacekeepers.

The observers are unarmed officers who visit an area in small numbers simply to watch. Then they report back to the UN. They wear blue helmets or berets. The jeeps and other vehicles that accompany them are white marked with large, black *UN*s. Observers monitor situations such as an election or a **cease-fire**—a pause in fighting. For example, in the 1990s the UN sent observers to Nicaragua in Central America to witness the change from civil war to a democratic government.

Refugees are leaving the capital of Rwanda.

Lightly armed soldiers do the actual peacekeeping. They often do not have tanks and heavy weapons. They sometimes do their job by coming between warring parties. Either side must first attack UN soldiers to get to its enemy. The UN soldiers also act as **mediators,** or go-betweens, to settle disagreements between enemies. Both kinds of peacekeeping are often necessary to maintain a cease-fire.

Understanding a Photo   Pictures often contain as much information as words do. Look at the photo on page 73. It shows people fleeing the capital of Rwanda where warring groups were battling for control of the government in 1994. What does this photo suggest about the UN's goals in Rwanda?

   a.   UN troops were hoping to stop the fighting.
   b.   UN troops were trying to help people flee from Rwanda.

Early Missions in the Middle East and Africa

On several occasions, UN troops have stepped in to make peace in the Middle East. One of the earliest instances was the Suez Crisis in 1956. The United States and Great Britain had offered to help pay for the Aswan High Dam project in Egypt. But Egypt's President Gamal Nasser also asked the Soviet Union for money. The Americans and British distrusted the Soviet Union and withdrew their offer. On July 26, 1956, an angry President Nasser responded by claiming that the Egyptian government owned the Suez Canal.

The Suez Canal was an important shipping lane. Until Egypt seized the canal, a company half-owned by the British ran it. So with the help of its **allies,** France and Israel, Britain tried to retake the canal by force. Israel attacked Egypt from the air on October 29, and British and French troops landed on its Mediterranean shore on November 5.

President Nasser requested help from the UN. Members of the Security Council were **deadlocked**—unable to agree on what to do. So the General Assembly voted to send troops. A cease-fire took effect on November 6, and Great Britain, France, and Israel withdrew from Egypt. Six thousand UN troops guarded the borders after the withdrawal.

On this mission, none of the troops were from Great Britain, France, the United States, or the Soviet Union. For the first time, an international police force took action without a major power involved. Since then, United Nations peacekeepers have gone several more times to the Middle East. To this day, UN observers continue to monitor borders there.

In the 1960s, the Congo crisis brought UN peacekeepers to Africa. The Congo declared independence from Belgian rule in 1960 and renamed itself Zaire. But the new central government could not control the far-flung parts of the country. Katanga and other **provinces**—regions similar to states in the United States—tried to pull out and establish their own countries.

Check your answer on page 235.

Zaire's Prime Minister Patrice Lumumba requested aid from the UN. In 1962 UN forces arrived to keep order. Despite their presence, Zaire collapsed into **civil war,** and the most that the 20,000 UN soldiers could do was to protect **civilians,** or nonmilitary persons.

In 1988 the United Nations peacekeeping forces received the Nobel peace prize. This award recognized the growing importance of international forces. In the 1990s, the UN definition of "keeping peace" became broader. Some missions, like the one in Somalia, focused on saving a country's people rather than its government.

Saving Somalis

Siad Barre was the ruler of Somalia. For years his harsh treatment of the people had caused revolts. Several groups of rebels came together in the United Somali Congress (USC) and overthrew Siad in 1991.

Groups in the USC then quarreled about who would take Siad's place. Heavy fighting broke out in a major grain-growing region of the country. The fighting drove out the farmers. Harvests had already fallen off because of a drought that began in 1989. As a result of the drought and the fighting, the country had almost no food.

By spring of 1992, civil war had killed about 30,000 Somalis. However, ten times more people had died from hunger. In June about 3,000 people were dying each day.

Agencies from all over the world flew in food. But the warring groups hijacked the food before the Red Cross and similar nongovernmental organizations (NGOs) could distribute it. So the UN Security Council approved a peacekeeping force to help deliver the food. Over six months, American planes flew 28,000 tons of food to Somalia, and 500 UN peacekeepers from Pakistan arrived to protect it. Still the food could not reach central Somalia, where people needed it most.

Relief to the hungry took many more soldiers. On December 12, 1992, thousands of troops from Canada and France began arriving to protect the trucks that would deliver the food. More soldiers spread out to the relief stations where the food would be distributed to the people. American soldiers and sailors began building and improving roads to the stations.

By February 1993, food and other aid was being distributed in all parts of the country. Famine was no longer a danger, and convoys full of supplies were rolling along on new or improved roads. Cooperation among governments, UN agencies, and NGOs had accomplished a truly humane mission.

Getting Meaning from Context   Sometimes you can figure out the meaning of an unfamiliar word from its context, or the sentences around it. Find the word *famine* in the last paragraph and choose the definition that fits the word's context.

    a.   a scarcity of food
    b.   a lack of rainfall

Thinking About the Article

Practice Vocabulary

The terms below are in the passage in bold type. Study the way each term is used. Then complete each sentence by writing the correct term in the blank.

charter	**neutral**	**cease-fire**	**mediator**
deadlocked	**provinces**	**civilians**	

1 The peacekeeping officer acted as a _____ between leaders of Somali groups.

2 The United States was _____ in the Bosnia conflict, and so American troops were included in the UN force sent to Bosnia.

3 The new secretary-general scanned the _____ for a description of his duties.

4 When the Security Council was _____, the General Assembly approved the use of UN troops in Egypt.

5 The rebels in Katanga and other _____ declared a _____ so they could discuss their demands with Zaire's prime minister.

6 In Somalia, the UN tried to help innocent _____.

Understand the Article

Write the answer to each question.

7 How does a UN observer differ from a UN peacekeeper?

_____

_____

_____

8 Why was the Suez Canal important to Great Britain?

_____

_____

_____

9 Why did Somalis have so little food in 1992?

_____

_____

Check your answers on page 236.

Apply Your Skills

Circle the number of the best answer for each question.

10 Look again at the photo on page 73. What might you conclude based on clues in the picture?
   (1) All Rwanda's men were engaged in the fighting.
   (2) More than half the refugees were women and children.
   (3) UN soldiers were indifferent to the refugees' hardships.
   (4) Most Rwandans could afford cars or trucks.
   (5) The UN soldiers in Rwanda were only observers.

11 Find the term *civil war* in the first paragraph on page 75. Then reread the paragraph as well as the paragraph before it. Which of the following meanings best fits *civil war* in the context of the two paragraphs?
   (1) a quarrel among staff members
   (2) war according to international rules
   (3) fighting between people of the same country
   (4) a disagreement about private rights
   (5) violence among people out of uniform

12 Find the word *allies* in the second paragraph under "Early Missions in the Middle East and Africa." Then choose the meaning that best fits *allies* in the context of the paragraph.
   (1) living things with similar traits
   (2) countries that help each other
   (3) assistants to government officials
   (4) mixtures of different things
   (5) narrow streets behind buildings

Connect with the Article

Write your answer to each question.

13 "The UN peacekeeping mission to Zaire was a failure." Do you agree or disagree with this statement? Explain your answer.

_____

_____

14 If you were going to be a mediator in a disagreement between two friends, why would it be important that you remain neutral in the dispute?

_____

_____

_____

_____

History at Work

Service: National Historic Park Guide

Some Careers in Service

Park rangers enforce laws and safety rules and provide assistance to visitors

Site managers supervise staff, organize special activities, and oversee the budget for the maintenance of the site

Visitor assistants tally visitor fees, answer questions, and provide assistance to visitors

Preservation specialists maintain and repair historic buildings and relics, help prepare site exhibits

Guides help guests enjoy their visits to America's historic parks.

Some people enjoy studying and talking about history, sharing information with others, and helping others appreciate our nation's cultural resources. If that describes you, a job in one of the U.S. national historic parks may be just what you are looking for.

Every year, millions of U.S. residents and foreign visitors tour America's 360 national historic parks and sites. Park guides help visitors learn about and enjoy these historic sites and areas. National historic parks such as Ellis Island and the battlefield at Gettysburg have a rich history that guides enjoy sharing with visitors.

Park guides must have a good understanding of the historic events related to their specific park. They are expected to be well read and know interesting facts about the people, times, and places associated with the site.

Guides must have good personal skills. They need to be patient and resourceful in order to answer people's questions. They must also have good public speaking skills since they often need to make presentations to groups.

Look at the *Some Careers in Service* chart.

- Do any of the careers interest you? If so, which ones?
- What information would you need to find out more about those careers? On a separate piece of paper, write some questions that you would like answered. You can find more information about those careers in the *Occupational Outlook Handbook* at your local library.

National park guides need to read information about the history of the park or site in which they work. **Use the excerpt below from an informational brochure about Liberty Island National Park to answer the questions that follow.**

The Statue of Liberty

It now stands as the ultimate symbol of immigration and welcome to the U.S. But in the beginning, "Liberty Enlightening the World," (better known as the Statue of Liberty), was a gift from the French to the people of the United States. This 151-foot-tall gift celebrated the partnership of these two countries in the American Revolution and America's independence from England.

It was presented on October 28, 1886, at Bedloe Island. Thousands of invited guests witnessed the incredible unveiling ceremony of the world's tallest freestanding statue and New York's tallest structure. The statue's artist, Frèdèric-Auguste Bartholdi, was given the honor of releasing the French flag draped across Liberty's 14-foot-long face.

Today the copper-covered Statue of Liberty is no longer the tallest structure in New York. However, it is among the top New York sites visited by Americans and tourists from around the world.

1 "Liberty Enlightening the World" is a(n)
  (1) building.
  (2) statue.
  (3) country.
  (4) island.
  (5) national park.

2 The Statue of Liberty was a gift from which country?
  (1) England
  (2) the United States
  (3) France
  (4) Italy
  (5) Canada

3 List four facts a guide at Liberty Island National Park should be expected to know about the Statue of Liberty.

_____

_____

_____

_____

Russia Struggles with Democracy

Russians have been taking lessons in democracy. Because they have had a long history of rule by one person, they have found the lessons difficult. Before the 1400s, princes ruled different parts of what is now Russia. In the 1400s, Ivan the Great conquered the parts and formed an empire. Only for a few months in 1917, immediately after the Russian Revolution, did rebels set up a government "by the people."

The Communist party, however, quickly took control of Russia and its empire. The Communists formed the Soviet Union, which survived for about 70 years. By 1991, however, peoples in the Soviet Union who were not Russians wanted to rule themselves. Russia also exchanged communist government for a more democratic system in 1991.

With little experience in democracy, Russians had to start at the beginning. First they created words in their language for *democracy, president,* and *constitution.* Then citizens voted for leaders. In the first seven years of the republic, Russians went to the polls five times to vote for a president and parliament, their law-making body.

Yet four years after democracy began, many Russians thought they may have been better off under communism. While their leaders tried to start an American-type economy, many Russians were without jobs or food. Even people who had money could not meet their needs because food and medicine were in short supply. In 1996 more than 75 percent of Russians said that "order" was more important than "democracy."

Still, many Russians have made some gains with democracy. Once their society was made up of the powerful rich and the very poor. Today the rich and poor still exist, but the poor have more freedom of expression and freedom of choice. The Russian people are getting a hands-on course in the ups and downs of democracy.

Circle the number of the best answer.

1 What is the main idea of this article?
   (1) Communists ruled Russia more years than emperors did.
   (2) Russians have had little experience with democracy.
   (3) Russia no longer has groups of rich and poor.
   (4) The new democratic government is struggling.
   (5) The Russian Revolution was unsuccessful.

Check your answer on page 236.

Write the answer to each question.

2 What does the bear represent in the cartoon? What does the pan represent?

_____

_____

3 Why is the pan on fire?

_____

_____

4 What is the main idea the cartoonist communicates in this cartoon?

_____

_____

Circle the number of the best answer.

5 Russians indicated in the 1996 survey that they valued order more than democracy. What values must a society hold to be successful with democracy?
  (1) respect, honesty, courage in battle
  (2) citizenship, loyalty, uniformity of beliefs
  (3) wealth, military power, order at all costs
  (4) authority, law, strength of purpose
  (5) freedom, open-mindedness, give and take

Check your answers on page 236.

The Spanish Empire Tumbles

By 1588 Spain had built the world's largest empire. It included land on nearly every continent. But this was not enough for Spain's King Philip II. He had his eye on England and its Protestant queen, Elizabeth I. Under Elizabeth's rule, English sea pirates had been raiding Spanish ships and stealing the treasures they carried from Spain's colonies. So Philip planned to attack the island nation.

The Spanish king built a magnificent fleet of ships, which the Spanish called an **armada.** Many of its 150 ships were huge, with enough space for mules, horses, food, weapons, and hundreds of soldiers. Each ship bore the name of an apostle or saint. To command the armada, Philip chose a high-ranking nobleman who had no experience at sea. The more than 25,000 soldiers on the armada considered this attack a mission to bring England back into the Catholic Church.

England's navy could not defend the nation by itself. Elizabeth asked the Dutch for help. She also called upon English merchant ships to join the Royal Navy. Nearly 200 ships met the armada, but they were only half the size of the Spanish ships.

In July 1588, fierce storms and rough seas tossed the two fleets in the English Channel. England's small ships were light and fast, and their sailors moved them expertly through the rough waters. After two days of heavy fighting, the English set fire to eight of their ships and sent them, loaded with ammunition, toward the armada.

The Spanish Empire 1588

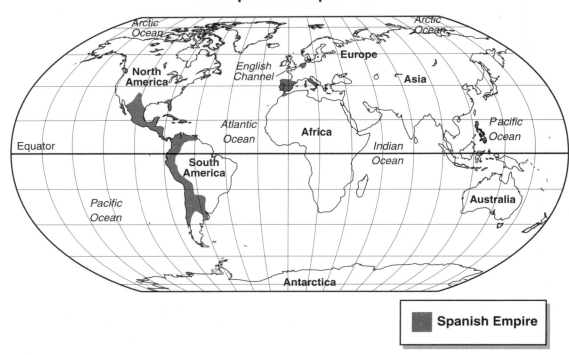

The Spanish ships headed north to dodge the attack, but even more English ships chased them. Wild storms wrecked 17 Spanish ships along Ireland's coast. Only a few hundred Spaniards returned home. England had defeated the grand Spanish armada.

Spain's empire was never the same. Its power seemed to sink with its ships. The next great power in Europe would be England.

Write or circle the answer to each question.

6 Reread the first two paragraphs of the article on page 82. From the context, what does *armada* mean?
(1) naval commander
(2) Spanish empire
(3) raiding sea pirates
(4) fleet of ships
(5) treasure ships

7 Which part of Philip's plan to attack England is the best example of faulty logic?
(1) He told his soldiers they were winning England back into the Catholic Church.
(2) He named an inexperienced nobleman as fleet commander.
(3) He named the ships after apostles and saints.
(4) He brought 25,000 soldiers.
(5) He set fire to his smaller ships.

8 Explain what was faulty about Philip's decision.

_____

_____

_____

Look at the map on page 82. Then read and answer the question.

9 Why do you think so many areas under Spanish control were along coastlines?

_____

_____

_____

Social Studies Extension

Think about a person with whom you often disagree. Choose an issue over which you have disagreed. List points you made in the disagreement, and then list the other person's points. Compare and contrast them. What values do you share? What values are yours alone? What opposite values does the other person hold? What seems to be the reason that you disagree?

Social Studies Connection: World History and Life Sciences

The Impact of Antibiotics

Before World War II, soldiers had to fight an unarmed enemy that was too small to see. These invisible enemies often posed a greater threat to a soldier's life than guns, bombs, or battleships. Soldiers who met these enemies faced disease and almost certain death. These enemies still exist today. We know them as bacteria or germs.

The weapons we use to fight them are called antibiotics. These are powerful tools that changed history forever. Sir Alexander Fleming discovered the first antibiotic, penicillin, in England in 1928. Fleming's interest in the treatment of wounds began when he worked as a medical captain in World War I. There he observed the high death rates that resulted from infections of wounds.

Although Fleming is credited with discovering penicillin, it took ten more years to get the antibiotic into a usable form. Scientists Howard Florey and Ernst Chain created the process that led to the production of penicillin in large quantities.

The need to focus England's resources on World War II caused the transfer of penicillin production from England to the United States. There, the process was perfected and the antibiotic was mass-produced. By the late 1940s, antibiotics were used to treat the general public. The first war in which antibiotics were used on a wide basis was the Korean War (1950–1953).

How do antibiotics work? Different antibiotics work in different ways. Some destroy bacteria by interfering with the bacterial cells' ability to divide. If they can't divide, they can't reproduce. So the infection can't spread. Other antibiotics stop bacteria from making the proteins they need to reproduce. A third type of antibiotics works by preventing protective cell walls from forming on the new bacterial cells. Unfortunately, overuse of antibiotics has created serious problems. New bacteria have appeared that resist the antibiotics that have been developed.

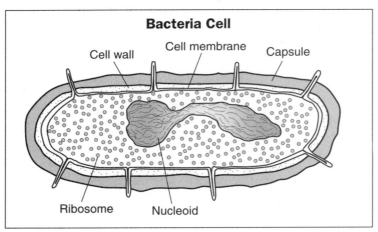

Bacteria Cell

Cell wall Cell membrane Capsule

Ribosome Nucleoid

Some antibiotics prevent cell walls from forming on bacterial cells.

Use the material on the previous page to answer the questions below.

1 Sir Alexander Fleming became interested in treating wounds
    (1) before World War I.
    (2) during World War I.
    (3) during World War II.
    (4) during the Korean War.
    (5) after the Vietnam War.

2 Why was the mass production of antibiotics moved from England to the United States?
    (1) Sir Alexander Fleming discovered penicillin in the United States.
    (2) World War II was not being fought in the United States.
    (3) There was no mass production in England.
    (4) England needed to focus on the war effort.
    (5) The Korean War had started.

3 Describe 3 ways in which antibiotics work.

a. _____
   _____

b. _____
   _____

c. _____
   _____

4 According to the diagram, the outside of a bacterial cell is called the
    (1) cell wall.
    (2) membrane.
    (3) DNA.
    (4) cytoplasm.
    (5) ribosome.

5 Items listed in a particular order is called a sequence. Order the following events in a sequence that moves from <u>the earliest event to the most recent</u>. Use the space in front of the event to number the events from 1 to 5. The first event has been labeled for you.

_____ World War II begins.

___1___ World War I begins.

_____ Fleming discovers penicillin.

_____ Florey and Chain invent the process of mass-producing penicillin.

_____ Mass production of penicillin moves to the U.S.

UNIT 3

American History

As you look at the sections in this unit, you will notice that half of the titles refer to a war. What does this tell you about the history of the United States? One thing it says is that Americans have faced many conflicts in our short history as a nation.

Also, you might already know that one way to look at a nation's history is by reviewing its "biggest" events. Obviously when the U.S. went to war, the nation changed in some very important ways. Yet between wars, Americans continued to make progress in the ways they worked, treated newcomers, and built a free and democratic nation.

◯ What will you look for as signs of progress as you read about our nation's history?

◯ How have the many periods of war changed Americans? How have they changed the nation as a whole?

SECTIONS

⑩ **Establishing Colonies**

⑪ **The American Revolution**

⑫ **The U.S. Civil War**

⑬ **The Reform Movement**

⑭ **World War II**

⑮ **The Cold War and the Vietnam War**

⑯ **Communicating in the New Millennium**

10 Establishing Colonies

Setting the Stage

The first people to come to North America traveled east from Asia long before written history. Some settled in one place, while others traveled farther and farther inland as they hunted and gathered food. They spread all across the continent and to the tip of South America. They became the original Americans, which is why they are called Native Americans. Many thousands of years later, Europeans traveled west across the Atlantic Ocean. Spanish explorers, looking for gold and silver, conquered Native Americans in southern North America. Later, in the 1600s, other Europeans built settlements along North America's eastern coast. The cultures of all these people eventually combined to create the United States of America.

PREVIEW THE ARTICLE

Begin to think about what you will read. Look at the title of the article, the headings (subtitles) within the article, and the map. Write two ideas about what you can expect to learn from this article.

_____

_____

RELATE TO THE TOPIC

This article is about the Americans who lived here first and the ones who came after. Think about your own background. Where did each of your parents' families originally come from? Are early family members from two or more countries? Write a sentence about how your family background has affected your life.

_____

_____

VOCABULARY

immigrants   migrated   pueblos

conquistadors   missions   indentured servants

Check your answers on page 237.

Native and New Americans

The United States is a land of **immigrants.** Immigrants come to a region or country where they were not born in order to live there. Scientists believe that the original Americans came at least 27,000 years ago. They may have walked from Asia to North America across land that today is underwater. Nearly five hundred years ago, Europeans sailed to the eastern shores of what would become the United States of America. Even today immigrants from many parts of the world travel to America.

The Original Americans

Small bands of Asian hunters followed animals across a land bridge where water now separates Siberia and Alaska. These people and their descendants **migrated,** or gradually moved, across the continent from the Pacific Ocean to the Atlantic Ocean and south to South America. Over thousands of years, the hunters changed to fit their environment. They learned to farm and settled in villages. Groups in different areas developed their own crafts, language, and religion.

One group in North America was the Anasazi. From 100 B.C. to about A.D. 1300, these people lived in what is now the southwestern United States. They managed to raise corn, squash, and beans in a very dry climate. They built large apartment-like **pueblos**—buildings made of sandy clay called *adobe*. These buildings are now considered to be the oldest in North America.

By the 1400s, some groups of Native Americans in what are now Mexico and Central America had empires with elaborate cities. The cities had canals, pyramids, temples, and markets. The Aztec people built the great city of Tenochtitlán, which was located where Mexico City stands today. In 1500, this Aztec city had about 300,000 people, which was twice the number of people that lived in London, England, at the time.

In the eastern woodlands of North America, many nations of American Indians shared the region's thick forests and rich soil. Groups often disagreed over farmland and hunting grounds. In what is now New York, Indians from five nations often trespassed on one another's land. Trespassing led to fighting. Tired of war, the nations finally decided to work together. About 1570 they formed the Iroquois League. Each nation governed itself but also chose members to serve on a Great Council. The council made decisions on important matters, such as trade and war.

European Explorers and Traders

The first Europeans to visit North America were sailors from Scandinavia. They reached Newfoundland about A.D. 1000 but did not stay. European exploration and settlement of the Americas did not really begin until Spain sent Christopher Columbus on a voyage in 1492. He was looking for a sea route from Europe to Asia. He wanted to trade for Asian spices. Instead he found the Americas, or what Europeans called the New World.

Europeans soon realized that the New World was full of riches. Spanish **conquistadors** (conquerors), fired by dreams of gold and silver, looted the rich empires of Mexico and South America. At first the Native Americans did not resist because they thought the Spaniards were gods. Later the Native Americans were unable to resist because so many had died from European diseases.

In North America the explorers found little gold. Nevertheless, Roman Catholic priests who came with the Spanish explorers built missions in what is now Mexico, Texas, California, and Florida. A **mission** is a settlement centered around a church. The priests who ran the missions were called missionaries. The Spanish missionaries invited Native Americans into their missions and taught them about Christianity. Many missionaries thought the Native Americans were savages and tried to make them give up their ways.

The English, French, and Dutch also searched for a water route through the Americas to the markets of Asia. In this search, they explored the northern regions of North America. By 1610 France had a profitable fur trade with Native Americans in what is now Canada.

Reading a Historical Map A map can show how different groups moved from one place to another. A map key can indicate when each move took place. Look closely at the map below. How many years before the English did the Spanish establish a settlement in what is now the eastern United States?

a.   42 years   b.   55 years

Some European Voyages to North America

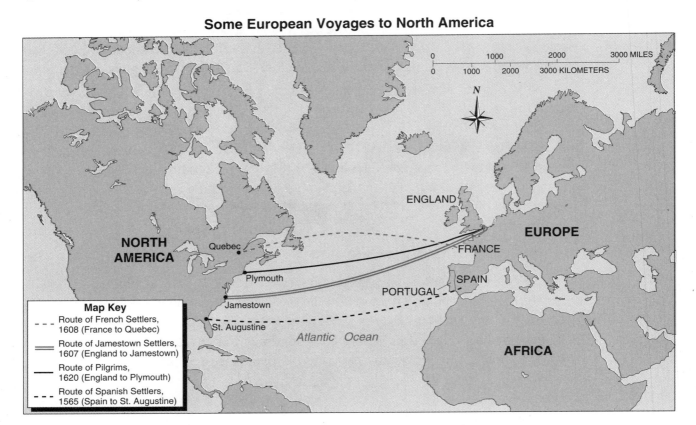

Check your answers on page 237.

New Americans

The English began their settlement of North America in the early 1600s. Their colonies lasted longer and grew larger than many other European settlements. Most English who settled in North America came for religious, political, or economic reasons.

The first long-lasting English settlement in North America was Jamestown, Virginia. Three ships carrying 144 settlers landed there in 1607. That first winter, the settlers faced disease, starvation, and attacks by Native Americans. In time, however, they learned to grow food crops and tobacco.

In 1620 the *Mayflower* set sail from Plymouth, England, with 73 men and boys and 29 women and girls. They were seeking religious freedom from the official Church of England. Their ship landed along the coast of Massachusetts. These settlers, who called themselves Pilgrims, also had a difficult first year. Almost half of them died. But a Native American named Squanto taught the survivors how to plant corn, catch fish, and find their way in the wilderness.

Later a religious group known as Puritans started the Massachusetts Bay Colony. They permitted only followers of their religion to live in their settlements. So some colonists who wanted religious freedom left Massachusetts and set up the colonies of Rhode Island in 1644 and New Hampshire in 1662. Quakers, another religious group, founded Pennsylvania in 1681. They welcomed Spanish Jews, Irish Catholics, and German Lutherans.

As news of these colonies returned to England, more people came to North America looking for land and freedom. Those who had no money to pay their way became **indentured servants.** They promised to work for two to seven years in exchange for their passage to the colonies. Convicted criminals served their sentences in the colonies as indentured servants. Africans were kidnapped and also forced to work in America as indentured servants. By the 1660s, however, colonies were passing laws that made slaves of African-American servants.

Gradually the 13 British colonies developed their own way of life. This strained their ties with England. By the 1770s some colonists were ready for independence.

Sequencing Events   The **sequence** of events is the order in which things happen. This is also called *chronological order.* Specific dates and words like *first, second, next,* and *finally* provide clues to the order of events. Reread the paragraphs under "New Americans." Then number the names of the colonies below in the order that they were established.

_____ Pennsylvania

_____ Massachusetts

_____ Virginia

_____ Rhode Island

Thinking About the Article

Practice Vocabulary

The terms below are in the passage in bold type. Study the way each term is used. Then complete each sentence by writing the correct term.

immigrants	migrated	pueblos
conquistadors	missions	indentured servants

1 The Spanish _____ came to America seeking wealth and adventure.

2 Europeans with little money became _____ to pay their way to America.

3 Scientists believe that over many generations the first Americans slowly _____ across North and South America.

4 Spanish priests invited Native Americans to live and learn at the _____ .

5 The _____ that the Anasazi built in the Southwest were two- and three-story buildings.

6 _____ from many parts of the world have moved to North America for a better life.

Understand the Article

Write the answer to each question.

7 Why did Asians first come to North America?

_____

8 Later settlers came from Spain, France, and Britain. Why did each of these groups come to North America?

_____

_____

9 What difficulties did settlers have in establishing a colony in Jamestown?

_____

_____

10 Why did some Massachusetts colonists found Rhode Island?

_____

_____

Check your answers on page 237.

Apply Your Skills

Circle the number of the best answer for each question.

11 Look at the map on page 90. Based on the map, which of the following statements describes the beginnings of European settlement?
   (1) European settlers moved west across North America over a long period.
   (2) Early English settlements lay north of Spanish settlements.
   (3) French settlers arrived about 40 years before the English.
   (4) The Spanish first landed in Asia on their way to North America.
   (5) The English settled before the Spanish.

12 Review the article, and then select the most recent event below.
   (1) The Anasazi Indians built large apartment-like buildings called pueblos.
   (2) The Aztecs in Mexico built an empire with a great city.
   (3) The first Americans migrated across a land bridge from Asia.
   (4) The English settled at Jamestown, Virginia.
   (5) Sailors from Scandinavia first arrived in Newfoundland.

13 Which of the following colonies was the last to be established?
   (1) Massachusetts
   (2) Virginia
   (3) Pennsylvania
   (4) Rhode Island
   (5) New Hampshire

Connect with the Article

Write your answer to each question.

14 The Pilgrims and Squanto were better neighbors than later colonists and Native Americans. Give two reasons why you think this was the case.

_____

_____

_____

15 At one time or another, members of your family moved to North America. Why do you think they came?

_____

_____

_____

The American Revolution

Setting the Stage

From 1688 to 1763, France, Spain, and Great Britain fought one another for control of Europe and the Americas. In 1763 Great Britain won a seven-year war with the French in North America. Now one of the largest empires in the world, Great Britain was deep in debt. British King George III decided that his colonies must help pay the bill. The colonists disagreed and started down the road to war with Great Britain.

PREVIEW THE ARTICLE

Begin to think about what you will read. Look at the title of the article, the headings (subtitles) within the article, and the timeline. What are two things you expect to learn from the article about the conflict between Great Britain and its colonies?

_____

_____

_____

RELATE TO THE TOPIC

This article is about the conflict between Great Britain and its American colonies. Describe two ways in which this kind of conflict could be similar to conflicts between parents and their teenage children.

_____

_____

VOCABULARY

exports	**legislature**	**boycotted**
repealed	**imports**	**minutemen**

The Fight for Independence

After Great Britain's long war with France, the British Parliament became more involved in its American colonies. The colonists, who had done as they pleased for many years, did not welcome this new interest. Parliament pushed and the colonists pushed back. In time, the disagreements grew more serious. They led to a war known as the American Revolution.

Growing Disagreements

Great Britain faced a huge bill after the war with France. Nearly half the debt was from the fighting in North America. Therefore Parliament decided that Americans should help pay the bill because they shared the benefits from the victory over France. Britain's **prime minister,** or head of the Parliament, realized that enforcing some old trade laws in the colonies might help the Treasury.

The money raised from these laws was still not enough to pay the bill. More taxes would raise money, but people in Great Britain already were paying high taxes. So in 1765 Parliament passed the Stamp Act. Colonists who bought certain items or documents had to buy stamps that proved they had paid the necessary tax. Without the stamp, the item was considered stolen or the document illegal. Marriage licenses, newspapers, diplomas, and playing cards were among the items that needed stamps.

The colonists were angry when they heard about the Stamp Act. In many colonies, mobs forced tax collectors out of town. The colonists knew the principles that British government followed. In Great Britain, people could not be taxed unless they had a representative in Parliament. The colonists did not have any representatives in Parliament. Therefore they believed that Parliament had no right to tax them. They felt that only a colony's **legislature,** or lawmakers, had that right.

Parliament said its members acted in everyone's interest, including that of the colonists. But the colonists did not accept this. They protested, "No taxation without representation." They **boycotted,** or refused to buy, British products. British merchants suffered when colonists refused to buy their **exports.** These were the products made in Great Britain and sold in the colonies. One year later, Parliament **repealed,** or did away with, the Stamp Act. Colonists celebrated with bonfires and parades.

Identifying Cause and Effect   Every event has at least one cause and one effect. The **cause** is *why* something happened. Words like *because, since,* and *reason* signal a cause. The **effect** tells *what happened* as a result of the cause. Words such as *so, therefore,* and *as a result* signal an effect. Reread the first paragraph under "Growing Disagreements." Then circle the letter of the effect of Great Britain's debt.

    a.   Parliament passed new taxes for the colonies.

    b.   Britain fought a seven-year war with France.

The next British prime minister still believed the colonists should be taxed. This time the money raised would help pay the salaries of royal governors and judges in the American colonies. Parliament passed a new law in 1767 that taxed imports to the colonies such as glass, lead, paper, silk, and tea. **Imports** are goods brought into a country from another country. The colonies protested the new taxes, and Great Britain sent troops to the colonies to enforce the law.

British soldiers and American colonists did not get along. On March 5, 1770, in Boston, Massachusetts, about sixty colonists taunted ten British soldiers. Colonists knocked down two soldiers. The squad opened fire on the colonists. The British killed three colonists and wounded eight others. Two of the wounded colonists later died. This clash is called the Boston Massacre.

A Tea Party in Boston

A month after the clash in Boston, Parliament repealed all the taxes except the tea tax. British lawmakers wanted to remind the colonists that Parliament had the right and power to tax them. Unexpectedly, the colonists boycotted tea. Parliament lowered the price of tea but kept the tax. The British were sure the colonists would buy tea again. Nevertheless, on the night of December 16, 1773, a group of colonists in Boston dressed up like Native Americans. They boarded British ships and dumped more than three hundred chests of tea into Boston's harbor. This protest against the tea tax became known as the Boston Tea Party.

The British were outraged. In 1774 Parliament passed new laws to punish the colonists. One law closed Boston's harbor until the colonists paid for the tea. Another law strengthened the power of the king's governor in Massachusetts. Still another law required the colonists to provide housing for British soldiers. Colonists called the laws the Intolerable Acts because Americans thought the laws made life unbearable.

Events Leading to the American Revolution

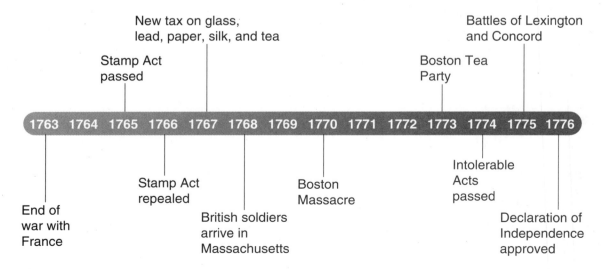

Because of the Intolerable Acts, representatives from 12 of the 13 colonies met in Philadelphia, Pennsylvania, in 1774. They called the meeting the First Continental Congress. The delegates were still willing to remain part of Britain. But they wanted the harsh laws repealed. The colonists also wanted Parliament to know it could not tax them. The delegates voted to meet again in May 1775. The American Revolution began before that meeting was held.

The Battles of Lexington and Concord

Few colonists wanted a war. Nevertheless, some farmers, blacksmiths, and other workers trained for battle. They called themselves **minutemen** because they were ready to fight at a minute's notice.

The British also prepared for war. British troops in Massachusetts planned to capture two colonial leaders, John Hancock and Samuel Adams, and to raid the colonists' military supplies. The supplies were stored in the small town of Concord, about twenty miles from Boston.

Paul Revere and other colonists learned of the British plan. On the night of April 18, 1775, they rode ahead of the British troops to alert the minutemen. The next morning when the British soldiers arrived at Lexington, a town near Concord, the minutemen were waiting.

The minutemen and the British soldiers were under orders to hold their fire. Nevertheless, someone opened fire and the shooting began. Eight minutemen were killed. The battle gave Hancock and Adams time to get away.

Next the British marched to Concord. There they found only a few weapons. Just outside Concord, three British soldiers and two minutemen died during a brief battle. At about noon, the outnumbered British soldiers headed back to Boston. Minutemen hid behind fences, barns, and farmhouses along the road. They fired at the soldiers. By the time the British reached their camp near Boston, 73 more soldiers had died. Another 200 were wounded or missing.

The American Revolution had begun. In the weeks that followed, the fighting spread. On July 4, 1776, the Second Continental Congress officially approved the Declaration of Independence. It told the world why the 13 colonies were fighting to be free of British rule. Americans' fight for independence continued until 1781.

Reading a Timeline   A **timeline** shows when a series of events took place. It also shows the order of events. It helps you figure out the time between events as well as cause-and-effect relationships. Look at the timeline on page 96 and answer the questions below.

1 In what year did the colonists begin paying taxes to Britain? _____

2 In what year were protesting colonists killed in Boston? _____

3 Was the Declaration of Independence approved before or after the Battles of Lexington and Concord? _____

Thinking About the Article

Practice Vocabulary

The terms below are in the passage in bold type. Study the way each term is used. Then complete each sentence by writing the correct term in the blank.

exports	**legislature**	**boycotted**
repealed	**imports**	**minutemen**

1 Colonists protested the Stamp Act by refusing to buy British

_____.

2 Parliament _____ the Stamp Act in 1766.

3 Each colony had its own _____, which made laws for its people.

4 _____ were waiting for the British soldiers when they came to Lexington.

5 Tea, glass, and silk were some of the _____ on which colonists had to pay taxes.

6 British trade was hurt after the colonists _____ goods from Great Britain.

Understand the Article

Write the answer to each question.

7 How did the colonists react to the Stamp Act?

_____

8 Why did the colonists throw the Boston Tea Party?

_____

_____

9 What is the Declaration of Independence about?

_____

_____

10 How did the minutemen manage to shoot so many British while the soldiers retreated to Boston?

_____

_____

Check your answers on pages 237–238.

Apply Your Skills

Circle the number of the best answer for each question.

11 Which of the following was <u>not</u> a cause of the American Revolution?
  (1) the tax on tea
  (2) the Declaration of Independence
  (3) Parliament's enforcing the old trade laws
  (4) the Intolerable Acts
  (5) the Boston Massacre

12 Which of the following was an effect of the battles of Lexington and Concord?
  (1) The colonists planned the Boston Tea Party.
  (2) The First Continental Congress met.
  (3) Parliament passed the Intolerable Acts.
  (4) Parliament passed the Tea Act.
  (5) The American Revolution began.

13 Look again at the timeline on page 96. How many years passed between the end of Great Britain's war with France and the beginning of its war with the American colonies?
  (1) 7
  (2) 10
  (3) 11
  (4) 12
  (5) 15

Connect with the Article

Write the answer to each question.

14 How do you think news of the American Revolution affected American colonists ruled by Spain?

_____

_____

_____

15 Using the American Revolution as an example, how do you think people today might react if laws are enforced unfairly over a long period of time?

_____

_____

_____

The U.S. Civil War

Setting the Stage

In the early 1800s, the United States doubled its territory. Each region—the North, the South, and the new West—developed a certain character of its own. In the North, many farm workers headed for cities where textile mills were hiring. In the South, plantation owners had African slaves work long hours to supply cotton to the mills in the North and Europe. Other Americans moved to new western lands and built towns, farms, and plantations of their own. The ways of life in the country's regions became different from one another. These differences grew into disagreements so serious that they threatened to tear the United States apart.

PREVIEW THE ARTICLE

Read the first two paragraphs on page 101. What are two things you can expect to learn from this article?

_____

_____

RELATE TO THE TOPIC

This article is about why Americans during the 1860s fought one another in a war that nearly broke the country into two. Recall a situation when you and a brother, sister, or close friend had opposite viewpoints on an issue of great importance to you both. Describe the steps the two of you took to resolve your difference. If the issue is unresolved, describe the feelings you still have about the disagreement.

_____

_____

VOCABULARY

cash crop	Union	Confederacy	abolitionists
Emancipation Proclamation		discrimination	regiment

Check your answers on page 238.

Differences Lead to War

In the North many people were leaving farms to become factory workers. Textile mills, where workers wove cotton and wool into cloth, were among the first factories in the North. Thousands of job-seeking immigrants arrived through northern seaports. By 1860 the North's population was nearing twenty million.

The South's eleven million people included four million enslaved African Americans. Many white Southerners depended on slave labor to grow cash crops, such as tobacco and cotton. A **cash crop** is grown to be sold rather than for personal use. Most Southerners did not hold slaves, but those who did were the South's leaders.

The Many-Sided Slavery Issue

In Congress and in newspapers throughout the country, Americans debated the issue of slavery. Many Northerners saw slavery as immoral. Southerners saw it as necessary for their economy. In coastal regions of South Carolina and Georgia, enslaved African Americans made up 50 to 75 percent of the population. Many plantation owners feared financial ruin if slavery was outlawed.

The most heated debates centered on whether new states in the West should allow slavery. Congress created plans in 1820 and 1850 to answer this question. Each plan tried to satisfy both the North and the South. But in the end, neither was satisfied. Abraham Lincoln, who was against slavery, was elected the United States President in 1860. Several states soon left the United States to form a new nation. In 1861 the Civil War began.

The Civil War was fought between 23 northern states, called the **Union,** and 11 southern states, called the **Confederacy.** Southerners in the Confederacy no longer wanted to be part of the United States. Most Northerners did not think the South had a right to declare itself a separate country. They were willing to fight to keep the nation together. African Americans hoped the Civil War would end slavery.

Before the war started, people held slaves in 15 states. Four of these slave states stayed in the Union. They are called the *border states.* When Lincoln asked for volunteers to fight for the Union, thousands of free African Americans rushed to sign up. But Lincoln thought the Union might lose the four border states to the Confederacy if he allowed African Americans to fight. He did not want people in these states to think the Union was fighting to end slavery. So the armed forces turned away African-American volunteers. Lincoln explained his war goals in a letter to the owner of a New York newspaper:

> My paramount object in this struggle is to save the Union, and is not either to save or destroy slavery. If I could save the Union without freeing any slave I would do it; and if I could save it by freeing all the slaves, I would [do] it; and if I could do it by freeing some and leaving others alone, I would also do that.

Understanding the Main Idea   The main idea of a paragraph is often stated in a sentence called the **topic sentence**. It is usually the first sentence in a paragraph but is sometimes the last. It tells what the paragraph is about. Underline the topic sentence from Lincoln's letter. Then circle the letter of the statement below that best describes his main idea.

a.   The Civil War must save the Union.
b.   The Civil War must destroy slavery.

The Emancipation Proclamation

Lincoln wanted a quick end to the war, and **abolitionists**—people opposed to slavery—were pressuring him to act. They wanted him to free enslaved African Americans.

Lincoln thought he should wait for a Union victory before announcing any decision. The North won a battle at Antietam, Maryland, in September 1862. Five days later, Lincoln issued a written statement. It said that on January 1, 1863, all slaves in states fighting against the United States would be "forever free." This statement was called the **Emancipation Proclamation.** Lincoln was still concerned that the border states might leave the Union. He was very clear that he had not freed the enslaved people in those states. But the war took on a new meaning. African Americans and white Northerners who were against slavery celebrated.

The proclamation did not end slavery in the Confederacy. Lincoln knew that the South would have to be defeated before all the people there would be free. The proclamation also did not end discrimination. **Discrimination** is the unequal and unfair treatment of a person or group. Even free African Americans in the North did not enjoy the same rights that Whites enjoyed. In most states African Americans could not vote or attend public schools. Many states did not allow them to own property. However the Emancipation Proclamation opened the door for African Americans to join the military. By the end of the war, about 200,000 African Americans served in the Union army and navy. Many had escaped from slavery in the South.

African-American soldiers faced discrimination. They were not allowed to fight beside white soldiers or to be officers. At first they were paid only half as much as white soldiers. But by the war's end, both groups were paid the same amount.

African Americans' Proud Record

Massachusetts was one of the first states to form African-American regiments, including the famous 54th regiment. A **regiment** is a large military group. In July 1863 the 54th attacked Fort Wagner near Charleston, South Carolina. Nearly fifty percent of the regiment was killed.

The fighting record of African-American soldiers in the Civil War was outstanding. Only the bravest members of the armed forces receive the Congressional Medal of Honor. Twenty-three African Americans received this honor during the Civil War.

Check your answers on page 238.

At the war's start, African Americans gave their support in other ways besides fighting. They acted as camp cooks, barbers, gravediggers, messengers, nurses, scouts, and spies. In 1862 a small group of enslaved African Americans in South Carolina took over a Confederate steamer named *The Planter*. Robert Smalls led the group. He had been forced as a slave to serve in the Confederate Navy. He sailed the ship out of Charleston harbor and turned it over to Union forces. Later he said:

> Although born a slave I always felt that I was a man and ought to be free, and I would be free or die. While at the wheel of *The Planter* . . . it occurred to me that I could not only secure my own freedom but that of numbers of my comrades.

Another one-time slave, Harriet Tubman, had been helping African Americans escape from the South since the 1830s. During the war, she helped the Union forces as a nurse, scout, and spy.

The South surrendered in April 1865, ending the Civil War. African Americans had won their freedom. However, the fight to end discrimination in the United States was just beginning.

The 54th Massachusetts Volunteers Regiment attacks Fort Wagner in Charleston, South Carolina, on July 18, 1863.

Identifying Point of View Everyone has a point of view. Writers express their point of view using words. Artists use pictures to show how they feel. Look at the picture above. It shows the Union's 54th Regiment attacking Fort Wagner in South Carolina. Which detail in the picture suggests that the artist sided with the North?

   a. The American flag is at the center of the picture.

   b. The Confederate fort looks strongly fortified.

Check your answer on page 238.

Thinking About the Article

Practice Vocabulary

The terms below are in bold type. Study the way each term is used. Then complete each sentence by writing the correct term in the blank.

cash crop   **Union**   **Confederacy**   **abolitionists**

Emancipation Proclamation   **discrimination**   **regiment**

1 Eleven southern states left the Union and formed the

_____.

2 In 1862 President Lincoln issued the _____.

3 _____ tried to persuade President Lincoln to end slavery.

4 Even free African Americans in the North suffered from

_____.

5 Massachusetts formed a _____ of African-American soldiers.

6 Abraham Lincoln's major concern was preserving the

_____.

7 An example of a _____ is tobacco.

Understand the Article

Write the answer to each question.

8 Why did plantation owners defend slavery?

_____

9 Why did the Union hesitate to enlist African Americans as soldiers?

_____

10 What were two ways African Americans supported the war before they were allowed to fight?

_____

_____

11 How did the Union discriminate against African-American soldiers during the Civil War?

_____

Check your answers on page 238.

Apply Your Skills

Circle the number of the best answer for each question.

12 Which description best expresses the main idea of the picture on page 103?
 (1) African-American soldiers fought bravely for the Union.
 (2) Confederate soldiers won the 1863 battle.
 (3) African-American soldiers pushed back Confederate soldiers as the Confederates attacked the fort.
 (4) Union ships supported the attack on Fort Wagner.
 (5) The American flag is at the center of the picture.

13 Who was least likely to view Robert Smalls as a hero?
 (1) Abraham Lincoln
 (2) Harriet Tubman
 (3) an abolitionist
 (4) a plantation owner
 (5) a European who opposed slavery

14 Which of the following statements expresses the main idea of the Emancipation Proclamation?
 (1) All enslaved African Americans were freed.
 (2) The Union was winning the war.
 (3) Enslaved persons in the border states were freed.
 (4) African Americans would have the same rights as whites.
 (5) Freeing slaves in the Confederacy was a Union goal.

Connect with the Article

Write your answer to each question.

15 In what two ways did the North and South differ before the Civil War began?

_____

_____

_____

16 What is a problem of discrimination in your community? Write a three-step plan to help fight this problem.

_____

_____

_____

_____

_____

The Reform Movement

Setting the Stage

In colonial times, a family worked as a team. Each family member, even the children, did his or her share of the work. They tended to animals, planted crops, and harvested together. They chopped wood, cooked meals, and cleaned the house and barns. Children worked from sunup to sundown, six days a week. Few children went to school.

During the early 1800s, business people began building factories to make products with the latest machines. A growing number of Americans left their farms. They moved to cities and factory towns. Factory owners encouraged their workers to have their children join them at work. In fact, owners preferred to hire workers with several children.

PREVIEW THE ARTICLE

Read the first two paragraphs on page 107. What are two things you can expect to learn from this article?

_____

_____

RELATE TO THE TOPIC

This article is about how some Americans in the early 1900s wanted to pass laws that limited the hours children could work. Write a few sentences explaining your early work experiences. How old were you when you first earned money? At what age did you hold your first part-time job? How many hours did you work each day? On what did you spend your wages?

_____

_____

VOCABULARY

child labor	**apprentice**	**master**
reformers	**literate**	

Check your answers on page 239.

Child Labor

As factories spread throughout the United States, so did the practice of **child labor,** or in other words, using children as workers. By 1890 a million children had jobs. In the South most child laborers worked in textile mills, where cotton was made into cloth. In Chicago many children worked in the meat-packing industry. In New York they worked in the garment industry. By 1900 more than 1.7 million Americans under 16 years of age had jobs.

Learning a Trade

Child labor was not a new idea. Learning from skilled masters was a common practice in ancient Egypt, Greece, and Rome. It was still the way young people learned a trade in Europe when the American colonies were founded.

During colonial times, many children were working as apprentices by the time they were 12 years old. An **apprentice** is someone who learns a trade, or skill, from an expert called a **master.** Apprentices learned how to make clothing from master tailors. They learned how to make shoes from master cobblers. Artists, hatmakers, blacksmiths, and silversmiths all trained apprentices. Apprentices worked long, hard days. Being an apprentice was an opportunity for a boy to get ahead. Girls, on the other hand, rarely had the chance to become apprentices.

At the age of 12, Benjamin Franklin became an apprentice to his older brother, James. The older brother was a printer. James agreed to teach Benjamin how to become a good printer. He also provided Benjamin with food, clothing, and a place to live. He promised to take care of Benjamin if he became ill. In return Benjamin had to work hard for five years. He also had to promise not to give away any of his master's printing secrets.

When Franklin finished his apprenticeship at age 17, he had valuable skills. His skills made him capable of contributing to a business. Because he had a trade, he would earn more wages than someone with no special skills. When he could not find work in Boston or New York, he moved to Philadelphia. Within weeks, he was working for a printer. By the time he was 22, he had enough experience to start his own printing shop. Franklin became one of Philadelphia's most respected business leaders.

Comparing and Contrasting. To **compare** people, events, or things is to show how they are alike. The words *also, as well as,* and *like* signal a comparison. To **contrast** is to show how people, events, or things are different. Words that signal a contrast include *however, on the other hand, unlike, although,* and *yet.* Reread the second paragraph under "Learning a Trade." In one sentence, the phrase *on the other hand* signals a contrast. Which two persons are being contrasted?

    a.   an apprentice and a master

    b.   a boy and a girl

A Child's Life

Factory owners in the 1800s had jobs that needed little or no training. A ten-year-old child could often handle the work. In fact, some factory owners hired only children. They claimed that children could do certain jobs better than adults. Children ran errands, helped machine operators, and cleaned. Factory owners also paid children less than adults. Unskilled adult workers made about a dime an hour, which came to one dollar for a ten-hour day. Children worked for as little as fifty cents a day.

By the mid-1800s, many states had free public schools. In 1850 nearly 3.3 million children went to elementary schools. Most parents wanted their children to go to school. But because factory jobs paid so little, some parents needed their children to work. Before 1900 most workers made only about $400 to $500 per year. Yet the basic cost of living was about $600. Many parents could not pay their family's living expenses without the money their children earned. They could not afford to let their children go to school.

Children did not work only in factories. Some worked in coal mines. Others worked in country stables. Some worked on city sidewalks, selling newspapers or shining shoes. Many children still worked on farms. They harvested berries, tobacco, sugar beets, and other vegetables. However, children in factories and mines worked under the most dangerous and unhealthy conditions. In paint factories child workers breathed in toxic fumes. In the garment industry, young laborers hunched over sewing machines and developed curved spines. In coal mines boys as young as nine years old inhaled coal dust all day.

Children worked in canneries in the early 1900s.

The Push for Reform

People who work to change things for the better are called **reformers.** In the 1890s and early 1900s, many Americans worked hard to improve the lives of children. These reformers wanted laws that set a minimum working age. They wanted to limit the number of hours children could work. They felt children should be kept out of dangerous jobs. Most reformers believed that every child should have the chance to go to school.

Reformers worked to make people aware of the conditions that children faced in the workplace. Some reformers created the National Child Labor Committee. This group hired people to investigate factories and mines. One of these investigators was Lewis Hine. He wrote about the children he met and took photos of them at work. In 1910 he took the photo shown on page 108.

Factory owners hired guards to keep Hine away. The owners did not want anyone to take pictures of their workers. They were afraid to let people see what conditions were like. But Hine found ways to get inside the factories. He often disguised himself as a Bible salesman or a fire inspector. Sometimes he pretended to be a photographer eager to take pictures of the latest machines. He always kept his notebook hidden in a pocket. He used his notes to write many articles. His photographs, however, were more powerful than any words he wrote.

Several states passed laws to protect children as the result of the work of Hine and others. For example, the Illinois Factory Act of 1893 stopped employers from hiring children under 14 to work more than eight hours a day. By 1914 every state but one had child-labor laws with a minimum age limit. The age was 12 in several states in the South, 15 in South Dakota, and 16 in Montana. Most laws also banned children from working until they were **literate,** or could read and write.

Often states failed to enforce their laws. As a result, many Americans demanded a national law that the United States government and its federal agents would enforce. But business people across the nation disapproved of any such law.

Several times Congress passed child-labor laws, but the Supreme Court ruled them unconstitutional. In 1925 reformers even proposed a Constitutional amendment that would limit child labor. However, the amendment failed to win enough support. Finally, in 1938 Congress passed a national child-labor law. The law made it illegal for most businesses to hire children under the age of 16. Children under the age of 18 could not work at dangerous jobs. But the law failed to protect all children. For example, it did not include farm workers. It also failed to stop child labor during World War II. When adults left their jobs to join the armed forces, states ignored the law and allowed young teenagers to work long hours.

Understanding a Photo   As proof of the need for laws to protect children, Hine used photos like the one on page 108. Which charge would the details in the photo support?
- a.   Child workers lack adult supervision.
- b.   Children work in unhealthy conditions.

Thinking About the Article

Practice Vocabulary

The terms below are in the passage in bold type. Study the way each term is used. Then complete each sentence by writing the correct term.

child labor   **apprentice**   **master**

reformers   **literate**

1. _____ was common from the nation's beginning.

2. Other _____ at the turn of the century worked to gain women the right to vote and to help the poor in cities.

3. From ancient times, the best way for a young person to learn a skill was to study under a(n) _____.

4. In the early 1900s, many immigrants moved to the United States and needed to become _____ in English.

5. A(n) _____ spent years learning a trade from an expert.

Understand the Article

Write the answer to each question.

6. How was Benjamin Franklin's master like a parent?

_____

_____

7. Why did some parents send their children to work?

_____

_____

8. Why did many factory owners hire children?

_____

_____

9. Why did factory owners try to keep Lewis Hine from visiting their factories?

_____

_____

Apply Your Skills

Circle the number of the best answer for each question.

10 Which statement is an example of a comparison?
  (1) Work in garment factories as well as in coal mines posed health hazards for children.
  (2) Hine often disguised himself as a Bible salesman or as a fire inspector.
  (3) Several states passed laws to protect children as the result of the work of Hine and others.
  (4) As a result, many Americans demanded a national law that the United States government and its federal agents would enforce.
  (5) A boy could learn a trade, but a girl, on the other hand, rarely had the chance to become an apprentice.

11 Look again at the photograph on page 108. Which phrase best describes the working conditions?
  (1) no fresh air
  (2) crowded workplace
  (3) dangerous tasks
  (4) unsafe machinery
  (5) loud noises

12 Which sentence states a true contrast between apprentices in colonial times and child workers in the early 1900s?
  (1) Both apprentices and boys in coal mines worked long hours.
  (2) Masters and factory owners supplied their workers with clothing.
  (3) An apprentice earned better wages than a child worker in a factory.
  (4) An apprentice learned more valuable skills than a factory worker.
  (5) Factory owners taught young workers to read while masters did not.

Connect with the Article

Write your answer to each question.

13 There is an old saying that "one picture is worth a thousand words." How does this saying apply to Hine's photograph on page 108?

_____

_____

14 Many teenagers have part-time jobs in which they work 20 to 30 hours a week during the school year. To help protect young workers, suggest two guidelines for an employer of teenagers.

_____

_____

World War II

Setting the Stage

Only 21 years after World War I, the world was fighting again. By the late 1930s, Germany, Italy, and Japan had built up their armed forces and were threatening their neighbors. As in World War I, the United States was not involved at the beginning of World War II. The nation was still recovering from serious economic problems of the Great Depression. President Franklin D. Roosevelt had created programs that helped people to hold onto their farms, to get jobs, and to stay in business. Putting people to work boosted the economy, but World War II helped American industry regain its strength.

PREVIEW THE ARTICLE

Begin to think about what you will be reading. Look at the title of the article, the headings (subtitles) within the article, the caption under the picture, and the title of the line graph. What are two things you can expect to learn from this article?

_____

_____

RELATE TO THE TOPIC

This article is about how Americans fighting overseas and working in factories at home helped to win World War II. Write a sentence or two about being a member of a team. Have you been a member of a sports team or any other type of group effort? What united the team? Why do you think your team accomplished what it did?

_____

_____

VOCABULARY

Allies	**defense industry**	**defense contracts**
labor union	**stock market**	**labor force**

The Search for New Workers

On December 7, 1941, Japanese planes bombed the American fleet in Pearl Harbor, Hawaii. The next day the United States declared war on Japan. Thousands of young workers left their jobs to join the armed forces. This meant fewer workers in factories. Yet war production required millions of skilled workers.

American factories had to make military supplies for American troops and the rest of the **Allies**—the British, the French, and the Soviets. The Allies fought together against the Germans, the Italians, and the Japanese. Enemy bombs had destroyed many weapons factories in other Allied countries. As a result, the American defense industry had more work than ever. The **defense industry** produced weapons, planes, and other military supplies.

The Doors Open

For years American employers had discriminated against African-American workers. Many companies in the defense industry had policies against hiring any African Americans. Others had labor unions that did not welcome African-American members. **Labor unions** are organizations that workers create to protect their interests. Unions help workers get higher wages and better work rules from employers.

African-American leaders wanted to end discrimination in the workplace. They planned a march on Washington, D.C., in 1941 to get the attention of President Roosevelt and the nation. Leaders of the march wanted to convince Roosevelt that African Americans had a right to be treated as most white Americans were treated.

One week before the scheduled march, Roosevelt issued a presidential order. It was the first time since Abraham Lincoln's Emancipation Proclamation that a presidential order involved civil rights. The order required that factories working on defense contracts end discrimination in hiring and promoting employees. **Defense contracts** are agreements that a government makes with companies so that they will produce goods needed by the military. To keep their defense contracts, these companies could no longer refuse to hire or promote workers because of race or religion. An African-American woman who found a job in a shipyard described the change:

> As the manpower in the country was getting pulled into the service, all of the industries were wide open. So they decided, "Well, we better let some of those blacks come in." Then, after the source of men dried up, they began to let women come in.

Summarizing Information   When you **summarize**, you shorten a large amount of information into its major points. Reread the text under the heading "The Doors Open." Which of the following statements best summarizes that information?
  a.   A need for workers during World War II opened doors for minorities and women.
  b.   Women faced discrimination in the defense industries before World War II.

Check your answer on page 239.

Soldiers Without Guns

The United States government helped the defense industry by recruiting workers for the industry. The government hired advertising experts in New York City and Hollywood to work on an advertising campaign. The ads encouraged Americans to join the war effort. They showed how people could help win the war by taking factory jobs. Government posters and movies called defense-industry workers "soldiers without guns."

Only lucky Americans had jobs during the Great Depression. This was the period that started after the United States stock market crashed in 1929. The **stock market** measures how much business the companies in the United States are doing. After the crash, businesses failed, and millions of people lost their jobs. For many years, the economy was in major trouble because the country was producing very few goods. World War II renewed the American economy. The war gave American workers jobs and hope.

Early in the war, the advertising campaign created a poster for an airplane company. The ad showed a woman named Rosie working as a riveter. Riveters joined large metal sections with fasteners called rivets. The idea of a woman putting together an airplane was new to Americans. The poster was an overnight success. Songs were written about Rosie. She appeared in movies and on the cover of a magazine. Rosie became a symbol of all the women who worked in the defense industry. The number of women in the industry increased 460 percent from 1940 to 1945.

When the war began, women made up about 25 percent of the labor force. The **labor force** consists of all the people capable of working. Before the war most women had low-paying jobs in offices, shops, and factories.

The war opened the door to higher paying jobs. Some women helped build airplanes and ships. Others worked in steel mills. Women began driving buses, trucks, and trains. They flew airplanes from factories to battlefields. By the end of the war, women made up 36 percent of the labor force.

A Changing Labor Force

World War II brought great changes to the United States labor force. Americans produced twice as many military supplies as Germany, Italy, and Japan combined. During 1939 American workers made about six thousand planes. In 1944 they made almost one hundred thousand planes. American workers made military supplies in less time than ever before. The time for making an aircraft carrier was cut from 35 months to 15 months. Factories were open day and night.

World War II affected the wages of American factory workers. Women and African Americans earned more than they had before the war. Yet women still earned about sixty percent less than men who were doing the same job. Women were often placed in unskilled jobs even though they had the skills for higher paying jobs.

American workers were a critical part of the war effort. Working for the Allies' victory was an experience many workers would never forget. A welder in New York explained the change. She said: "Rosie the Riveter was the woman who got up early in the morning when it was still dark and went to work and came in smiling, drinking coffee, working hard, finding herself as a new person."

Yet many of these new workers were unemployed within a year after the war ended. Soldiers returned from the war, and employers were eager to place the war heroes back in their old jobs. About four million women either lost or left their jobs between 1944 and 1946. Three-fourths of the women workers during the war were married, and many husbands did not want their wives working outside the home.

Neither women nor African Americans were willing to return to the way things were before the war. They now knew what it was like to have good jobs. They had enjoyed the benefits of a good wage. An African-American woman years later recalled the feeling:

> A lot of blacks . . . decided they did not want to go back to what they were doing before. They did not want to walk behind a plow. They wouldn't get on the back of the bus anymore.

Women contributed to the war effort.

Women in the Labor Force, 1940–1950

Source: Statistical Abstracts, 1951

Reading a Line Graph   A **line graph** usually shows how information has changed over time. According to the graph above, which statement best sums up what happened between the beginning of World War II and the height of the war in 1943?

  a.   The number of women in the labor force increased.
  b.   The number of women in the labor force decreased.

Thinking About the Article

Practice Vocabulary

The terms below are in the passage in bold type. Study the way each term is used. Then complete each sentence by writing the correct term.

Allies	defense industry	defense contracts
labor unions	stock market	labor force

1 The government got the weapons and military supplies that it needed

through _____ with private companies.

2 Advertisements sponsored by the United States government helped the

_____ attract more workers.

3 The wartime _____ included many women and
African Americans.

4 The _____ crash began a downturn in the American
economy.

5 The _____ included the Americans, British, French,
and Soviets.

6 For years many _____ did not welcome African-
American members.

Understand the Article

Write the answer to each question.

7 Why were Americans eager to join the wartime labor force?

_____

8 What are two reasons the wartime advertising campaign was so effective?

_____

_____

9 How did the workplace change when former soldiers returned to their
jobs in the United States?

_____

10 Why were African Americans unwilling to return to the way life was
before the war?

_____

Check your answers on page 239.

Apply Your Skills

Circle the number of the best answer for each question.

⑪ President Roosevelt issued a presidential order in 1941. Which statement best summarizes why it was important?
   (1) It ended all discrimination against African Americans in the workplace.
   (2) It ended racial and religious discrimination in all American factories.
   (3) It protected the rights of women in the workplace.
   (4) It raised the pay for women and African Americans.
   (5) It ended discrimination in companies with national defense contracts.

⑫ Look at the line graph on page 115. Which statement best summarizes what the changes on the graph show?
   (1) Many women were unwilling to return to the way life was before the war.
   (2) World War II affected the wages of American factory workers.
   (3) Former soldiers returned to their old jobs after the war.
   (4) No job seemed too tough for women.
   (5) The number of women in the work force continued to decrease five years after the war ended.

⑬ Which of the following phrases best summarizes what Rosie the Riveter symbolized during the war?
   (1) women driving trucks, buses, and trains
   (2) women acting in the movie industry
   (3) women putting together airplanes
   (4) women working in the defense industry
   (5) women modeling for magazines

Connect with the Article

Write your answer to each question.

⑭ World War II marked the end of serious problems for the American economy. Do you think war is "big business?" Explain your answer.

   _____

   _____

⑮ If you had lived during World War II, how would you have helped the war effort? Describe the job you would have wanted.

   _____

   _____

   _____

Setting the Stage

The Soviets and the Americans, along with the other Allies, had joined forces during World War II to fight Hitler and the Nazis. After the war their leaders clearly showed that they had very different ideas about how to treat Germany. The Soviet Union took over East Germany. Great Britain, the United States, and France controlled West Germany. The Allies even divided Berlin, Germany's capital. The Soviet Union wanted control over even more of Europe. The other Allies wanted all European countries to become independent. These differences of opinion created two opposing sides. Thus the Soviet Union and the United States began a long-standing struggle for world power.

PREVIEW THE ARTICLE

Begin to think about what you will read. Look at the title of the article, the headings (subtitles) within the article, and the map. What two things can you expect to learn from this article?

_____

_____

RELATE TO THE TOPIC

This article is about how world politics changed after World War II and led to the Cold War and the Vietnam War. Think about what you have heard about the Vietnam War. Write one fact you know about the war and one question you would like answered about the war.

_____

_____

VOCABULARY

communism	containment	Cold War
guerrilla	draft	deferment
civilians		

Check your answers on page 240.

The Race for World Power

World War II had left much of the Soviets' western lands in shambles. The Soviet people were starting over. Many had lost not only family members but also their homes during the war. With so much destruction, the Soviet leaders and people were bitter. They wanted to punish Germany. The Soviets believed that a weak Germany was their best protection against another war. So they stripped East Germany of its factories and other resources. The Soviets also wanted to control their eastern European neighbors, some of whom had once belonged to Russia.

The Cold War

After World War II, the United States, Great Britain, and France were still allies. They believed that a rich Germany was the best protection against another war. These Allies worked to return West Germany to normal. Americans gave West Germans financial help to rebuild their shops, factories, and homes.

The Soviet Union had a different point of view. It wanted to force its communist system on all of eastern Europe. **Communism** is both a political system and an economic system. A small group of people, those who lead the Communist Party, run the government. The party also controls the economy and most property.

Eventually the Soviets gained control of Poland, Czechoslovakia, Hungary, Romania, Bulgaria, and Albania. They made sure each country, including East Germany, had a communist government. In 1949 the West made West Germany an independent nation. The Soviets soon made East Germany an independent nation, too, but they continued to control its leaders and those of other eastern European countries. The Soviets also helped Communists in China, the Soviets' neighbor to the east. The Chinese Communists gained control of China in 1949.

Some Americans feared that the Communists might take over the world. In 1947 the United States announced a policy called **containment.** This policy was designed to stop communism from spreading without going to war. Instead, the United States sent military and economic aid to help threatened countries fight the Communists themselves.

From 1945 to 1989, the United States and the Soviet Union struggled for world power in what has been called the **Cold War.** The two countries' military forces never fought each other directly, even though tensions were often high.

The Vietnam War

The Soviet and Chinese Communists had their eyes on Southeast Asia. Vietnam was a French colony before World War II. The Japanese conquered Vietnam during the war. When the war ended, the French tried to return after the Japanese left. But the Vietnamese wanted independence. In 1946 the French went to war against the Vietnamese, who were backed by Soviet and Chinese Communists.

The American containment policy was put to its greatest test in Southeast Asia. American generals thought that if Communists came to power in Vietnam, all of Southeast Asia eventually would become communist. At first, the United States sent supplies to the French. In 1954 the Vietnamese defeated the French forces. Vietnam was then divided. North Vietnam had a communist government. South Vietnam was to become a democratic nation after it had elections.

The United States sent military advisors in 1955 to help Ngo Dinh Diem, the new South Vietnamese leader. He was against communism but did not allow free elections. More and more people in South Vietnam thought communism might be a better way. These people formed the Viet Cong and rebelled against Diem. North Vietnam supported the Viet Cong. By 1960 the Viet Cong had ten thousand soldiers. They began attacking Diem's bases. U.S. military support to Vietnam increased year after year. By 1963 more than sixteen thousand United States military advisors were in South Vietnam.

Southeast Asia During the Vietnam War

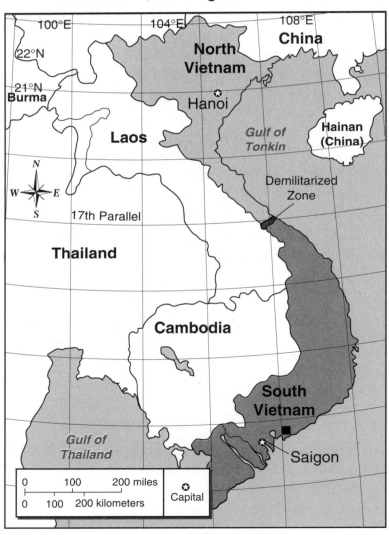

By 1964 the Viet Cong had taken control of about 75 percent of South Vietnam's population. In 1965 the first U.S. combat troops went to South Vietnam. Many American soldiers believed they were fighting against communism and defending freedom. As the war dragged on, the United States sent more and more soldiers and weapons to South Vietnam.

American forces struggled to fight effectively in the South Vietnam countryside. The land is mostly mountainous with many forests, except along the coast. Temperatures were hot, and the rain was heavy. Because the Viet Cong were part of the South Vietnamese people, American troops could not tell who the enemy was. The Viet Cong used **guerrilla** tactics. Small units of Viet Cong fighters hid in forests and attacked villages as well as military targets. As a result, many innocent **civilians,** or nonmilitary people, suffered.

From Glencoe's *American History: The Early Years to 1977,* p. 691

Reading a Political Map   Maps that focus on showing boundaries between countries are called **political maps.** The map on page 120 is a political map. Its key shows the symbol that stands for a capital. North Vietnamese Communists set up camp in another Southeast Asian country. Which country gave them better access to South Vietnam's capital?

    a.   Laos   b.   Cambodia

The Controversy Over the War

As more United States troops headed to Vietnam, many Americans began to question the war. Every night on TV, people watched pictures of soldiers dying, villages burning, and children crying. A peace movement sprang up and used demonstrations and educational programs to spread its message. At the same time, other Americans believed that all citizens should support their government. These people reacted to the peace movement with anger and resentment.

Some Americans who opposed the war did not want U.S. soldiers fighting halfway around the world. Others felt the United States should not interfere in another nation's politics. Some thought the war's cost in money and lives was too high. Money spent on the war meant that less money was available for Americans who needed help at home.

Many who opposed the war were also against the **draft**—a system of required military service. If men were in college, they could get a **deferment,** which meant they could avoid military service until after they completed school. Those who did not go to college were drafted. As a result a high percentage of the American troops were young men from low-income families, who could not afford college. African Americans made up a large part of the American soldiers in Vietnam.

Many demonstrations against the draft and the war took place on college campuses. Most protests were peaceful. But in May 1970 National Guard troops shot into a crowd of antiwar protesters at Kent State University in Ohio, killing four students. The antiwar movement grew dramatically after the deaths.

As a result of growing opposition to the war, American troops withdrew from Vietnam in 1973. American military aid was cut, too. Within two years South Vietnam fell to communist forces. About fifty-eight thousand Americans, more than a million South Vietnamese, and nearly a million North Vietnamese died in the war.

Drawing Conclusions   To draw a **conclusion,** you must identify what facts about a subject are important. Then you judge or decide what the facts tell you about the subject. A judgment made from examining facts is a conclusion. Which of the following facts supports the conclusion that the Vietnam War was splitting the American people?

    a.   Some parents and children didn't speak to each other for years because of differing positions on the war.

    b.   The people who opposed the Vietnam War had different reasons for their opposition.

Thinking About the Article

Practice Vocabulary

The terms below are in bold type in the passage. Study the way each term is used. Then complete each sentence by writing the correct term.

communism	containment	Cold War
guerrilla	draft	deferment

1. In the _____, Soviets and Americans opposed each other without any direct military conflict between them.

2. Americans thought that the _____ policy was the answer to stopping the spread of communism.

3. During the Vietnam War, young males faced the

   _____ .

4. A student could get a _____ until after he finished college.

5. Under _____ one political party controls the government.

6. The Viet Cong used _____ tactics such as shooting from the cover of forests.

Understand the Article

Write the answer to each question.

7. Why did the Soviets try to control other European countries?

   _____

8. Why did the United States begin to send help to Vietnam?

   _____

   _____

9. What were two reasons why Americans opposed the war in Vietnam?

   _____

   _____

10. How did the peace movement try to spread its message?

   _____

   _____

Check your answers on page 240.

Apply Your Skills

Circle the number of the best answer for each question.

11 Which conclusion about the Vietnam War can be drawn from facts presented in the article?
   (1) The United States should have sent combat troops to help the French fight the Vietnamese.
   (2) Holding elections in South Vietnam would have stopped any North Vietnamese influence.
   (3) Most South Vietnamese favored democracy.
   (4) Guerrilla tactics made the job of American soldiers difficult.
   (5) The Viet Cong were members of the North Vietnamese Communist Party.

12 Look closely at the map on page 120. What feature formed the approximate boundary between North Vietnam and South Vietnam?
   (1) the Mekong River
   (2) the 104° E meridian
   (3) the 17th parallel
   (4) the Gulf of Tonkin
   (5) the Ho Chi Minh Trail

13 Look again at the map on page 120. What fact about South Vietnam might you conclude gave the nation its best advantage in defending against North Vietnamese attack?
   (1) South Vietnam has a long western border.
   (2) South Vietnam is narrow and close to the South China Sea.
   (3) Mountains and forests cover most of North and South Vietnam.
   (4) South Vietnam is farther away from China than North Vietnam.
   (5) South Vietnam's capital is a far distance from North Vietnam.

Connect with the Article

Write your answer to each question.

14 Why do you think the United States and the Soviet Union had different attitudes toward Germany after World War II?

_____

_____

15 If you were advising the President, what would you recommend about sending troops to another country? What are some good reasons? What are reasons to be avoided?

_____

_____

Communicating in the New Millennium

Setting the Stage

In the late 1700s, people invented machines that manufactured products faster and at lower costs. This began the Industrial Revolution. As a result, many people turned from farming to factory work. Also in the 1700s, an inventor discovered a way to use steam power. In time this discovery helped change sailboats to steamboats and stagecoaches to railroads. This began the Transportation Revolution. As a result, people and products moved from one place to another more quickly and easily. Today we are in the middle of another major change, which is called the Information Revolution.

PREVIEW THE ARTICLE

Begin to think about what you will be reading. Look at the title of the article, the headings (subtitles) within the article, and the title of the bar graph. What are two things you can expect to learn from this article?

_____

_____

RELATE TO THE TOPIC

This section is about the ways we get and share information and how the information affects our lives. What kinds of machines have you used in the past 24 hours for getting and sending information?

_____

_____

_____

VOCABULARY

technology	communicate	telecommunications	transistors
laser	Internet	World Wide Web	

Technology Changes the Way We Live

Technology has a way of changing the world. **Technology** includes the tools and methods used to increase production. Over the past 150 years, the world has witnessed great changes in communications and information technology. We can communicate faster, at lower cost, to a greater number of people than ever before. This revolution has made a huge difference in the ways people learn and work.

The Information Revolution

The Information Revolution is actually a series of inventions that changed the way we **communicate,** or send and receive information. The revolution started with American Samuel Morse's telegraph, which sent electrical impulses through a cable. By 1844 the telegraph used a dot-and-dash code for the messages. In 1876 another American, Alexander Graham Bell, invented the telephone. It sent voice messages over wire. In 1901 the first communication was sent without wires, and radio was born. Each invention led to improved **telecommunications,** or ways to send messages over long distances using either wires or radio waves.

In the early 1900s, adding telephone technology to radio technology led to voice radio **broadcasts.** These sent messages far distances over invisible radio waves. Radio stations soon sprang up across the United States. Not long after came television, which sent pictures as well as sounds over radio waves. By 1948 about one million American families had televisions in their homes.

The Development of Computers

Other important technology came from the work of two American engineers. In 1930 Vannevar Bush invented a "mechanical brain," which could calculate quickly and solve math problems. In 1944 Howard Aiken designed a machine that could store large amounts of information. Today's computers combine the technologies of these two types of machines. **Computers** are electronic machines that process, store, and recall information. The early computers of the 1940s and 1950s were huge. Just one might fill a large room and weigh as much as 30 tons.

The invention of the transistor in 1947 greatly changed computers and telecommunications. A **transistor** is a tiny device that controls the flow of electricity in electronic equipment. Transistors' small size and light weight made possible the launching of communication satellites into space. These satellites enable sound and pictures to be easily sent from one part of the world to another.

Computers have become smaller, more reliable, more powerful, and less expensive because of transistors and microchips. A **microchip** is a tiny electrical circuit that carries messages. It is the computer's "brain." Scientists keep making microchips smaller, which means the microchips fit more easily in small or complex machines. Today microchips power artificial legs and arms as well as robots that weld or paint automobile parts on an assembly line.

Computers are also changing the world by increasing the speed at which things happen. This is because computers help people share information more quickly. Before modern telecommunications, scientific discoveries were slow to spread. For example, an Irish scientist first discovered the effects of temperature and pressure on gases in the 1600s. It took 150 years for someone else to find a practical application of that early research—the first steam engine.

Modern scientists take much less time to put a new theory to a practical use. For example, two scientists first proposed the idea of a laser in 1958. A **laser** is a narrow beam of intense light. Only ten years later, American astronauts placed a laser reflector on the moon to measure the precise distance to Earth. Today lasers help surgeons remove tissue. Lasers also help artists to clean centuries-old artwork and supermarket checkers to scan prices at the checkout counter.

Computers have changed the way we learn. Students read lessons on a computer instead of in a book. Libraries store their book titles on computers instead of in card catalogs. Teachers instruct students in different locations instead of in just one classroom.

Computers have changed the way we work, too. In factories computerized robots complete tasks that workers once had to do over and over. Fast-food restaurant workers take orders on a touch-screen ordering system. Mechanics at the repair shop hook a car to a computer to find out what is wrong with the engine.

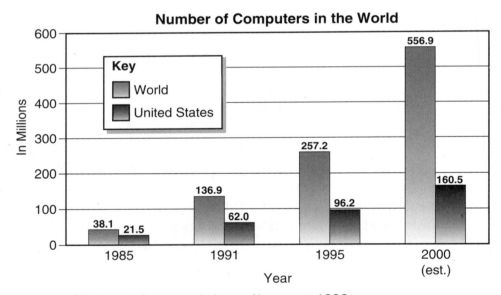

Source: *8th Annual Computer Industry Almanac* © 1996

Reading a Bar Graph   A **bar graph** is often used to make comparisons. The title tells what information the graph displays. The labels along the side and bottom of the graph tell the categories of this information. Look at the bar graph on this page. Compare the numbers of computers in the world and in the United States by looking at the bars. Circle the letter before the year when Americans owned more than one-half of the world's computers.

    a.   1985   b.   1991

Exploring the Internet

Another new communications technology is the Internet. The **Internet** is a network that connects many thousands of computers all over the globe through telephone lines. The idea of the Internet came out of the Cold War. In the 1960s the United States government was afraid that the Soviet Union would launch missiles to destroy its military bases. American leaders wanted to be sure that, even if some bases were hit, the others could communicate with one another. Scientists developed a way for computers to communicate without going through a central switchboard. A **switchboard** connects, controls, and disconnects the many phone lines in one building or location.

In 1985 the National Science Foundation (NSF) set up five supercomputer centers at large universities. It wanted to give science researchers an easier way to share research data. Using the government's technology, NSF linked these centers. It also helped connect other computer centers to the supercomputer centers. Computer users on the network found they could quickly send messages through electronic mail, or **e-mail,** and share documents.

In 1992 the network's capabilities grew. Swiss scientists created a single computer language that all computers could use for text on the Internet. Later, graphics were added. Now from any computer on the Internet, a person can find information stored in this language on computers all over the world. The **World Wide Web** is all the stored information available through the Internet. Anyone with an Internet connection can search the Web and find documents, pictures, and sounds related to a particular topic.

In its short life, the Internet has shown many benefits. It encourages people from different cultures to exchange ideas. It removes distance and the high cost of travel as roadblocks to communication. It offers a visual way of learning. Internet users swap messages, share jokes, check the weather, debate politics, play games, look for job openings, and read newspapers. People can also buy and sell things on the Internet, do scientific research, and study any subject they want.

In time many more people will have access to computers at home and at work. Many Americans already have several home phone lines, a cellular phone, a fax machine, a car phone, and an Internet connection. With an Internet connection and a computer, many people work at home and send their work electronically to their company's office. Some home builders have even included telecommunications centers with large-screen televisions and computer components in new homes.

Applying an Idea to a New Context   Ideas are often presented in one particular situation or **context.** You have just read about how scientists applied the Internet to a new situation or context. However, the Internet itself has created a need for new ideas. For example, some Internet users want to limit the messages they receive on their computers. Which telephone technology might be applied so that the user can decide who communicates with him or her over the computer?

   a.   call waiting   b.   caller identification

Check your answer on page 241.

Thinking About the Article

Practice Vocabulary

The terms below are in bold type in the passage. Study the way each term is used. Then complete each sentence by writing the correct term.

technology   communicate   telecommunications   transistors

laser   Internet   World Wide Web

1 The _____ gives researchers access to information using computers around the world.

2 Advances in _____ often change the way people live and work.

3 _____ made communication satellites possible.

4 The _____ connects computers around the world.

5 The telegraph was among the first uses of _____ technology.

6 Astronauts placed a(n) _____ reflector on the moon to measure the precise distance to Earth.

7 To _____ is to send and receive information.

Understand the Article

Write the answer to each question.

8 How did the development of telecommunications help people to communicate?

_____

_____

9 What is one way that computers have changed learning?

_____

10 What is one way that computers have changed working?

_____

11 In what two ways has the Internet changed communication?

_____

_____

Check your answers on page 241.

Apply Your Skills

Circle the number of the best answer for each question.

12 Look at the bar graph on page 126. What do the numbers along the vertical axis represent?
  - (1) the years that computers have been available
  - (2) the number of computers in each country
  - (3) the prices of computers over the years
  - (4) the percentages of computers in use
  - (5) the surface areas occupied by computers

13 Look again at the bar graph. Which of the following general statements does the data support?
  - (1) The United States leads in computer use among the world's nations.
  - (2) The estimated figure for the number of computers in the world in 2000 is low.
  - (3) In the first 10 years, the number of computers in the United States went up 400 percent.
  - (4) In 2000 the rest of the world has as many computers as the United States.
  - (5) In 1995 the United States had more than one-half the world's computers.

14 The National Science Foundation applied technology used by the United States government in a new context and created the Internet. Which technology is a comparable blend of telephone and radio technologies?
  - (1) television
  - (2) voice broadcasts
  - (3) laser reflectors
  - (4) transistors in satellites
  - (5) facsimile machines

Connect with the Article

Write the answer to each question.

15 Why do you think scientific ideas turned into practical new technologies more quickly during the late 1900s than during the late 1800s?

_____

_____

16 Computers have changed the way we learn. Are you using a computer to help you prepare for the GED exam? If so, how is it helping you?

_____

_____

History at Work

Service: Sales Associates

Some Careers in Service

Education Aide
prepares activities and assists museum visitors and groups with the activities

Security Guard
monitors exhibits and visitor traffic; provides information as needed

Tour Guide
leads visitors through museums and historic sites; makes presentations and conducts demonstrations

Museum Library Aide
assists patrons in finding requested information, using library facilities, and obtaining desired material

Museum store workers help customers choose souvenirs.

You find them at museums and many other places of interest. Over the past decade, they have become one important way for many museums to help fund their operations. They are the museum stores and gift shops you see at historic places you visit. The sales associates at these stores are important to the financial success of the stores and the satisfaction of the customers.

Sales associates have many responsibilities. They must be familiar with all the goods for sale in the store. They see that the displays are attractive and well stocked and that objects are placed in appropriate arrangements. They also handle sales, returns, and exchanges.

Because a sales associate assists customers, he or she should know how the goods in the store relate to the focus of the museum or historic place. A sales associate must also have good communication skills and a pleasant personality and appearance. Sales associates may be called on to write notes to fellow workers or provide written follow up to a customer's request. Strong math skills and a working knowledge of computers are also expected for sales and inventory management.

Look at the chart of Some Careers in Service.

- Do any of the careers interest you? If so, which ones?

- What information would you like to find out about those careers? On a separate piece of paper, write some questions that you would like answered. You can find out more information about those careers in the *Occupational Outlook Handbook* at your local library.

Use the material below to answer the questions that follow.

Coleman is a sales associate in the gift shop at the Smithsonian Institution's Museum of American History in Washington, D.C. He is showing a shopper objects that are on sale in the gift shop.

Coleman: Here we have a copy of an iron from the colonial days. Notice the size of this iron compared to the irons of today. Today's irons are much larger. They are made of plastic and metal; their handles are plastic and the base is metal. This colonial iron is made completely of metal and is about one-third the size of a modern iron. Hot coals were used to heat the colonial iron. The little door at the back of the iron was opened and hot coals were put inside. The door was closed and the coals heated up the metal. Before the iron could be used, a damp cloth was wrapped around the handle so the person ironing wouldn't get burned.

1 Which of the following materials was used to heat the colonial iron?
(1) electricity
(2) plastic
(3) hot coals
(4) a damp cloth
(5) hot metal

2 Which of the following is not a true statement?
(1) Colonial irons were one-third larger than modern irons.
(2) Colonial irons were one-third smaller than modern irons.
(3) Colonial irons were made of metal.
(4) Modern irons are made of metal and plastic.
(5) Modern and colonial irons have metal bases.

3 Why would it be important to close the door of the colonial iron before using it?
(1) to prevent the coals from cooling off too quickly
(2) to prevent the coals from spilling onto the material
(3) to help the iron heat up more quickly
(4) all of the above
(5) none of the above

4 Many of the objects we use today were invented years ago, like the colonial iron demonstrated by Coleman. Compare and contrast an object or invention we use today with its predecessor. Use a separate piece of paper to discuss how they are the same and how they are different.

The St. Augustine Colony

Juan Ponce de León, a young Spanish noble, was one of the first Europeans to explore the Americas. He was part of Christopher Columbus's 1493 return voyage. The Spanish king had heard of gold in Puerto Rico, and in 1508 he sent Ponce de León to explore. Within a year the island was inhabited by settlers, who made the Native Americans dig for gold. The king appointed Ponce de León governor of Puerto Rico.

Legend says that Ponce de León went in search of the "Fountain of Youth." In 1513 he sailed north to a land that he named La Florida. Ponce de León was the first European to set foot on the North American mainland. During the next several years, Ponce de León tried to colonize La Florida. But at each site Native Americans drove him out.

In 1564 the king of Spain learned that a group of French Protestants had started a colony in northeastern Florida. The king was angry because he believed all of La Florida belonged to Spain. The king sent his most experienced admiral, Pedro Menéndez de Avilés, to destroy the French colony. Menéndez de Avilés and his soldiers surprised the French colonists and killed them all. Then the Spanish built a colony called St. Augustine near the place where their fleet had landed.

By the time the first English colony in America was founded, St. Augustine was already 40 years old. It became an important military base for the Spaniards. The soldiers guarded the Spanish ships carrying gold and silver from Mexico to Spain. They also kept out French and English colonists. St. Augustine now has its place in history as the oldest permanent European settlement in what is now the United States.

Circle the number of the best answer for each question.

1 Why did the king of Spain want to build a colony in La Florida?
(1) to protect Spain's claim to La Florida
(2) to help the French build a colony
(3) to prove to Ponce de León that La Florida had gold
(4) to beat the English and French to the Americas
(5) to prove that Menéndez de Avilés was his best admiral

2 Which reason best summarizes why Menéndez de Avilés was sent to Florida?
(1) to find the Fountain of Youth
(2) to guard the Spanish ships going from Mexico to Spain
(3) to protect St. Augustine
(4) to remove the French colonists
(5) to search for gold

Check your answers on page 241.

The United States in 1862

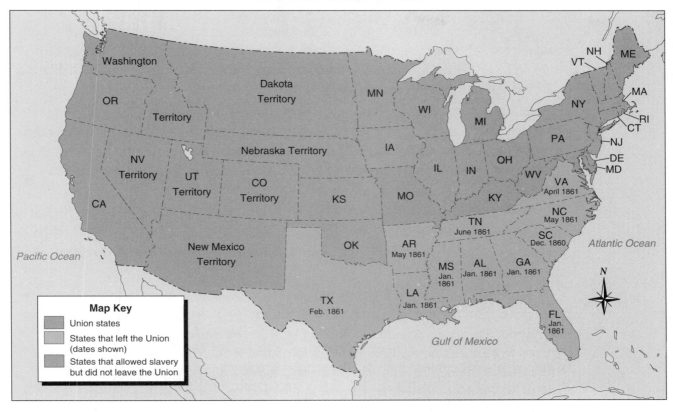

Map Key
- Union states
- States that left the Union (dates shown)
- States that allowed slavery but did not leave the Union

Correctly complete each statement.

3 The first state to leave the Union was _____ .

4 The last state to leave the Union was _____ .

5 The number of states that left the Union was _____ .

Circle the number of the best answer for the question.

6 Why were states that allowed slavery but did not leave the Union called border states?
(1) They all lay along the southern border of the United States.
(2) They formed the northern border of the United States.
(3) They all separated the rest of the states from the western territories.
(4) They separated the Union and the Confederacy.
(5) They all lay along the Ohio River.

The Internment of Japanese Americans

After Japan's attack on Pearl Harbor, the United States government feared that Japanese Americans would become spies for Japan. In January 1942 President Franklin D. Roosevelt ordered all **aliens,** or people who were not American citizens, to register with the government.

In March, officials began arrangements to move Japanese Americans from their homes in west coast states. More than 120,000 Japanese Americans were forced to sell their homes and most of their belongings. About seventy-seven thousand of these Japanese Americans were American citizens. Many had been born in the United States. But that did not seem to matter.

Then the Japanese-American families were interned. **Interned** means to be forced to live in camps away from home. Families were rounded up and taken to out-of-the-way places, often in the middle of a desert. Internment camps were in Colorado, Utah, and Arkansas.

Yet Japanese Americans remained loyal to the United States. In 1943 Japanese Americans were permitted to enlist in the Army. More than twelve hundred men from the internment camps signed up. Although the Japanese-American soldiers' war records were outstanding, their families remained in the camps. The last Japanese Americans at the camps were not allowed to leave until six months after the war ended. No Japanese American was ever convicted of spying.

In 1988 the United States government under President Ronald Reagan formally apologized to sixty thousand surviving Japanese Americans who had lived in the internment camps. The government gave each survivor $20,000 as **reparations,** or payment for damages.

Circle the number of the best answer for each question.

7 Why were Japanese Americans interned?
  (1) The government wanted Japanese workers in defense industries.
  (2) The government feared that Japanese Americans were responsible for World War II.
  (3) The government feared that Japanese Americans might be spies for Japan.
  (4) The government feared that Japanese Americans would refuse to join the armed forces.
  (5) The government feared that Japanese Americans would move to Japan.

8 Which conclusion does the article support best?
  (1) Japanese Americans were spies for Japan.
  (2) The internment of Japanese Americans was an injustice.
  (3) Japanese Americans didn't mind the internment camps.
  (4) The United States won the war with Japan.
  (5) Japanese Americans should have joined the Japanese army.

American Workers and Labor Unions

Union Membership in the United States, 1930–1995

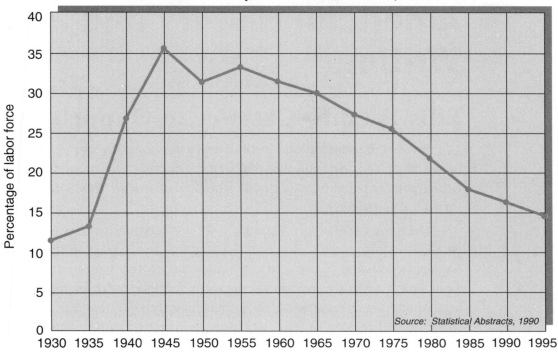

Source: Statistical Abstracts, 1990

Y-axis: Percentage of labor force

X-axis: 1930 1935 1940 1945 1950 1955 1960 1965 1970 1975 1980 1985 1990 1995

Write the answers to each question.

9 Union membership kept increasing until what year? _____

10 What happened after union membership increased in 1955?

_____

11 What might explain the steep rise in membership from 1935 to 1945?

_____

Circle the number of the best answer for each question.

12 Which statement is accurate according to the graph?
   (1) Union membership was greater in 1995 than in 1930.
   (2) Union membership grew rapidly from 1965 to 1970.
   (3) Union membership remained the same after 1950.
   (4) Union membership continued to increase after 1955.
   (5) Union membership was at its highest in 1955.

Social Studies Extension

For the next two weeks, collect the front sections of daily newspapers and read the headlines. Which news items indicate progress for your town or our nation? Which indicate conflict? Which will have lasting impact and make history?

Social Studies Connection: American History and Personal Writing

Ellis Island—Gateway to Opportunity

It was the most famous point of entry into America for millions of immigrants between 1892 and 1954. Whether wealthy or poor; English, Irish, Italian, German, or Greek; man, woman or child, those who arrived at New York's harbor had to pass through Ellis Island.

More than twelve million immigrants passed through Ellis Island during these years. For many, the hours endured during the processing into the U.S. were relatively painless compared to the uncomfortable days of their journeys at sea. Yet others, who were sick or unable to communicate, were detained for days and sometimes weeks. Still, some were turned away, never making it through the great immigration station. Others proudly spoke of their persistence—how they returned to Ellis Island time after time, until they were successfully admitted into America.

The stories of those who came through Ellis Island are as varied and unique as the people themselves. Many events and situations motivated these immigrants to leave the people and countries they loved. Over the years, discrimination and persecution, two world wars, the rise of fascism and communism, lack of jobs, famine, and poverty contributed to the constant flow of brave individuals into the United States.

Personal Writing: The Story of William Reinhart

Born: June 29, 1905

Emigrated: 1910, Age 4

Passage on the *Rotterdam* (Hamburg-American Line vessel)

My father came here first. He was an engraver, and our family history in that business dates back to 1611. My two oldest brothers were both officers in the German army, and they told him about the imminence of World War I. They suggested to my father if he wanted to leave, now was the time. That was 1909. So my father came to this country to get a home for us and establish us.

We came the following year. My mother must have been a saint, because she had the courage to bring eight children by herself to America. Her voice was so soft. When she scolded you, it hurt more than a physical punishment.

We had very bad weather crossing the Big Pond, as I got to call it in later years. And it took twenty-one days. I was the first one to get seasick, because we were cooped up. We had the lowest cabins in the ship.

Then at some point, we docked, and they told me we were at Ellis Island. The Health Department came aboard, and we received vaccinations. We didn't know a word of English. Then we took a small ferry from Ellis Island to the Battery. As we got off the ferry, our father met us. And it was just overwhelming. We hadn't seen our father for more than a year, and I really got to know him that first day. It was both exciting and wonderful.

Use the material below and on the previous page to answer the questions that follow.

I've heard stories of the roughness [of the inspectors] . . . the roughness consisted of somebody who did not make it. That was tough. That was worse than killing them. But we had to be honest enough. We had to go by the law . . . the ordeal they went through was not with the inspectors. It was with the doctors.

Jacob Auerbach, Immigration Inspector at Ellis Island, 1930–42

1 Ellis Island is located in
(1) England.
(2) Ireland.
(3) Italy.
(4) The American west.
(5) New York.

2 Upon arrival at Ellis Island, immigrants received
(1) a job.
(2) an inspection.
(3) a passport.
(4) a ferry ride.
(5) a hospital visit.

3 Which of the following best expresses William Reinhart's feelings about his entry into the U.S.?
(1) sad to have left his German homeland
(2) frightened to be leaving the *Rotterdam* ship
(3) embarrassed by his mother's scolding
(4) excited to be reunited with his father
(5) nervous to be meeting the immigration doctor

4 Which of the following best expresses the way Jacob Auerbach feels about the processing experience he observed at Ellis Island?
(1) compassion for those who did not pass the inspection
(2) dislike for the sick and weak who did not pass the inspection
(3) admiration for the doctors who inspected the immigrants
(4) disgust for inspectors who roughed up the immigrants
(5) fear of the inspectors and doctors

5 Personal writing can take many forms. Journals, biographies, and letters are just some of the forms we use to express our thoughts and feelings. Imagine that you must leave your family and homeland and travel to a strange, new country. Use a separate piece of paper to write a paragraph about the personal thoughts and feelings you might have. If you have actually had this experience, write about your immigration experience.

Check your answers on page 242.

UNIT 4

Government and Civics

Many Americans use the remote control to flip quickly past C-Span and the local cable channel when they see government meetings. Their inner voices shout "Government is boring!" And yet some of the most popular television programs in the United States today are about lawyers and detectives, wise-cracking judges, and "real" police in action. Americans like those parts of government.

Government plays many roles in American life and exists at several levels. Americans have local government close to home, government for their states, and a national government in Washington, D.C. At all levels government protects Americans' rights and freedoms.

○ What freedoms and rights are you guaranteed by living in the United States?

○ In what ways are you involved in your local government? In what ways could you be more involved?

SECTIONS

State and Local Governments

Setting the Stage

Your paycheck stub shows what share of your wages goes to federal, state, and city taxes. **Taxes** are one way that governments raise funds to pay for services to the people. But why are we taxed more than once?

The explanation actually starts back in the early days of the United States. The nation's first leaders did not want all the power of their new government in one place. They knew what that was like because Great Britain demanded all sorts of taxes from its colonies in America.

The leaders wanted decision-making power in the hands of all Americans. But they asked themselves if all Americans should decide about taxes spent in only one part of the country. The leaders reasoned that only the people who lived in that part of the country should decide. As a result, the writers of the Constitution created different levels of government that share the power to tax.

PREVIEW THE ARTICLE

Begin to think about what you will be reading. Look at the title of the article, the headings (subtitles) within the article, and the title of the table. What are two things you can expect to learn from this article?

_____

_____

RELATE TO THE TOPIC

This article tells how state and local governments get rid of trash. Do you recycle cans, plastic, glass, newspapers, paper, or junk mail? Why or why not?

_____

_____

VOCABULARY

Constitution	ordinances	hazardous wastes
landfill	groundwater	recycling

     Check your answers on page 242.

Taking Care of Everyday Needs

The **Constitution** is the basic law for American citizens. It describes the parts of the government and spells out the powers that belong to each part. These powers are shared between smaller, regional governments and a central, national government. The national government is in Washington, D.C. It is called the **federal government.** The regional governments are all over the nation. They are in states, cities, towns, counties, and villages and are called state and local governments.

The Constitution lists which powers the federal government has and which powers it cannot have. The Constitution also lists powers that state governments have and cannot have. However, many of the powers of state and local governments are not listed in the Constitution. If the Constitution does not ban the states from having a certain power, and it does not give the same power *only* to the federal government, then that power belongs to the states. States, for example, decide how old you must be to get a driver's license. That age varies from state to state.

Handling Trash

Many powers of state and local governments deal with the basic services people need every day. Local government, in particular, affects the quality of life. Cities and counties, for example, pave streets, treat and supply water, manage law enforcement and fire protection, and collect trash.

Today local governments face a trash crisis. Between 1960 and 2000, the amount of trash people produced increased by 136 percent. Americans throw away more than 200 million tons of trash each year.

Local governments have four choices in getting rid of this trash. They can burn it, bury it, compost it, or recycle it. But first they must sort it. Glass, metal, and other solid materials are separated from garbage, which decays by itself. Most local governments have **ordinances,** or laws, that require people to separate hazardous wastes from the rest of their trash. **Hazardous wastes** are those items that harm the environment. They include old batteries, motor oil, and certain kinds of paint.

Some counties and towns have furnaces that burn trash. It is burned under carefully controlled conditions. Burning reduces the volume of some trash by 90 percent, leaving only ash. The ash is then buried.

Most trash is not burned but buried in landfills. A **landfill** is a plot of land that is reserved for trash. It is often in areas away from neighborhoods. Trash is buried in the landfill between thin layers of soil. The United States had eight thousand landfills in 1988. Five thousand had closed by 1996. Many were older landfills that closed because they were full. Other older landfills closed because they became dangerous. As garbage decays, it forms poisons that can seep into the soil. The poisons pollute **groundwater,** which is an underground source of water. Groundwater feeds wells, springs, ponds, and **aquifers.** About half of the country's drinking water comes from groundwater.

Taking Responsibility

In many states, state and local government officials have worked together to solve their trash problems. They looked at all their options. As a result, some states passed laws that encourage recycling.

Recycling is reusing trash for the same or new purposes. To be used again, recyclable trash must often be processed into a new form. Some places require people to separate recyclable materials, such as aluminum, from their trash. Towns may get people to recycle by charging for trash pickup by the can or bag. Those who produce more trash pay more. One citizen said of the charges, "I've been [recycling] for years, but many of my friends and neighbors said they couldn't be bothered. But now they bother because it's hitting them in the pocketbook."

by Don Landgren; *The Landmark;* Holden, Mass. Reprinted with permission.

Reading a Political Cartoon   A **political cartoon** expresses an opinion on an issue. The cartoonist uses exaggerated drawings and symbols to express his or her views. It is important to know what the symbols mean and understand why they are used. What idea is the cartoonist expressing by having the man toss the globe as shown?

    a.   By not recycling, the man can have more fun.

    b.   By not recycling, the man is sacrificing the planet.

Some communities practice composting. Composting is letting plants and food waste decay on their own. These materials are then turned into rich soil. More than 2,000 communities have set up leaf-and-yard-waste compost centers.

Some states have laws that set requirements for new landfills. Towns and cities can no longer build their landfills near aquifers or lakes. The new landfills are also designed to be safer. The pits are lined with layers of sand, plastic, and clay. These linings prevent poisons, formed as trash decays, from oozing into the ground outside the pits. Also, pumps remove dangerous liquids from decaying trash. Many communities are cleaning up old landfills. When landfills are full, some local governments recycle the land and build golf courses and parks there.

The table below shows how some states have disposed of their trash. Each one (with its local governments) has made different decisions. Keep in mind that some states have more land available for landfills than others. Most landfills in the eastern half of the United States are full or will be within a few years. These states are more densely populated. A place that is densely populated has many people living within a square mile. Most land in these states is already in use.

How Different States Dispose of Their Trash

	California	Texas	Minnesota	Indiana	Georgia	Florida	New York	New Jersey	Maine
Landfilled	72%	85%	25%	69%	66%	38%	52%	34%	28%
Recycled	26%	14%	46%	23%	33%	40%	32%	43%	33%
Burned	2%	1%	29%	8%	1%	22%	16%	23%	39%

Source: *Municipal Factbook,* Environmental Protection Agency, 1997

Zero Waste

Since the 1980s, recycling has increased an average of 27 percent nationwide. But high costs stop local governments from recycling more than about thirty percent of their trash. New technology has helped lower the costs of recycling and burning trash, yet landfills are still the cheapest form of trash disposal. It costs about $35 a ton to bury trash, $70 a ton to burn it, and $125 a ton to recycle it.

Some trash experts suggest that manufacturers start designing their products with trash disposal in mind. These experts want companies to create ways for customers to reuse, recycle, or compost products and packaging. They hope to reach a goal of "zero waste." One expert says that local governments can clean and sort all trash into 12 categories. Recycling facilities would process these materials and create new goods from them.

Finding the Implied Main Idea   The **topic sentence** of a paragraph tells the main idea of the paragraph. Sometimes a paragraph has no topic sentence. So the main idea is not stated, but it is implied. The reader must determine the main idea from the details in the paragraph. Reread the first paragraph under the heading "Zero Waste." Which sentence best describes the main idea of the paragraph?

    a.   Recycling is an expensive way for local governments to dispose of trash.

    b.   More local governments are recycling trash than ever before.

Thinking About the Article

Practice Vocabulary

The terms below are in the passage in bold type. Study the way each term is used. Then complete each sentence by writing the correct term in the blank.

Constitution	**ordinances**	**hazardous wastes**
landfill	**groundwater**	**recycling**

1 A _____ is likely to be located away from densely populated areas.

2 Most local governments have _____ that require people to separate their trash.

3 Hawaii has no curbside program for _____, whereas New York has 1,472 such programs.

4 Old landfills may leak poisons into the _____, polluting water supplies.

5 The _____ lists the powers of the federal government.

6 _____ include old batteries, motor oil, and certain kinds of paint.

Understand the Article

Write the answer to each question.

7 Why do American citizens pay taxes more than once?

_____

_____

8 What are the four ways that local governments dispose of trash?

_____

_____

9 What are two reasons that landfills have been closing lately?

_____

_____

10 How are recycling and composting different?

_____

_____

Check your answers on page 242.

Apply Your Skills

Circle the number of the best answer for each question.

11 Look at the cartoon on page 142. Which opinion does it express?
(1) Americans are too lazy to recycle.
(2) Americans should clean up their homes.
(3) Americans' trash smells.
(4) The United States needs more landfills.
(5) Americans should recycle tires, sinks, and newspapers.

12 Reread the second paragraph under the heading "Taking Responsibility" on page 142. Which sentence states the paragraph's implied main idea?
(1) Most Americans refuse to recycle.
(2) Individuals and all levels of government must deal with the trash crisis.
(3) Recycling is the answer to the trash crisis.
(4) Getting cash refunds is a popular way to recycle.
(5) Local governments have set up different ways to get people to recycle.

13 Some cities now charge people for trash pickup according to how much trash they produce. Which opinion does the success of these programs support?
(1) Only individuals can end the trash crisis.
(2) People take local government's basic services for granted.
(3) People care about trash when it hits their pocketbooks.
(4) Nobody wants his or her trash picked up.
(5) The trash crisis is the government's problem.

Connect with the Article

Write your answer to each question.

14 Based on the table on page 143, what general statement can you make about the ways state and local governments dispose of trash?

_____

_____

_____

15 What are you doing now to help your community dispose of trash? What more could you do?

_____

_____

_____

The Constitution of the United States

Setting the Stage

The writers of the United States Constitution used ideas from European thinkers. One source was the French writer Baron de Montesquieu. In 1748 Montesquieu wrote a book praising Great Britain's government. In the book he explained that the British balanced the power of government among three branches. Parliament made the laws. The courts interpreted the laws. And the monarch and his or her ministers carried out the laws. Under such a system, Montesquieu wrote, "power should be a check to power."

Montesquieu's ideas became very popular in Great Britain's American colonies. Many colonial leaders agreed that government should be divided into branches. They used Montesquieu's ideas in the Constitution.

PREVIEW THE ARTICLE

Read the first two paragraphs on page 147. What are two things you can expect to learn from this article?

_____

_____

RELATE TO THE TOPIC

This section is about the way the Constitution divides the government's power among three branches. Recall when you last heard about the Congress, the President, or the Supreme Court taking action. Describe how you felt—shocked, angry, or grateful, perhaps—and whether you agreed with the action.

_____

_____

_____

VOCABULARY

legislative branch	**executive branch**	**judicial branch**
checks and balances	**separation of powers**	**bill**

Separation of Powers

In the United States, three branches of the federal government share power. Each branch has a specific job. The **legislative branch** makes laws. The **executive branch** carries out laws. The **judicial branch** decides what the laws mean. The Constitution spells out each branch's powers. The three branches work together to govern the nation.

Because each branch has responsibility for one key job of government, no one branch can become too powerful. This idea is called **separation of powers.** The writers of the Constitution also gave each branch ways to make sure the other two branches do not act beyond their power. Each branch has a certain amount of authority over the other branches. This balances the power among them and makes them equal partners in running the government. This idea is called **checks and balances**. The writers of the Constitution were the first to form a government that combined these two ideas.

Checks and Balances in the Executive and Legislative Branches

The President and Vice President lead the executive branch of the federal government. They make sure that the laws Congress passes are carried out. This branch is the only one in charge of enforcing laws. It has many departments to help. For example, the Labor Department enforces laws about workers, and the Defense Department carries out laws that deal with defending the United States from its enemies.

The executive branch has powers that check the legislative branch. For example, the President may **veto,** or reject, bills. A **bill** is a proposed law. Without a President's support and signature, a bill usually dies.

The executive branch also has a power that checks the judicial branch. The President appoints Supreme Court justices and other federal judges. The judges' decisions reveal their political views. The President often appoints people who share the President's views.

Congress is the legislative branch of the federal government. This legislature is made up of two houses, the House of Representatives and the Senate. American voters elect the members of each house. Together both houses of Congress make laws. This branch is the only one in charge of making laws.

The legislative branch has powers that check the executive branch. Although the President may veto a bill, the Constitution allows Congress to vote on the bill again. If two-thirds of both houses vote in favor of the bill, it becomes law. This action is called an **override** of the veto. The Constitution also gives Congress the power to approve government spending. To check the President, Congress can deny funds to pay for the President's favorite programs. The legislative branch can check the judicial branch, too. It sets federal judges' salaries and has the power to impeach judges.

Reading a Diagram   A **diagram** shows how a system works. Look at the diagram below. Follow the arrows from each branch of government and read what checks it has over the other branches. Which branch determines if a law is constitutional?

    a.   legislative branch   b.   executive branch   c.   judicial branch

The System of Checks and Balances

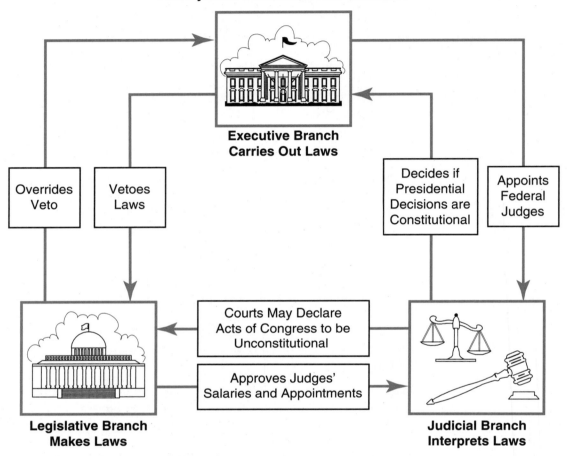

Checks by the Judicial Branch

The judicial branch of the federal government makes certain that the government follows the Constitution. At the head of the judicial branch is the Supreme Court. It has many lower courts to help it. If citizens object to a decision made in a federal court, they can **appeal,** or bring the case to another federal court called the appeals court. If citizens are unsatisfied with the appeals court's ruling, they can go to the Supreme Court.

The judicial branch checks both the legislative and executive branches in a similar way. It uses its power of **judicial review.** This means the Supreme Court and lower federal courts can determine whether a law passed by Congress follows the Constitution. If the Court rules that a law is unconstitutional, the executive branch stops enforcing the law.

Check your answer on page 243.

A Case Study in Checks and Balances

Government officials are sometimes frustrated with checks and balances. The following example is a case in which the judiciary checked both the executive and legislative branches. It shows the system of checks and balances in action.

In 1997 Congress passed the line-item veto law. Before this law, the President could reject only an entire spending bill or tax bill. The President could not accept some parts of the bill and reject others. The line-item veto law allowed the President to veto only specific parts of a bill.

Surprisingly, Congress was in favor of this law, which gave the President more power. Lawmakers thought the law would be a good way to control wasteful spending. They hoped it would encourage presidents to lower the huge **federal deficit.** This is the amount of money the government has to borrow each year. Congress knew that governors in 44 of the 50 states had line-item veto power. Governors who had used this power had some success in limiting spending in their state budgets.

Other people thought that giving the President a line-item veto was a bad idea. They said that the Constitution gave the power to control spending to Congress, not to the President. They believed the line-item veto weakened the separation of powers between these two branches of government.

When the new law took effect, President Bill Clinton praised it as "a powerful tool to protect taxpayers." Many presidents before him had wanted more power to curb government spending. Members of the executive branch saw the passage of the law as their victory.

In 1998 the Supreme Court ruled that the line-item veto law was unconstitutional. In the written decision, the justices quoted George Washington, who wrote that a president cannot change the text of a bill by Congress. In addition, the Constitution allows a president to veto a bill, but it does not say if the President can veto only parts of it. The Court decided that Congress could not give this power to the executive branch.

President Clinton was unhappy about the Supreme Court's decision. "The decision is a defeat for all Americans," he said. "It deprives the President of a valuable tool for eliminating waste in the federal budget."

Senators who favored the line-item veto were also unhappy with the decision. Usually Congress combines many kinds of spending in one bill. These unhappy senators threatened to include only one type of spending in each bill. If lawmakers used this method, the President would have to sign or veto thousands of spending bills each year.

Distinguishing Fact from Opinion   A **fact** states something that can be proved. An **opinion** expresses what a person or group thinks or believes. Which statement is a fact?

a.   The Constitution's writers gave the executive branch the power to veto bills.

b.   The judicial branch is the most powerful branch of government.

Check your answer on page 243.

Thinking About the Article

Practice Vocabulary

The terms below are in the passage in bold type. Study the way each term is used. Then complete each sentence by writing the correct term in the blank.

> legislative branch   executive branch   judicial branch
>
> checks and balances   separation of powers   bill

1 Determining whether the federal government acts according to the Constitution is the main job of the _____.

2 A(n) _____ does not usually become a law until the President signs it.

3 The _____ includes many departments that help enforce laws.

4 The writers of the Constitution used the idea of _____ by creating three branches of government to run the United States.

5 The Constitution gave the _____ control over government spending.

6 The idea that each branch of government has a certain amount of power over the other branches is called _____.

Understand the Article

Write the answer to each question.

7 What is an example of a check that the President has on Congress?

_____

8 What is a check that the Supreme Court has on the President?

_____

9 Why did the President and some people in Congress favor the line-item veto?

_____

_____

10 Why did the Supreme Court declare the line-item veto law to be unconstitutional?

_____

_____

Apply Your Skills

Circle the number of the best answer for each question.

11 Look at the checks and balances diagram on page 148. Which fact is supported by the information in the diagram?
  (1) The legislative branch is the most powerful because Congress makes laws.
  (2) Each branch of government checks the power of the other branches.
  (3) The veto power gives the President great power over Congress.
  (4) The Supreme Court has lower federal courts to help it interpret laws.
  (5) Congress is made up of the Senate and the House of Representatives.

12 What opinion did President Clinton hold about the line-item veto?
  (1) Presidents had been trying since the 1870s to gain the line-item veto.
  (2) President George Washington would have supported the line-item veto.
  (3) Putting each government expense in a separate bill would overload the President.
  (4) Some governors had the power to veto specific lines in a spending bill.
  (5) The line-item veto was a powerful tool to protect taxpayers.

13 According to the Supreme Court, how did the line-item veto disrupt the balance of power among the branches of the federal government?
  (1) It gave power to state governors that the executive branch should have.
  (2) It gave power to the executive branch that the state governors should have.
  (3) It gave power to Congress that the executive branch should have.
  (4) It gave too much power over Congress to the executive branch.
  (5) It did a poor job of limiting government spending.

Connect with the Article

Write your answer to each question.

14 How is the idea of separation of powers different from the idea of checks and balances?

_____

_____

15 Do you think it is in your best interest for the President to have a line-item veto? Explain your answer.

_____

_____

Setting the Stage

After the Constitution was written in 1787, several states were reluctant to approve it. These states wanted a list of rights in the document. They wanted it to say that the federal government would protect certain rights of citizens. Many of the Constitution's framers saw no need for such a list, because most states had these rights in their state constitutions already. But Virginia, in particular, was determined. Its leaders asked that a list of rights be added to the Constitution. These Virginians wanted to be sure the new American government would protect an individual's rights.

PREVIEW THE ARTICLE

Begin to think about what you will be reading. Look at the title of the article, the headings (subtitles) within the article, the chart, and the photograph of the document. What are two things you can expect to learn from this article?

_____

_____

RELATE TO THE TOPIC

This section is about the constitutional amendments that protect Americans who have been accused of a crime. Imagine that you are falsely accused of shoplifting and you cannot afford to hire a lawyer. Describe two disadvantages you would have in preparing to appear before a judge without a lawyer's help.

_____

_____

_____

VOCABULARY

amendment	**Bill of Rights**	**due process**
probable cause	**warrant**	**landmark**

Guarding Our Rights

Voters in Virginia elected James Madison as a representative to the first United States House of Representatives. Madison knew how important a list of individual rights was to Virginians. In the first session of Congress in 1789, Madison introduced 17 amendments to the Constitution. An **amendment** is an addition or change. These amendments were the list of rights that Virginia and other states wanted in the Constitution. In 1791 the states approved ten of the amendments that Madison suggested. These first ten amendments to the Constitution are called the **Bill of Rights.**

Guarantees of Freedom and Justice

The Bill of Rights protects freedom and justice for Americans. The First Amendment is the main guarantee of freedom. This amendment allows Americans to talk and write about their beliefs and opinions. It also allows them to meet with other people and to worship freely.

The Fourth through Eighth Amendments guarantee justice. They require that a person who is accused of a crime receives due process. **Due process** is the set of steps that officials who work in law enforcement and in the courts must follow to protect the rights of the accused. Below is a summary of the five amendments that are related to due process. Together these amendments protect the rights of the accused person.

Fourth Amendment A person has the right to be safe and secure. Police and other agents of the government cannot search a person's body, house, automobile, papers, or other belongings without a reason. They must show a judge that there is **probable cause,** or a significant link between the person and a criminal act. The judge then signs a **warrant**—a legal document that permits a search.

Fifth Amendment A person cannot be tried for a crime unless **indicted,** or formally charged with a crime. The accused cannot be tried twice for the same crime. A person cannot be forced to testify against himself or herself. The government cannot take a person's life, freedom, or property without due process. This means the government cannot jail, fine, or execute an accused person until he or she has gone through the proper steps in the legal process.

Sixth Amendment People accused of crimes have a right to a speedy and public trial. Government officials must tell them what the charges are. They are entitled to a lawyer. They also have the right to question anyone who testifies against them and to call witnesses in their defense.

Seventh Amendment A person is entitled to a trial by jury.

Eighth Amendment Fines and **bail,** or money given to the government for the temporary release of an accused person before trial, cannot be unusually large. Punishments cannot be cruel or unusual.

The Gideon Case

In June 1961 Clarence Gideon was charged with "breaking and entering" in Bar Harbor, Florida. Later that summer, he was tried and found guilty. He could not afford a lawyer. At that time in Florida, the state gave free legal help only to those persons accused of a crime punishable by death. Because the charges against Gideon were not that serious, he had to act as his own lawyer. Gideon believed that, as a result, he did not get a fair trial. He believed he had been denied his rights, which were guaranteed in the Bill of Rights.

Applying an Idea to a New Context   When Gideon read the Constitution, he applied what he read to his situation. He considered how each idea might affect his case. Reread the descriptions of the amendments on page 153. Which amendment did the state ignore in its treatment of Gideon?

   a.   Fourth

   b.   Sixth

Gideon believed that the Bill of Rights applied to his case. He thought it was wrong that he had to act as his own lawyer. The judge in the Florida trial court disagreed. In time Gideon's case reached the nation's highest court, the United States Supreme Court. The final decision about how the Constitution applies to a particular case is made by Supreme Court justices. A **justice** is a judge who serves on the Supreme Court.

The diagram on page 155 shows how cases reach the Supreme Court. Thousands of cases go through this process each year. However, the Supreme Court can hear only a few cases. Still Gideon felt he had nothing to lose by trying. He sent the Supreme Court justices a handwritten letter on prison stationery. In the letter Gideon asked the Court to release him from prison because the state should have provided him with a lawyer. Because it did not, Gideon claimed that he did not get a fair trial.

The Supreme Court agreed to hear Gideon's case. The Court felt that his case was a clear constitutional issue. Many states had strong feelings about the matter. Twenty-two states asked the justices to rule in Gideon's favor. Three states, including Florida, asked that the Court rule against Gideon.

Making Inferences from a Diagram   A diagram can show steps in a process. Making an **inference** means figuring out something based on the information you know about a subject. Look at the diagram on page 155. Considering what you know about Gideon's case, which court heard his case directly before it went to the Supreme Court?

   a.   highest state court

   b.   U.S. Court of Appeals

   c.   U.S. Court of Appeals for the Federal Circuit

How Cases Reach the United States Supreme Court

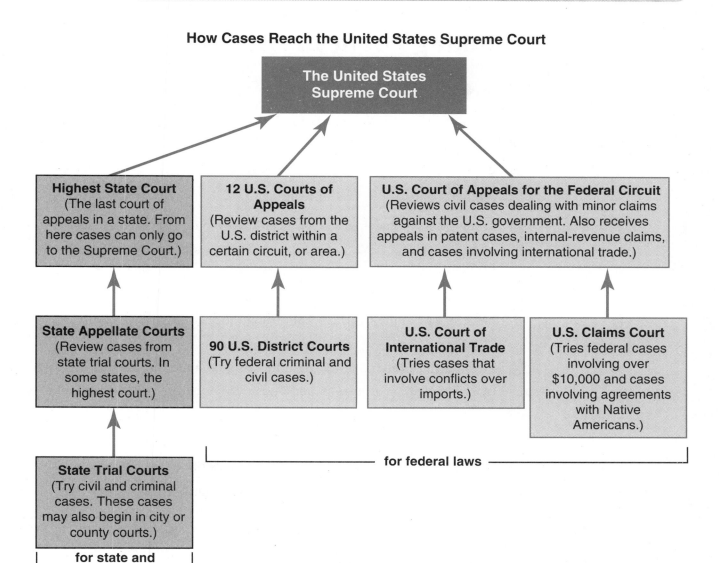

The United States Supreme Court

Highest State Court
(The last court of appeals in a state. From here cases can only go to the Supreme Court.)

12 U.S. Courts of Appeals
(Review cases from the U.S. district within a certain circuit, or area.)

U.S. Court of Appeals for the Federal Circuit
(Reviews civil cases dealing with minor claims against the U.S. government. Also receives appeals in patent cases, internal-revenue claims, and cases involving international trade.)

State Appellate Courts
(Review cases from state trial courts. In some states, the highest court.)

90 U.S. District Courts
(Try federal criminal and civil cases.)

U.S. Court of International Trade
(Tries cases that involve conflicts over imports.)

U.S. Claims Court
(Tries federal cases involving over $10,000 and cases involving agreements with Native Americans.)

for federal laws

State Trial Courts
(Try civil and criminal cases. These cases may also begin in city or county courts.)

for state and local laws

A Landmark Decision

The nine justices disagreed among themselves on how to decide Gideon's case. They discussed the case a great deal. Finally on March 18, 1963, the justices ruled in Gideon's favor. To explain their ruling, they quoted from a case the Court heard in 1932:

> (The accused) requires the guiding hand of counsel (a lawyer) at every step in the proceedings against him. Without it, though he be not guilty (even though he is not guilty), he faces the danger of conviction because he does not know how to establish his innocence.

The Gideon ruling was a **landmark** Supreme Court decision. This means that it changed the way government works. Today anyone accused of a crime has the right to a lawyer. If the person cannot afford a lawyer, the court must appoint one without charge.

Thinking About the Article

Practice Vocabulary

The terms below are in the passage in bold type. Study the way each term is used. Then complete each sentence by writing the correct term in the blank.

amendment	Bill of Rights	due process
probable cause	warrant	landmark

1. When police think a person has been involved in a crime, they must obtain a(n) ———————————— from a judge to search the person's home or car.

2. James Madison satisfied Virginians by introducing a list of rights that became part of the Constitution through the ———————————— process.

3. The Fourth through Eighth Amendments guarantee that a person accused of a crime will receive ———————————— from the government.

4. A(n) ———————————— decision changes the way the government works.

5. The ———————————— guarantees freedom of speech to Americans.

6. A good reason for thinking a person is guilty of a crime is called ————————————.

Understand the Article

Write the answer to each question.

7. Which amendment guarantees an individual's basic freedoms?

   _____

8. Which amendments guarantee justice to a person accused of a crime?

   _____

9. What does *due process* mean?

   _____

10. Why do you think Florida provided a lawyer only to persons accused of crimes punishable by death?

   _____

   _____

Check your answers on page 244.

Apply Your Skills

Circle the number of the best answer for each question.

11 In 1990 the Supreme Court heard an appeals case in which a preschool teacher was convicted of child abuse. The accused said her rights had been violated during the trial process. The child who brought the accusation testified about the case outside the courtroom through a one-way closed-circuit television. The judge, jury, and the accused with her attorney watched the testimony in the courtroom. Which amendment did the court ignore in this case?

(1) Fourth Amendment
(2) Fifth Amendment
(3) Sixth Amendment
(4) Seventh Amendment
(5) Eighth Amendment

12 Which statement can you infer from the diagram on page 155?

(1) Every criminal case goes to the Supreme Court.
(2) All cases begin in the state trial courts.
(3) The Supreme Court must hear all the cases from the U.S. Court of Appeals.
(4) At least two courts must hear any case before it moves to the Supreme Court.
(5) The President appoints Supreme Court justices.

13 After the Supreme Court's decision, Gideon was retried in 1963. This time he had the help of a lawyer. The jury found him not guilty. What lesson did Gideon teach other Americans?

(1) Know your rights under the law.
(2) You have the right to be safe.
(3) A person can be tried only once for a crime.
(4) You are entitled to a trial by jury.
(5) You have the right to express your beliefs.

Connect with the Article

Write your answer to each question.

14 Most state governments guaranteed individual rights, but Virginians wanted a list of these rights in the Constitution. Why do you think they wanted this?

_____

15 If you were unjustly accused of a crime, would you feel confident that a court-appointed lawyer would prove your innocence? Explain your answer.

_____

Elections

Setting the Stage

Each year voters in the United States go to the polls. There the people choose their representatives in government. Every four years Americans elect the President of the United States. Every two years they elect all their state's members in the House of Representatives, and every six years they elect one of their state's two senators. Voters also choose governors, mayors, judges, sheriffs, and many other government leaders.

People vote for or against issues as well as candidates on election day. They may vote to approve the local school budget or a new tax for enlarging the public library. By voting, people directly decide important matters of government.

PREVIEW THE ARTICLE

Read the first two paragraphs on page 159. What are two things you can expect to learn from this article?

_____

_____

RELATE TO THE TOPIC

Describe the last public issue or person running for office about whom you felt strongly for or against. What about the issue or person made you feel the way you did? If you can vote, did you act on your feelings by voting? Why or why not? If you cannot vote, do you think voting would have been a good outlet for your feelings? Why or why not?

_____

_____

VOCABULARY

politics	political party	campaign	primary election
media	political action committees		general election

Check your answers on page 244.

The Election Process

The right to vote is one of the most important rights of a citizen. It is a right that many groups of Americans have worked hard to win. White men who did not own land could not vote in the early 1800s. Women could not vote until 1920. Native Americans, who voted on tribal decisions, did not vote in U.S. elections until 1924. African Americans could not vote in some Southern states until the 1960s. And eighteen-year-olds did not gain the right to vote until 1971.

American Voters

Americans must meet certain requirements to vote. Voters must be citizens and at least 18 years old. Most Americans are citizens because they were born in the United States. Others came to this country, studied English and U.S. history, and became citizens. Voters also must have lived in a state a certain length of time before they can vote. Most states require people to live there at least thirty days before they are eligible to vote. Other state laws also bar some people from voting. No state allows people who are in a mental institution to vote. Most states will not allow people convicted of serious crimes to vote. Some states disqualify homeless persons.

Voters learn about **politics,** or the ideas and actions of government, at a very young age. As children, they hear their parents talk about issues and leaders. In time the children form opinions. About two of every three Americans have the same political beliefs as their parents. Often they express these beliefs by joining a political party. A **political party** is a group that **nominates,** or chooses, candidates. A **candidate** is a person who runs for public office. People in the same political party often share the same views on one or more issues. If their party's candidate wins the election, the members of the party assume that the candidate will promote their political goals.

The Democratic and Republican parties are the major American political parties. Almost every election has candidates from one or both of these parties. Other political parties have fewer members. These parties have too little support to run candidates for every political office.

Supporting Conclusions   To draw a **conclusion,** you must identify which facts about a subject are important. Then you judge or decide what the facts tell you about the subject. The judgment you make after examining facts is called a conclusion. The facts on the subject should support your conclusion.

Reread the first paragraph under the heading "American Voters." One conclusion you might draw is that all voters are not American born. Which fact in the paragraph supports that conclusion?

a.   Most states require people to live there at least thirty days before they can vote.

b.   Others came to this country, studied English and U.S. history, and became citizens.

Persuading the Voters

Before an election, a candidate takes part in a series of events called a **campaign.** The goal of the campaign is to persuade people to vote for the candidate. If several members of a political party want to run for the same office, the party chooses its candidate by committee, convention, or a **primary election.** This is an election in which voters choose the party's candidate for the office.

In a presidential election year, many states hold primary elections in the spring. In the summer the delegates, who were selected in the primary, attend the party's national convention. There they nominate the party's candidate for President in the **general election** in the fall. Because of this process, a candidate's campaign can last for many months. Candidates must first campaign within their party to get the nomination. Then, if they are successful at the national convention, they must campaign for all the voters' support in the general election.

Many Americans learn about election candidates and issues from the media. The **media** include radio, television, newspapers, and magazines. Reporters present news stories and other information about a campaign. The people who run a campaign also use the media. They run ads to persuade people to vote a certain way. Television has become the key means of gaining support for candidates. To be successful, candidates must get their point across in television ads and compete for the American voters' attention.

The media are on hand to cover campaign events.

Political ad writers use the same methods to win votes that advertisers use to sell products. In recent years many political ad writers have taken a negative approach. They want their candidate's opponents to look like poor choices. Their ads often reveal only some of the facts and may mislead voters.

In 1992 the Democrats blamed America's economic problems on Republican Presidents Ronald Reagan and George Bush. In response the Republicans ran a series of ads against the Democratic party. The Republican party hoped the ads would help Republicans win more seats in the House of Representatives. On page 160 read the transcript from one of the Republican party's television ads.

Distinguishing Fact from Opinion   Political ad campaigns mix opinions with facts. They do this in order to help the candidate put forth the best image he or she can.

Circle the letter of the opinion below.

a.   Our candidate is the best person to speak for our state's concerns.

b.   Our candidate has supported children's rights in her work as a defense attorney.

c.   Our candidate has worked in the governor's office for 10 years.

Financing Campaigns

When George Washington ran for President some two hundred years ago, he did not spend any money. But campaigns today are expensive. Running a TV ad just once can cost hundreds of thousands of dollars. In the last week of the 1996 campaign, President Clinton spent about $1.2 million a day on TV advertising.

Raising money has become an important task of political parties. Some money comes from individuals. However, most of it comes from **political action committees** (PACs). Special interest groups, such as the American Association of Retired Persons and the National Rifle Association, set up PACs. The PACs give money to candidates who share their political beliefs about certain issues.

PACs also do a good job of getting members of special interest groups to vote. Election experts know that PACs can help a candidate win. PACs also may help defeat candidates who oppose their views.

In the 1970s Americans became concerned about the high cost of running for office. Many people said that the system favored wealthy candidates over poorer ones. As a result, members of Congress passed laws that demanded better records of contributions and created a public fund that all candidates could use. Congress gave the power to enforce these laws to the Federal Election Commission.

After the 1992 presidential election, the public campaign fund was nearly empty. Too few Americans were contributing to the fund. However, advertising costs were so high that candidates soon reached their spending limits. For these reasons many Americans are working on proposals for new and fairer ways to finance political campaigns.

Thinking About the Article

Practice Vocabulary

The terms below are in the passage in bold type. Study the way each term is used. Then complete each sentence by writing the correct term in the blank.

> **politics** **political party** **campaign** **primary election**
>
> **general election** **media** **political action committees**

1 Television advertising is an important way that candidates communicate

with voters during a _____.

2 Candidates use all kinds of _____ to communicate
with the American voters.

3 Special interest groups called _____ support
candidates who promote political beliefs similar to their own.

4 The family is a major influence on Americans' attitudes toward

_____.

5 The Democratic candidate who wins the _____ in the
spring runs against the Republican candidate in November.

6 Democrats belong to the same _____.

7 In the United States a _____ is held in November.

Understand the Article

Write the answer to each question.

8 What three qualifications must an American meet to vote?

_____

_____

9 Why might a candidate's political campaign last for many months?

_____

_____

10 Name one way elections have changed since George Washington was
President.

_____

_____

                    Check your answers on page 245.

Apply Your Skills

Circle the number of the best answer for each question.

11 Which of the following examples <u>best</u> supports the conclusion that the media sometimes take sides in political campaigns?
(1) A newspaper article describes both sides of a campaign issue.
(2) A television network broadcasts a debate between candidates.
(3) A radio announcer points out factual errors in political ads.
(4) A magazine includes information about only one candidate for senator.
(5) A newspaper runs political ads about all the candidates for mayor.

12 Ann is running for the state assembly. She promises that if she wins the election, she will vote to repeal a law that requires motorcyclists to wear helmets. Ann's opponent runs a campaign ad stating that if Ann wins, deaths due to motorcycle accidents will increase. Which of the following statements points out the faulty logic in this ad?
(1) Ann may not be elected to the state assembly.
(2) Ann probably will vote to repeal the helmet law if she is elected.
(3) The number of deaths due to motorcycle accidents probably will increase if the helmet law is repealed.
(4) Ann will not be the only assembly member deciding whether or not to repeal the helmet law.
(5) The number of deaths due to motorcycle accidents has nothing to do with whether people wear helmets.

13 Why is a special interest group most likely to form a PAC?
(1) to give money to the candidates who need it the most
(2) to support a candidate who shares the group's views
(3) to run political ads that present all views on the issues
(4) to encourage people to stay home instead of voting
(5) to support all the candidates running for office

Connect with the Article

Write your answer to each question.

14 Do you think television ads are a wise use of a candidate's campaign funds? Explain your answer.

_____

15 Most campaign finance laws have failed to hold down the cost of presidential campaigns. What two changes would you make if you were in charge of campaign spending?

_____

_____

Debating an Issue

Setting the Stage

Each year guns are involved in the death or injury of thousands of Americans. Many people think the nation needs tough laws to control the sale of guns. Others believe the Constitution's Second Amendment protects a citizen's right to own a gun.

Throughout the 1990s Americans debated the meaning of the Second Amendment. Because it is in the Bill of Rights, some Americans believe the amendment gives them the right to own guns. Other Americans think the amendment only allows weapons for a citizen army. The wording of the amendment is not easy to understand. So Americans have differences of opinion as to what this amendment means.

PREVIEW THE ARTICLE

Begin to think about what you will be reading. Look at the title of the article, the headings (subtitles) within the article, and the title of the bar graph. What are some of the things you can expect to learn from this article?

_____

_____

RELATE TO THE TOPIC

This section is about the opinions Americans have toward laws that stop them from owning certain guns. Think about what you know about this controversial issue. What kinds of guns do you think private citizens should be allowed to purchase for their personal use?

_____

_____

VOCABULARY

militia   **gun control**   **federal law**

self-defense   **permit**

Check your answers on page 245.

Limiting Guns

The 1980s was a violent decade for America. During that period people with handguns killed nearly 225,000 Americans. Gunshot wounds became the leading cause of death among African-American men. In 1981 a young man tried to kill President Ronald Reagan.

Many Americans reacted to all this violence by calling for tougher laws on buying guns. They pointed out that, by the late 1980s, some criminals were using assault weapons designed for use in war. Soldiers use these weapons in battle. These guns can kill many people at a time.

Other Americans disagreed with this solution. They argued that such laws only limit a person's freedom and will not stop violence. In their opinion the Second Amendment to the United States Constitution guarantees every American the right to own weapons.

Gun Control: Yes or No?

One role of the United States Supreme Court is to tell the people what the Constitution means. Americans have looked to the Court to interpret the Second Amendment. The Second Amendment states, "A well regulated Militia, being necessary to the security of a free State, the right of the people to keep and bear Arms shall not be infringed [taken away]."

The Court has failed to give people a clear-cut answer. In a 1939 ruling, the Court decided that the Second Amendment did not protect a person who used a sawed-off shotgun in a crime. The justices pointed out that a "well regulated militia" would not have used such weapons, so no protection should be granted. A **militia** is an army of citizens called to guard and protect only during emergencies. In other cases the Supreme Court justices said that the use of guns was not the federal government's concern. The Court ruled that states should make the laws concerning gun ownership.

Before the 1990s some state legislatures passed gun-control laws. **Gun control** sets legal limits on the sale of guns to the public. Cities and towns as well as states made these laws, so different places had different rules concerning the sale of guns. This meant that people would go to another city or state and buy guns they could not buy in their own hometown. Many Americans believed that only a tough **federal law,** or a law that applies to the whole country, could deal with the growing rate of violent crime.

Distinguishing Fact from Opinion   The paragraphs above contain both facts and opinions about guns and violence. You can check in reliable sources to be certain that facts are accurate. Opinions are people's beliefs and feelings about the facts. Which of the following statements is an opinion?
  a.   A tough federal law can stop the growing rate of violent crime.
  b.   State legislatures pass laws to limit the sale of guns.

The Argument Against Gun Control

For a long time, the National Rifle Association (NRA) has led the fight against gun-control laws. The group began more than one hundred years ago to teach safety and marksmanship to gun owners. Since the 1970s the NRA has worked to protect the right of every American to own a gun. The group believes that protecting the right to own guns ensures the protection of other rights.

Another reason the NRA resists gun-control laws is that its members believe people need guns for self-defense. **Self-defense** is defending oneself and one's property. The NRA stresses that most gun owners are law-abiding citizens. The group's members ask why an honest citizen should be deprived of a firearm for a gun collection, sport, or self-defense. After all, they argue, criminals can always obtain a gun, whether there is a law against purchasing guns or not. They simply would pay enough money to a person who deals in guns illegally.

Members of the NRA agree that violent crime is a problem in the United States. But the group does not believe that laws controlling guns will stop it. Its members reason that instead of gun-control laws, Congress should pass tougher laws to punish criminals. One senator who is a supporter of the NRA said, "Blaming guns for a criminal's violence makes no more sense than blaming automobiles for drunk driving."

In 1998 the NRA elected actor Charlton Heston as its president. Heston is best known for playing Moses in the 1956 movie *The Ten Commandments.* He has enlisted the support of many famous people to fight gun control.

David Horsey; © *Seattle Post-Intelligencer.* Reprinted with permission.

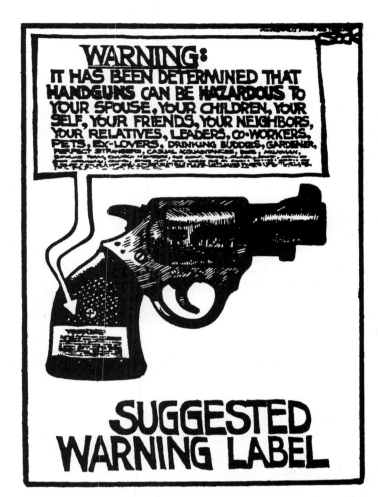

Steve Sack; *Minneapolis Star and Tribune.* Reprinted with permission.

The Argument for Gun Control

When Ronald Reagan was shot in 1981, James Brady, the President's press secretary, was also hit. Reagan made a full recovery, but Brady's injuries caused permanent disability. Brady and his wife, Sarah, began a long battle to get Congress to pass a federal gun-control law.

The Bradys and others who favor gun control say the issue is not whether the Second Amendment allows citizens to own guns. They point to the limits on many other rights that the Constitution protects. For example, the First Amendment gives Americans the right to hold parades. Yet most cities require groups of people to get a **permit,** or written permission, before parading down city streets. Supporters of gun control say that the right to own guns should be treated in a similar way. Only people with permits should own weapons.

Those who favor gun control say that guns owned by law-abiding citizens often end up in the hands of criminals. Burglars are just as likely to steal guns as anything else. In fact, they can get more money for a gun than for a television or stereo. Gun-control supporters also point to research that shows gun owners who keep guns for self-defense are more likely to kill someone they know than to kill a criminal.

In 1993 President Bill Clinton signed the Brady Handgun Violence Prevention Act. The law required licensed gun dealers to register handgun customers. Then customers waited five days before receiving their guns while local police checked to see if they had criminal records.

The law's provision for a five-day waiting period was only temporary. It expired in 1998. Now local police may enforce a three-day waiting period but often fail to do so. However, recent surveys show most police departments still check for criminal records.

Reading Political Cartoons A political cartoonist expresses an opinion about an issue through the cartoon's symbols and words. Which opinion does the cartoonist express in the cartoon above?

    a.   The cartoonist is against gun control.

    b.   The cartoonist is in favor of gun control.

Thinking About the Article

Practice Vocabulary

The terms below are in the passage in bold type. Study the way each term is used. Then complete each sentence by writing the correct term in the blank.

militia   **gun control**   **federal law**

self-defense   **permit**

❶ People against laws that set limits on owning guns believe that everyone has the right to own a gun for _____.

❷ Supporters of _____ believe that setting limits on owning guns will help decrease the number of violent crimes.

❸ The Supreme Court has interpreted the Second Amendment only as it relates to weapons and the _____.

❹ According to supporters of gun control, requiring that a gun owner get a _____ may help keep guns out of criminals' hands.

❺ Early supporters of gun control demanded a _____, which would apply to the whole country.

Understand the Article

Write the answer to each question.

❻ What does the Second Amendment say and why do people disagree about its meaning?

_____

❼ Why is the right to own a sawed-off shotgun not protected by the Second Amendment?

_____

_____

❽ What are two issues on which groups debating gun control disagree?

_____

_____

❾ What is one issue on which the groups for and against gun control agree?

_____

_____

Apply Your Skills

Circle the number of the best answer for each question.

10 Which of the following is a statement of *opinion* about gun control?
   (1) An honest citizen should not be deprived of a firearm for sport.
   (2) During the 1980s, people with handguns killed nearly 225,000 Americans.
   (3) Gun owners who keep guns for protection are more likely to kill someone they know than they are to kill a criminal.
   (4) The National Rifle Association was founded to teach safety and marksmanship to gun owners.
   (5) The vote in Congress for the Brady bill was very close.

11 Look at the cartoon on page 166. Which statement <u>best</u> summarizes the cartoon's main idea?
   (1) Tough gun-control laws follow the First Commandment.
   (2) The Constitution guarantees Americans the right to own guns.
   (3) Charlton Heston's fame will improve the NRA's image.
   (4) Owning a gun is a sacred right that cannot be taken away.
   (5) The Second Amendment is one of the Ten Commandments.

12 Look at the cartoon on page 167. Which statement <u>best</u> summarizes the cartoon's main idea?
   (1) Tough gun-control laws will not reduce violence.
   (2) Criminals buy guns in order to kill people.
   (3) Guns give families good protection.
   (4) Having a waiting period before buying a gun will decrease shootings of family members.
   (5) A gun kept for protection is more likely to kill someone the gun owner knows than an attacker.

Connect with the Article

Write your answer to each question.

13 Describe one benefit of a federal law requiring a five-day waiting period before a person may purchase a handgun.

_____

_____

14 Based on the arguments presented in this article, are you for or against gun control? Give reasons to support your opinion.

_____

_____

Civics at Work

Service: Community Worker

Some Careers in Community Service

Food Bank Worker collects and distributes needed food and other consumable products to community residents

Community Outreach Worker helps local residents organize for their rights or against unfair or discriminatory practices

Political Aide serves as a link between candidates, politicians, or political organizations and the rest of the community

Shelter Coordinator oversees providing shelter, clothing, food, and counseling to the homeless and to victims of domestic violence

Community worker discussing issues with a local resident

You find them in a variety of settings. They may work for environmental groups, political organizations, social service agencies, or neighborhood and grassroots organizations. Who are they? They're community workers.

Community service work is usually challenging, but it is also rewarding. There is often a lot of work to do, and the hours can be unpredictable. But if you care about the well-being of your community, then this may be the type of job for you.

A broad range of community service work exists. Some workers help clients obtain basic services such as housing assistance, job placement, medical care, and child care. Others may focus their efforts on community safety or environmental protection. Still other community workers may help residents speak up for their personal and political rights.

Community workers must be familiar with the laws and rules affecting the work they perform. While all community workers' rights to speech and assembly are protected by the U.S. Constitution, they also have to know state and local laws and regulations involved in their work. Community workers need to be good listeners and speakers. They also need to be able to put their ideas and the ideas of others into writing.

Look at the Some Careers in Community Service chart.

- Do any of the careers interest you? If so, which ones?

- What information would you need to find out more about those careers? On a separate piece of paper, write some questions that you would like answered. You can find more information about those careers in the *Occupational Outlook Handbook* at your local library.

Use the material below to answer the questions that follow.

> **MEMO**
>
> To: Evan, Project LINK Director
> From: Anita, Community Outreach Worker
> Re: Election Efforts
>
> Last Thursday evening I was distributing election flyers at Stone Elementary School. I was asked to leave the site by the school's principal and a police officer. When I asked them why, they gave no explanation. They grabbed me by my elbows and escorted me to my car.
>
> I know by now you have heard about this incident. I would like you to know that I followed all the laws that you explained to me. I stood more than 15 feet from the school's entrance. I did not give a flyer to anyone under the age of 18. I did not force anyone to take a flyer.
>
> This troubles me. I know that the First Amendment to the Constitution guarantees me the right to freedom of speech. I think this action violates my rights. Please let me know what I can do about this situation.

❶ Anita's assignment for Thursday evening was to
   (1) guard the entrance of Stone Elementary School.
   (2) help the principal at Stone Elementary School.
   (3) distribute election flyers at Stone Elementary School.
   (4) get arrested by the police at Stone Elementary School.
   (5) make sure no one under age 18 entered the school.

❷ Which of the following is <u>not</u> a right guaranteed Anita by the First Amendment?
   (1) the right to be on the school district's property
   (2) publishing a flyer about the upcoming election
   (3) telling adults over the age of 18 about the election
   (4) handing flyers about the election to interested adults
   (5) talking to local reporters about the election

❸ It is likely that Anita stood more than 15 feet from the entrance of the school because
   (1) she was able to talk to more people before they entered the school.
   (2) she was nervous that the principal would make her leave.
   (3) the local law specified she must be that distance from the entrance.
   (4) the First Amendment requires her to stand that distance from the entrance.
   (5) the principal and the police officer told her she should stand that far away.

The Miranda Decision

In March 1963 a man kidnapped and raped a young girl. Ten days later the police arrested Ernesto Miranda. After police questioned Miranda alone for two hours, he confessed to the crime. Prosecutors used Miranda's confession as evidence against him at the trial. The jury found Miranda guilty. In 1966 the Supreme Court overturned, or set aside, Miranda's conviction. The justices believed police had violated Miranda's constitutional rights. Police had not told Miranda that, as a suspect in a crime, he had the right to talk to a lawyer before they questioned him. This Supreme Court ruling is called the Miranda Decision.

As a result of the Court's ruling, police must tell people they arrest about three of their constitutional rights: First, people have the right to remain silent. Second, anything they choose to say can be used against them in court. Third, they have the right to have a lawyer present while police question them. These rights are known as the Miranda rights.

In 1986 another case about suspects' rights reached the Supreme Court. The New York City police chased a man suspected of rape into a store. When the officers checked to see if the man had a weapon, they found an empty holster. When police asked him where his gun was, the suspect told them. After police found the gun, they read the suspect his Miranda rights. The gun and the man's statement were used as evidence against him. The Supreme Court decided that "public safety outweighs the need for the rule protecting the Fifth Amendment's privilege against self-incrimination."

Write the answers to the question.

1 Name two ways the two cases described in the article are alike.

_____

_____

Circle the number of the best answer for each question.

2 Which conclusion is the best one to draw from the facts in the article?
  (1) The Supreme Court can reverse its decisions after time has passed.
  (2) When suspects threaten public safety, their rights are not fully protected.
  (3) The Supreme Court does not always side with criminals.
  (4) Reading Miranda rights makes it harder for police to make arrests.
  (5) The three Miranda rights that police read have been changed.

City Government

Two Plans of Mayor-City Council Government

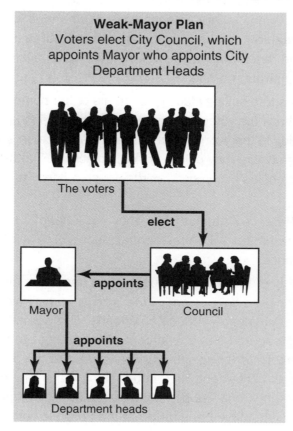

Weak-Mayor Plan
Voters elect City Council, which appoints Mayor who appoints City Department Heads

The voters
elect
Mayor
appoints
Council
appoints
Department heads

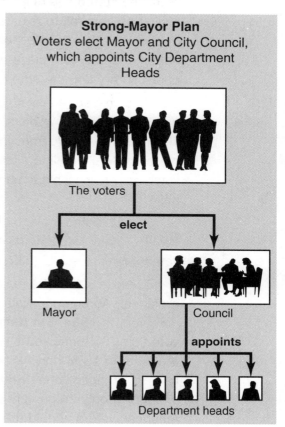

Strong-Mayor Plan
Voters elect Mayor and City Council, which appoints City Department Heads

The voters
elect
Mayor
Council
appoints
Department heads

Circle the number of the best answer for each question.

3 Which statement is supported by information in the diagram?
(1) Voters must go to the polls only for the strong-mayor plan.
(2) A weak mayor can reject decisions that the city council makes.
(3) The council chooses the mayor in the weak-mayor plan.
(4) The mayor has no direct voter support in the strong-mayor plan.
(5) The council appoints department heads in the weak-mayor plan.

4 Which idea about local government does the diagram imply most clearly?
(1) The power of voters is greatest in the strong-mayor plan.
(2) The council approves all mayoral decisions in the weak-mayor plan.
(3) The council must approve the strong-mayor's choices for department heads.
(4) Local government is weakest when voters elect both the council and mayor.
(5) Local government is most representative when most voters stay away from the polls.

Check your answers on page 246.

Voting Makes a Difference

Just before elections, the ads appear. "Don't forget to vote!" "Every vote counts." Many registered voters go to the polls on election day. However, many people who are eligible to vote fail to register. Almost every American citizen who is at least 18 years of age is eligible to vote. To **register** means to complete a form that tells the voter's name, address, and place and date of birth. These forms are often available at the public library and the auto registration office.

Each registered voter goes to a polling place close to his or her home on election day. There, election workers check the voter list to make sure the person is registered. This prevents people from voting in the wrong place or more than once. In some polling places, voters step into a booth where they pull levers on a machine. In other places, voters use a punchpin to punch holes in computer cards or use a pencil to mark a paper ballot.

Do the votes make a difference? Studies show they do. A handful of votes decides many elections. Even in nationwide presidential elections, a small number of votes have made a big difference.

Experts say that a majority of the voting-age population has never elected a president. Abraham Lincoln received 55 percent of the vote when he was reelected President in 1864. But Native Americans, African Americans, and women could not vote then. So those votes represented only 13 percent of the voting-age population at the time. In 1996 only 49 percent of voting-age Americans went to the polls. About 49 percent of these voters reelected President Bill Clinton. This means that he had the support of only 24 percent of the voting-age population—not even one-fourth of the American voters. Would the results have been different if all eligible voters had taken time to vote? No one will ever know.

Write the answer to each question.

5 Where can an eligible voter go to register to vote?

_____

6 Why is a person's date of birth important on the voter's registration form?

_____

Circle the number of the best answer for each question.

7 Which statement does the article support?
  (1) If you pay taxes, you must register to vote.
  (2) Registering is a way of helping people vote.
  (3) Most people register to vote.
  (4) More people would vote if they registered.
  (5) Votes can make a difference in all kinds of elections.

The Right to Privacy

Write the answer to each question.

8 What does the man on the left with the beard represent?

_____

9 The drawing on the right is of Bill Gates, the head of a major computer software company. What does he represent in the cartoon?

_____

Circle the number of the best answer for the question.

10 What does the cartoon imply about Americans' right to privacy in the world today?
  (1) Americans have little privacy because they are just numbers to government and big business.
  (2) Protecting the right to privacy is challenging because computers make information easily available.
  (3) The right to privacy is threatened because criminals can get information about Americans.
  (4) The right to privacy is guaranteed because the federal government and big business promise not to abuse this right.
  (5) Americans' right to privacy is safeguarded under the Constitution.

Social Studies Extension

Attend a meeting of your local city council, county commission, or school board. List all the topics the officials discuss and circle those that lead to a decision by the group.

Social Studies Connection: Government, Civics, and Math

Who Are We? Let's Take a Count!

As a nation, who are we? Where do we live? What do our families look like? What kind of work do we do? How have we changed over the years? The highest law of our land, the Constitution, requires that the federal government answer these questions every ten years. To obtain an accurate count of the population of our nation, the government uses a process called a **census.**

The information gathered in a census determines many things. For example, it determines how many representatives each state has in the U.S. House of Representatives. Since states have one representative for every 30,000 residents, changes in population, as reported by the census, affect whether states gain or lose representatives. Census information also determines the amount of federal funds that states receive for education, housing, welfare programs, and other public services.

Census takers help communities get an accurate count of their residents.

Math: Numbers in the Census Battle

Since 1790, the U.S. government has tried to get an accurate count of the people in our nation and their characteristics. It sends a survey form to every household. For households that don't respond to the survey, the Census Bureau sends workers to talk to the people. This method has been criticized as resulting in inaccurate census figures. Some communities are undercounted because of low response rates. It was estimated that the 1990 census undercounted the country's population of approximately 248,710,000 by as many as four million people.

Problems of undercounting and rising census costs led the U.S. Census Bureau to propose using a different method called *statistical sampling*. The sampling method would collect data from only some of the population. These data would then be used to make projections for the rest of the population.

Some people were pleased with this idea. They believed that it would provide a more accurate picture of the nation's people. Others feared losing political representation and government funding if previously uncounted people were added to the population figures of other communities. A lawsuit against the proposal made its way to the Supreme Court. The Court ruled that statistical sampling was unconstitutional and could not be used in the 2000 census.

Use the material on the previous page and the chart below to answer the questions that follow.

1990 U.S. Census Data–Race	
Universe: Persons	
American Indian, Eskimo, or Aleut	2,015,143
Asian or Pacific Islander	7,226,986
Black	29,930,524
White	199,827,064
Other Race	9,710,156

1 A census is conducted in the U.S. every
  (1)   1 year.
  (2)   3 years.
  (3)   5 years.
  (4)   10 years.
  (5) 100 years.

2 The Census Bureau suggested using a new counting method for the 2000 census because
  (1) it would be a good way to begin the new millennium.
  (2) the Constitution requires the government to do so.
  (3) the Supreme Court ruled they must do it.
  (4) the people of the U.S. asked them to do it.
  (5) the old method yielded errors and high costs.

3 If the appropriate correction was made to the figures from the 1990 census, the total population of the U.S. would have been approximately
  (1) 30,000 persons
  (2) 4,000,000 persons
  (3) 4,030,000 persons
  (4) 248,000,000 persons
  (5) 253,000,000 persons

4 Historically, minority groups have been among the most seriously undercounted populations. According to the chart above, which subpopulation is likely to be <u>most</u> affected by the undercounting problem?
  (1) American Indian, Eskimo, or Aleut
  (2) Asian or Pacific Islander
  (3) Black
  (4) White
  (5) Other Race

Economics

Have you ever said, "I *need* that CD!"? Actually, you *want* that CD. But most Americans, at one time or another, catch themselves spending money on things they want but don't need. These purchases—along with the electric bill, phone bill, or rent—are all economic choices that cost money Americans work hard to earn. Multiply a day's wants and needs by the more than 125 million American workers and you end up with a vast number of wants and needs. Yet the number of resources available to make products, develop services, and sell these to Americans and American businesses is limited. **Economics** is the study of how people satisfy their wants and needs by making choices about how to use limited resources.

◉ What economic choices do you make daily? Weekly? Monthly? Yearly?

◉ Would you describe yourself as a good money manager? A cost-conscious shopper? A saver?

SECTIONS

22 Free Enterprise

Setting the Stage

In the United States, individuals choose daily how they will spend the money they earn. Some will travel several miles, for example, to buy groceries from a supersized grocery-hardware-clothing store. Others will shop at the supermarket closest to their neighborhood. Such factors as price, convenience, and good service influence such decisions. Businesses make economic choices as well. They note which products are selling and which are not. They study which product supplier offers the lowest prices, the best quality, and the fastest delivery. Americans are free to buy, and American businesses are free to sell what they want.

PREVIEW THE ARTICLE

Begin to think about what you will be reading. Look at the title of the article, the headings (subtitles) within the article, the chart, and the photograph of the document. What are two things you can expect to learn from this article?

_____

_____

RELATE TO THE TOPIC

This section uses farming to explain how the economy in the United States works. Think back to your childhood and recall two specific food products or toys your parents bought you. Are they still available? Why do you think they remained available or did not remain available?

_____

_____

VOCABULARY

free enterprise system	**market**	**consumers**
demand	**efficiency**	**cooperative**

   Check your answers on page 247.

How Free Enterprise Works

The United States has an economic system called the **free enterprise system.** In this type of economy, **consumers,** or buyers, buy products and services from privately owned businesses. Producers determine the kinds, the amounts, and the prices of goods based on what consumers want to buy. In other words, Americans make economic choices based on opportunities in the market. A **market** means several related things. It could be a place where producers sell to sellers. It could be a place where people who buy products from producers sell to consumers. It can also mean all the potential customers for a particular product or service. For example, consumers of agricultural products make up a market. Farming is a good example of how free enterprise works in the United States.

Farming for a Market

How do farmers decide what crops to grow? How do they decide what animals to raise? How do farmers know how much to produce? Farmers try to find answers to these questions by watching consumers. For example, consumers today are buying more cheese than they did in the past. In 1996 people consumed 140 percent more cheese than they did in 1970. Increasing pizza sales and frozen dinners with cheese contributed to the rise. Over the years stores also ordered more cheese. As a result, dairy farmers raised more dairy cows, which produced more milk, which was made into cheese. On the other hand, during the same 26 years consumers bought 24 percent fewer eggs. Stores ordered fewer eggs. So chicken farmers raised fewer egg-laying hens.

Farmers have an **incentive,** or good reason, to produce the kinds of goods people want. Farmers want to make as much money as possible. By looking at what consumers buy, farmers learn what to produce and how much.

The amount of goods or services consumers are willing to buy at a certain price at a given time is called **demand.** If people prefer potatoes over beets, then demand is higher for potatoes. This gives farmers an incentive to grow potatoes. As a result, more farmers grow potatoes than beets.

An incentive for the consumer is price. The price of a product helps to determine how many people will buy it. Fewer people can afford high-priced goods. But if the price is low, more people can buy the goods.

Making Inferences   It is important to look for main ideas and details as you read. Sometimes you can use that information to figure out things that are not actually stated. This is called making an **inference.** Reread the first paragraph under the heading "Farming for a Market." Which inference can you make from details in the paragraph?

a.   The market determines what products are produced.

b.   Consumers will pay any price to get cheese and eggs.

How Competition Leads to Efficiency

Farmers sell their goods in a market where there is competition from other farmers. Because many buyers and sellers are in the market, no one buyer or seller sets the price. In a competitive market, sellers have an incentive to keep prices low. Suppose one farmer's price for corn is higher than another farmer's price. The consumer will buy the corn at the lower price. So the farmer has to sell at the lowest possible price. But the price must not be so low that the farmer cannot recover the costs of growing the corn, such as supplies, equipment, and labor. The farmer wants a price that allows him or her to make some money after paying expenses.

A competitive market requires efficiency. **Efficiency** means that the time, energy, and money put into a job results in a great deal of production without much waste. Over the years American farmers have become more efficient. In the 1850s one farmer produced enough food to feed five people. About fifty percent of Americans were farmers. Today the average farmer feeds 65 people. Only 2.8 percent of Americans today are farmers.

So few farmers can produce so much food because of **technology.** This includes the tools and methods used to increase production. Today farmers use more machines. They also have special seeds, fertilizers, and weed killers. As a result, it takes fewer farmers to produce a larger food supply.

The graph on page 183 shows that farms today are larger than they were in the past. But as the graph below shows, there are fewer farms. Many farms are now owned by corporations rather than by individuals. A **corporation** is a business that stockholders own. Each stockholder shares in the profits and the risks of the business. Since a corporation may consist of many people, it can raise large sums of money. Today large amounts of money and skill are needed to run a farm.

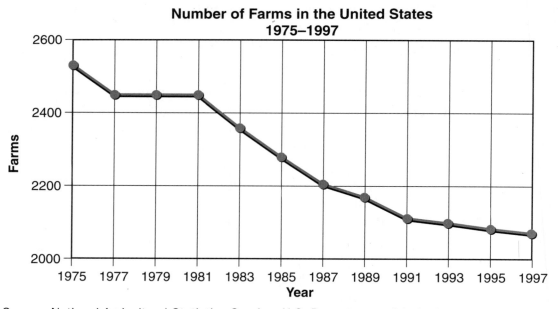

**Number of Farms in the United States
1975–1997**

Source: National Agricultural Statistics Service, U.S. Department of Agriculture

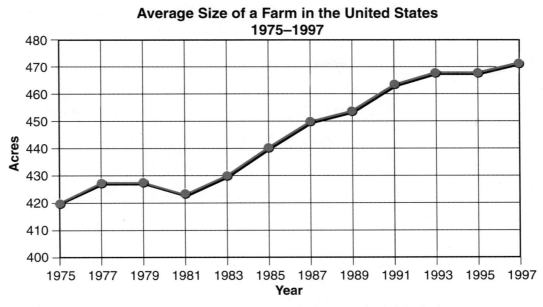

**Average Size of a Farm in the United States
1975–1997**

Acres (y-axis): 400, 410, 420, 430, 440, 450, 460, 470, 480

Year (x-axis): 1975, 1977, 1979, 1981, 1983, 1985, 1987, 1989, 1991, 1993, 1995, 1997

Source: National Agricultural Statistics Service, U.S. Department of Agriculture

Comparing Line Graphs   A **line graph** usually shows changes over time. A change may be an increase or a decrease. Look at the line graphs on page 182 and above. They show changes in the number and average size of U.S. farms over 22 years. During different periods farms changed in different ways. How did the farms change from 1977 to 1981?

   a.   The number of farms stayed the same while the size of farms decreased.

   b.   The number of farms decreased while the size of farms increased.

How Competition Affects Farmers and Consumers

Competition among farmers benefits consumers in many ways. In 1900 the average American family spent more than 45 percent of its income on food. They ate nearly every meal at home. Today the average family spends only about 14 percent of its income (after taxes) on food. About nine percent of that food budget is spent on meals at home. Americans spend the remaining five percent on meals away from home. Competition has kept food prices down and given consumers more choices in how to spend their food money.

However, individual farmers have a hard time competing with large, corporate farms. As a result, some individual farmers have left the market. Others sign contracts with canneries, frozen-food companies, and other food processors before they plant their crops. These farmers know in advance how much they will get for their crop. Still other individual farmers join cooperatives. A **cooperative** is formed by people who join together to ensure the best price for their products. Many orange and grapefruit growers in California and Florida belong to cooperatives. Some cooperatives advertise to encourage consumers to buy their products. For example, beef and pork cooperatives use ads to convince consumers that beef and pork are part of a healthful diet.

Check your answer on page 247.

Thinking About the Article

Practice Vocabulary

The terms below are in the passage in bold type. Study the way each term is used. Then complete each sentence by writing the correct term in the blank.

free enterprise system	market	consumers
demand	efficiency	cooperative

1 An economy in which the buyers and sellers determine what goods are produced is called a(n) _____.

2 A person who buys goods and services is a(n) _____.

3 A(n) _____ represents all the potential customers for a particular product or service.

4 If few consumers are buying a product, it has a low

_____.

5 Members of a farm _____ work together to get the best price for their products.

6 Farms in the United States are known for their _____, because they produce more farm products with fewer farmers than in the past.

Understand the Article

Write the answer to each question.

7 Why do farmers experiment with new methods of farming?

_____

_____

8 What is one way consumers benefit from competition?

_____

_____

9 What are the three definitions of market?

_____

_____

Check your answers on page 247.

Apply Your Skills

Circle the number of the best answer for each question.

10 Reread the third paragraph under "Farming for a Market" on page 181. Which statement might you infer from details in the paragraph?
  (1) Farmers earn more when they produce goods that are in demand.
  (2) The amount of goods consumers buy helps determine demand.
  (3) If people prefer potatoes over beets, then the demand is higher for potatoes.
  (4) Farmers have an incentive to grow potatoes.
  (5) More vegetable farmers grow potatoes than beets.

11 Look at the graphs on pages 182 and 183. What do the graphs suggest might be true by 2010?
  (1) Farms will be fewer but about the same size as in 1997.
  (2) Family-owned farms will be more numerous than in 1997.
  (3) Farms will be fewer but much larger than those in 1997.
  (4) Farms will be fewer than in 1997 but individuals will own most of them.
  (5) Farms will be more numerous and corporations will own almost all of them.

12 Read the last paragraph on page 183. Which sentence below states an inference based on details from the paragraph?
  (1) Competition has kept food prices down.
  (2) If there was less competition among farmers, food prices would be higher.
  (3) Competition gives consumers more choices in how to spend the money they budget for food.
  (4) Consumers eat out more often today than consumers did in 1900.
  (5) Consumers eat more chicken today than consumers did in 1900.

Connect with the Article

Write your answer to each question.

13 Why are products that are not readily available usually high in price? Why might such a product have a low price?

_____

14 How does competition among long-distance telephone companies help you choose which one to use?

_____

_____

Money Management

Setting the Stage

    People learn about money the same way they learn many other values—from their families. Some families guard every penny earned. They keep track of expenses carefully and rarely overspend. They have financial goals and save money to reach them. Other families enjoy spending. They may often give gifts to others as a way to show they care. They may buy a bigger house when a new baby arrives because they want the space. They feel sure that the money will be there when they need it. Some families are willing to take even more risks with their money. They like to invest if there is a chance to make even more money. Sometimes they get more. Sometimes they lose the money they invested. They figure, in the end, it all evens out. What people learn at a very young age about money influences what role money plays in their lives. It helps determine how they spend money and whether they take financial risks or not.

PREVIEW THE ARTICLE

    Read the first two paragraphs on page 187. What are two things you can expect to learn from this article?

_____

_____

RELATE TO THE TOPIC

    Reread "Setting the Stage". Which description most closely resembles your family? Describe one common practice of a family member as an example.

_____

_____

VOCABULARY

budget	**fixed expense**	**net income**	**flexible expense**
interest	**opportunity cost**	**annual percentage rate**	

Getting the Most for the Money

Few people have as much money as they would like. To get the most out of what they earn, people must become money managers. This requires that they use their money wisely. People who manage their money well follow similar rules. First, they create and follow a spending plan. Second, they consider all the costs involved in a purchase before deciding to buy something. Third, they do not borrow money often. And last, if they *must* get a loan, they borrow carefully.

Follow a Plan

People who manage their money make a budget. A **budget** is a detailed spending plan. It shows how much money comes in and goes out each month. To prepare a budget, first list your net income. The **net income** is money left after taxes are paid. It is generally called take-home pay. Then list all expenses, or money that is owed. Start with **fixed expenses,** which are payments that stay the same each month. Rent and car payments are fixed expenses. Next list expenses that vary from month to month. This kind of expense is called a **flexible expense.** Clothing is a flexible expense.

The chart below is an example of a budget. The amounts the family planned to spend in a month are in the left-hand column. The amounts actually spent are in the right-hand column. A budget contains categories of expenses. Utilities generally include electricity, natural gas, water, sewer, and trash removal. Transportation may include gasoline, bus fare, and an emergency auto repair fund.

Budget for the Rivera Family
Net Monthly Income $2,500

Fixed Expenses	Planned	Actual
Home mortgage	$ 500	$ 500
Car payment	$ 230	$ 230
Insurance	$ 260	$ 260
Flexible Expenses		
Utilities	$ 165	$ 165
Transportation	$ 205	$ 220
Food	$ 350	$ 355
Credit card debt	$ 200	$ 200
Medical/dental	$ 130	$ 150
Clothing	$ 140	$ 100
Entertainment	$ 160	$ 145
Savings	$ 100	$ 85
Other	$ 60	$ 90
Total	$2,500	$2,500

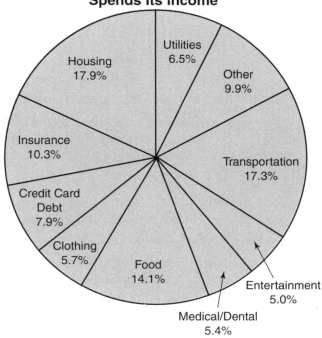

How the Average American Family Spends Its Income

Housing 17.9%
Utilities 6.5%
Other 9.9%
Transportation 17.3%
Insurance 10.3%
Credit Card Debt 7.9%
Clothing 5.7%
Food 14.1%
Medical/Dental 5.4%
Entertainment 5.0%

Source: *Statistical Abstract,* 1996

Fixed expenses are usually easy to budget. However, sometimes fixed expenses are due only a few times a year and are forgotten until the bill comes in the mail. Property taxes are an example of this type of periodic expense. It is important to set aside money each month for periodic expenses. Then bills can be paid when they are due.

Flexible expenses are harder to budget. The best way is to make a prediction. Base it on how much was spent during past months or years.

A budget helps people decide what they can and cannot afford. They see how a purchase could affect other things they want or need. They may find places where they can cut costs.

Many people are surprised when they prepare a budget. They see how much money they spend on things they do not really need. Some people give up smoking, drinking alcohol, or expensive entertainment after they realize how much income these activities use up.

Reading a Circle Graph   A **circle graph** is used to compare parts to a whole and to each other. Circle graphs are sometimes called pie charts. Each section of the graph looks like a slice of a pie. The sections can be compared to one another or to the whole amount. The larger the section, the greater the amount. Often a circle graph is presented using percents. The whole circle is always 100 percent. Look at the circle graph on page 187. It shows the percent of net income the average family spends on various goods and services. What expense takes up the largest percentage of the average family's income?
    a.   food
    b.   housing

Consider the Costs

It is important to look at all the costs involved before deciding on a purchase. The cost of a new pair of shoes is not just the price of the shoes. There is also an opportunity cost. **Opportunity cost** is the cost of choosing one thing over another. For example, as a result of buying shoes, the shopper may have less money for a new winter coat. Sometimes opportunity cost is called a trade-off. In making choices, a person knows that he or she gives up one thing in order to get something of greater value. Good money managers know what the results of most of their buying decisions will be.

Once the shopper decides to buy the shoes, he or she must decide how much to spend. A smart shopper makes this choice by asking what will be gained by buying a good pair of shoes rather than a pair of lesser quality. A smart shopper is willing to substitute one thing for another. The shopper may choose an inexpensive pair of shoes to save money. Or the shopper may choose a better brand that will last longer. Comparing prices of the same pair of shoes at several stores also may save money.

Check your answers on page 248.

The Riveras' budget allows only $140 a month for clothing, including shoes. Mr. Rivera needed work boots that cost $100. Mrs. Rivera must buy shoes for a party. To stay within her family's budget, the pair she chooses should cost no more than $40. If she chooses to spend $75 on a fancy pair of shoes, the opportunity cost of the shoes is that members of her family must spend less on something else to stay within the budget. For example, they might decide to rent videos rather than go to the movie theater.

Identifying Cause and Effect   Every event has at least one cause and one effect. The **cause** is *why* something happened. The **effect** is *what happened* as a result of the cause. Words like *because, reason,* and *since* suggest a cause. Such words or phrases as *as a result, cost,* and *for this reason* signal effects. Reread the paragraphs under the heading "Consider the Costs." What would be an effect of ignoring opportunity cost when deciding to buy something?

a.   The purchase would cost more than the budget allows.

b.   The family might have no money for something else it wants or needs.

Careful Borrowing

People do not always have enough cash on hand to pay for the things they want or need. They may decide to borrow the money now and pay for it later. Borrowing money can be more expensive than combining the price of the item and the opportunity cost. The loan's **interest,** or the fee for borrowing the money, must be considered, too.

Some experts suggest that a person should borrow no more than one-fifth of his or her net income. In other words, a person who takes home $20,000 a year should limit debts to $4,000. Borrowing includes anything bought on an installment plan, paid for with a credit card, charged at local stores, or borrowed from a bank.

Knowing the cost of borrowing helps people get the most for their money. Interest rates can vary greatly. A recent study of new-car loans showed that some lenders charged 10 percent more interest than others. Many loans had hidden costs. In some cases, borrowers had to pay a fee just to apply for the loan. In other cases, they had to pay extra money if payments were late. Some lenders charged a penalty if borrowers paid off their loans early.

A smart borrower never signs a loan agreement without reading and understanding the contract. By law, lenders have to tell people what a loan will cost. Borrowers have a right to know the interest rate on the loan. A borrower also needs to know the annual percentage rate. The **annual percentage rate,** or APR, is the percent of interest a lender charges per year for the money that is borrowed. By knowing the APR, borrowers can compare loans.

People who are good money managers take charge of their finances. They know what they spend their money on and how much they spend. They not only take advantage of opportunities, but they also make the most of those opportunities.

Thinking About the Article

Practice Vocabulary

The terms below are in the passage in bold type. Study the way each term is used. Then complete each sentence by writing the correct term in the blank.

budget   **fixed expense**   **net income**   **flexible expense**

interest   **opportunity cost**   **annual percentage rate**

1 The _____ of buying a new car is that a family may have to wait another year to go on vacation to Disney World.

2 Take-home pay is often called _____.

3 Unfortunately the rate of _____ that banks give for saving money is not as high as the rate they charge for lending money.

4 Before taking a loan, the borrower should know its

_____, or the amount of interest a lender charges each year.

5 An example of a _____ is a mortgage payment.

6 The first step in managing money is setting up a

_____.

7 A grocery bill is an example of a _____.

Understand the Article

Write the answer to each question.

8 What are two benefits of following a budget?

_____

9 What costs should someone consider before borrowing money to buy a used car that costs $7,000?

_____

10 List four rules that can help people become better money managers.

_____

_____

_____

_____

Check your answers on page 248.

Apply Your Skills

Circle the number of the best answer for each question.

11 Look at the chart of the Riveras' budget on page 187. They spent more on medical and dental expenses than they budgeted. What was the effect?
(1) They paid less to their credit card debt.
(2) Their housing and insurance expenses decreased.
(3) They had less money to put into savings.
(4) They spent more money on expenses in the "Other" category.
(5) The Riveras had to sell their car.

12 How might the Riveras cause a decrease in their fixed expenses every month?
(1) They might move to a more expensive house.
(2) They could pay off their credit card debt.
(3) They could switch to less expensive insurance.
(4) They might eat all their meals at home.
(5) They could cut their monthly savings.

13 What does the circle graph on page 187 show about the average American family's spending habits?
(1) It spends more on food than anything else.
(2) It spends one-half its income on housing, food, and entertainment.
(3) It spends about the same on medical and dental expenses as it does on life insurance.
(4) It spends the least on clothing.
(5) It spends less on electricity, gas, telephone, and other utilities than it does on credit card debt.

Connect with the Article

Write your answer to each question.

14 Why do you think some lenders charge a fee if a loan is paid off early?

_____

_____

15 People often buy things on the spur of the moment. This means they make the purchase without planning. What was the last item that you bought on the spur of the moment? What was the opportunity cost for this type of purchase? Explain your answer.

_____

_____

_____

Supply and Demand

Setting the Stage

Friday night trips to video stores can be frustrating. Families are all set to watch a movie they missed in the theaters. They scan the shelves, see the title, but find the case empty. "Why didn't the store order enough of these?"

The answer is not an easy one. The store owners may know that demand for a new video is likely to be high. But they cannot tell how high. They want to order enough of a new video to satisfy their customers but not so many that they lose money as the extra dozen copies sit on the shelves. This is an example of an economic choice that results in making money or losing it.

PREVIEW THE ARTICLE

Begin to think about what you will be reading. Look at the title of the article, the headings (subtitles) within the article, the table, and the photos of baseball cards. What are two things you can expect to learn from this article?

_____

_____

RELATE TO THE TOPIC

This section discusses basic principles of a free enterprise system—the laws of supply and demand. List the last item that was marked so low that you bought an extra one. Was this item a want or a need? Then list an item that you refused to buy because the price was too high. Was this item a want or a need?

_____

_____

VOCABULARY

inelastic demand	elastic demand	supply	profit
elastic supply	inelastic supply	scarce	

Check your answers on page 248.

It's All in the Cards

Two things determine the price of goods. One is the consumers' demand for the goods. The other is the **supply,** or the amount of goods and services sellers offer at certain prices at a given time. People who study the market economy look closely at how supply and demand affect each other.

A Changing Market

Ideally sellers would supply the same amount of goods and services that the consumers will buy. But just like the owner of the video store, business owners can only **estimate** how much to order or produce. Sometimes they are right, and sometimes they are wrong. Considering the past and their business knowledge, sellers learn to predict what and how much to sell. Stadium vendors predict how many fans a team will draw so they can order enough hot dogs. And grocery store owners predict how much candy corn to order for Halloween.

More sellers enter a market when prices are high. They have seen the success of other businesses and want to make money selling the goods, too. Sellers usually increase production when prices are high. In fact, that is what is happening with baseball cards.

Young people have been collecting baseball cards for decades. A photo of a baseball player appears on the front of each card. On the back are facts about the player. In the past, young people traded cards with friends to get a favorite player or a set of all the players on their favorite team. As these young card traders grew up, many lost interest in baseball cards. Others could not bear to part with their collections and they stored their cards away. Today more than half of all card collectors are adults. These people **profit,** or make money, by selling the cards at prices higher than the ones they paid.

Prices of old baseball cards were higher than ever in the late 1990s. Someone sold Yogi Berra's Bowman card for $6,000. This person paid one cent for the card in 1953. The value of old baseball cards can show how supply and demand affect each other.

A Matter of Supply and Demand

How a price change affects supply or demand is called elasticity. The supply and demand of certain products are either elastic or inelastic. An **elastic demand** means that a change in price affects the number of people who will buy the product. When steak goes up in price, for example, fewer people buy it. When the price drops, people buy more. A product has an **inelastic demand** if a price change does not affect the number of people who buy it. Products with an inelastic demand are generally things that are always needed. When the price changes for bread and milk, for example, shoppers still buy about the same amount. Because they need the product, its demand stays about the same despite a price change.

An **elastic supply** means that sellers can increase the supply of a product that has increased in price. Since the price of baseball cards is up, the sports-card companies are increasing supplies. This means the supply of new baseball cards is elastic.

On the other hand, an **inelastic supply** is limited. The supply of older baseball cards is inelastic. The supply cannot increase regardless of what happens to the price. For example, Topps, a sports-card producer, made a certain number of rookie baseball cards for Mark McGwire in 1985. At the beginning of the 1998 baseball season, McGwire's rookie card was worth $30. After McGwire broke Roger Maris's home-run record, the card's value rose to $200.

The law of supply says that if prices are high, suppliers will make more products for the market. If prices are low, they will cut back production. Prices go up if the demand is greater than the supply. So the prices for old baseball cards are rising. Below are the 1999 values for old baseball cards.

Reading a Table   A **table** organizes information in columns and rows. The title tells what kind of information is in the table. Look at the table below. For example, to find the 1999 value of a 1951 Willie Mays baseball card, read down the column under the heading "Player." When you come to *Willie Mays,* read across the row to the column labeled *Mid-1999.* The Willie Mays card is valued at $2,500. Which Mickey Mantle baseball card has a higher value?

    a.   the Topps edition   b.   the Bowman edition

Baseball Cards for Investment			R=Rookie Year	
Player	Card Year	Card Co.	Card No.	Mid-1999 Value
Musial, Stan	48 R	Bowman	36	$750
Williams, Ted	50	Bowman	98	$700
Mantle, Mickey	51 R	Bowman	253	$5,250
Mays, Willie	51 R	Bowman	305	$2,500
Mantle, Mickey	52	Topps	311	$16,000
Banks, Ernie	54 R	Topps	94	$695
Aaron, Hank	54 R	Topps	128	$1,250
Koufax, Sandy	55 R	Topps	123	$725
Clemente, Roberto	55 R	Topps	164	$1,650
Yastrzemski, Carl	60 R	Topps	148	$125
Carew, Rod	67 R	Topps	569	$210
Seaver, Tom	67 R	Topps	581	$650
Ryan, Nolan	68 R	Topps	177	$775
Jackson, Reggie	69 R	Topps	260	$275
Yount, Robin	75 R	Topps	223	$80
Brett, George	75 R	Topps	228	$125
Henderson, Rickey	80 R	Topps	482	$40
Ripken, Cal	82 R	Topps	21	$80
Gwynn, Tony	83 R	Topps	482	$60
Boggs, Wade	83 R	Topps	498	$20
Clemens, Roger	84 R	Fleer Update	U27	$240
McGwire, Mark	85 R	Topps	401	$200
Clemens, Roger	85	Donruss	273	$40
Bonds, Barry	87	Fleer	604	$20
Griffey, Jr., Ken	89 R	Upper Deck	1	$100
Sosa, Sammy	90 R	Upper Deck	17	$12
Ripkin, Jr., Cal	92	Donruss Elite	none	$375
Jeter, Derek	93 R	SP	279	$40
Rodriguez, Alex	94 R	Fleer Update	86	$45
Jordan, Michael	94 R	Upper Deck	19	$12
Griffey, Jr., Ken	95	Donruss Elite	54	$75
Wood, Kerry	97 R	Bowman	196	$20
McGwire, Mark	98	Fleer Diamond Standouts	15	$15
McGwire, Mark	98	Leaf	171	$20

Source: *Sports Cards Magazine and Price Guide,* May 1999

This 1909–11 Honus Wagner baseball card sold in 1996 for $640,500.

Mark McGwire's 1985 rookie card increased in value every month through his 1998 record-breaking season.

The Mickey Mantle 1951 rookie baseball card is scarce, and people are willing to pay a lot of money to get it. **Scarce** means that the demand for the item is greater than the supply. People are willing to pay even more money for cards that are extremely rare.

Scarcity and Price

In 1996 a baseball card of Honus Wagner sold for $640,500. Wagner was a shortstop for the Pittsburgh Pirates in the early 1900s. Why is his card so valuable? In the early 1900s, tobacco companies distributed baseball cards. Wagner was a nonsmoker. He objected to any connection with a tobacco product. So the company took his card off the market. Today only forty Wagner cards exist. Eight of them are in excellent condition. It was one of these cards that sold for $640,500. The value of a Wagner card is high because it is rare. A Wagner card in excellent condition is rarer still.

A controversial purchase shows what can happen when a rare card becomes one of a kind. A 13-year-old boy bought a 1968 Nolan Ryan rookie baseball card for $12 at a store. The card was worth $1,200, but the store clerk did not read the price correctly. The store had a big sign that read "All sales final," but the store owner took the boy to court anyway. He wanted the other $1,188 from the boy.

During the trial, the boy told the judge that he had already traded the Ryan card. He had traded it for two cards that were worth about $2,200. The judge ordered that the Nolan Ryan card be brought to court as evidence.

Predicting Outcomes   Trying to figure out what will happen next is called **predicting outcomes.** As you read, try to guess something based on what you have read so far. Use what you already know from past experiences to help make predictions. Reread the paragraphs above. How do you think the court case affected the value of the Nolan Ryan card?
   a.   The value of the card increased.
   b.   The value of the card went down.

The new owner agreed to bring the card to court. But he asked that the court's Exhibit 1 sticker remain on the card after the case was settled. The card, with the sticker, could be worth as much as $3,000. The trial and the sticker made the card one-of-a-kind, so it has increased in value.

Today many collectors continue to buy cards, hoping to find a rare one and strike it rich. Critics doubt that anyone will get rich from cards produced in the last few years. They say the supply of new cards is far too great. They point out that in 1951, only two major companies, Topps and Bowman, made baseball cards. By 1998 more than twenty companies make baseball cards.

Other baseball-card experts disagree with this idea. They believe that baseball cards will never lose value. One trader said, "As long as there are baseball fans, there will be baseball cards, and those cards will be worth something."

Thinking About the Article

Practice Vocabulary

The terms below are in the passage in bold type. Study the way each term is used. Then complete each sentence by writing the correct term in the blank.

inelastic demand	elastic demand	supply	profit
elastic supply	inelastic supply	scarce	

1 Mickey Mantle's baseball cards are an example of a(n)

_____ .

2 A collector who sells a rare baseball card is likely to

_____ .

3 If the amount of a product increases when its price goes up, the product

has a(n) _____ .

4 When the supply of a product is very low, the product is considered

_____ .

5 Products and services with a(n) _____ are generally
necessities.

6 Fewer people buy a product with a(n) _____ when its
price goes up.

7 A seller increases the _____ of a product when its
price goes up.

Understand the Article

Write the answer to each question.

8 How does decreased demand for a product often affect its price?

_____

9 Why is the word *elastic* used to describe products with a changing supply
or demand?

_____

10 Why do necessities such as milk and dish soap have an inelastic demand?

_____

Check your answers on page 248.

Apply Your Skills

Circle the number of the best answer for each question.

11 Reread page 195. Which prediction would the information in the paragraphs support?
(1) There is only one 1968 Nolan Ryan rookie card marked Exhibit 1.
(2) The Exhibit 1 sticker on the card will lower the card's value.
(3) The store owner received his $1,188 from the boy.
(4) The new owner of the Ryan card will make a profit.
(5) The boy was put in jail for trading the card.

12 Look at the table on page 194. Which best explains why the two Roger Clemens cards have different values?
(1) Clemens had a better year in 1984 than 1985.
(2) The demand for the 1985 Clemens card may increase over time.
(3) The demand for a Clemens card increased from 1984 to 1985.
(4) Clemens was traded to another team after the 1984 season.
(5) Clemens' Fleer card is in shorter supply than his Donruss card.

13 Based on information in the article and table, whose card would likely be worth the least a year from now?
(1) Hank Aaron
(2) Yogi Berra
(3) Mark McGwire
(4) Honus Wagner
(5) Kerry Wood

Connect with the Article

Write your answer to each question.

14 How do supply and demand cause companies that make a product to enter or leave a market?

_____

_____

_____

15 Would you advise someone to invest his or her money in baseball cards? Explain your answer.

_____

_____

_____

The Changing Nature of Work

Setting the Stage

Most early Americans worked as farmers. Decades later many of the nation's farmers left the farms for jobs in factories. In both instances they worked with their hands, which did not call for much education or training. But this country today is no longer an agricultural or a manufacturing society. Because of modern technology, Americans now live in a society based on creating and distributing information in many different forms. Now many people work more with their minds than with their hands. Most jobs with high wages are skilled, trained positions in business and industry. And this trend will continue. Workers today must learn more to earn more.

PREVIEW THE ARTICLE

Begin to think about what you will read. Look at the title of the article, the headings (subtitles) within the article, and the graph. What two things can you expect to learn from this article?

_____

_____

RELATE TO THE TOPIC

This article is about what jobs in the 2000s and how people must prepare for them. Think about the kind of work you would like to do. What kind of training do you think you will need to get a job in that field?

_____

_____

VOCABULARY

work ethic	**service industries**	**bachelor's degree**
apprenticeship	**internships**	**job shadowing**	**mentoring**

Check your answers on page 249.

Work in the Twenty-first Century

Work is a foundation stone of our society. But the American workplace has changed. New kinds of work skills and the ability to adapt to change are the tickets to success for workers in the 2000s.

Jobs Today

In the early 1900s, most Americans worked at unskilled jobs in farming and manufacturing, which required only manual labor. Today machines do most farm work. Computer-operated robots assist in manufacturing. Many workers who used to be on the assembly line now have been retrained. Some perform sophisticated tasks with computers. Modern technology is here to stay.

A great many jobs require technological literacy. This means, for example, that a person knows how to use computers. Most jobs in the United States today use technologies that process information. They demand specialized education and training. Workers in the best-paying jobs are those who are comfortable with technology. For example, medical workers must know how to use computerized health aids. Mechanics must know how to use computerized tools.

Yet the new workplace demands more than technological skills. Workers must be able to follow directions and work with a team or as a team leader. It also requires personal skills. Having a strong **work ethic** is important. Workers with a strong work ethic come to work on time, act responsibly, and use common sense in making judgments.

Workers must also be flexible. They must adapt to new ways of doing things as technology changes everyday tasks in a particular job. Many industries have adopted new high-performance work systems. These programs aim for efficiency through quality circles and job rotations. **Quality circles** are groups of employees who monitor the quality of a product or service they produce or perform. **Job rotation** means workers learn different jobs so that they can step in to help other workers when the need arises.

Learning to Earn

The U.S. Bureau of Labor Statistics predicts that job growth in the next decade will be highest in service industries. **Service industries** hire people who offer services. Education, banking, medicine, hotels, restaurants, and theme parks are all service industries.

One of the fastest-growing service industries is health care. The generation born between 1945 and 1960 make up a large part of the American population. Today they are aging and need more medical care. To cut expenses, many people today use outpatient facilities, nursing homes, and home health care rather than hospitals. Personal and home care aides are already in great demand. They care for the aging and people recovering from surgery and other serious health conditions.

Other quickly growing service industries are transportation, public utilities, and wholesale and retail trade. Examples of transportation jobs are air traffic controllers and creators of aircraft computer software. Telephone line workers and water quality testers are examples of jobs in public utilities. Wholesale and retail trade jobs include many sales positions.

The Bureau of Labor Statistics has identified occupations with potential for the fastest growth, highest pay, and lowest unemployment in the next decade. Of 25 such occupations, 18 require at least a **bachelor's degree,** which is a four-year college education. Workers in the future simply must learn more to earn more. People with education, work experience, and technological skills will all find jobs, but those with more education will get the better-paying jobs.

Education does not necessarily mean college, however. A number of occupations do not require a bachelor's degree, yet offer higher than average earnings. These include nurses, mechanics, carpenters, and various kinds of technicians. These careers require on-the-job training, advanced training in a technical or vocational school, or apprenticeships. An **apprenticeship** is a period of training that includes specialized classroom work as well as on-the-job training. All of these continuing education opportunities help workers prepare for more challenging and better-paying occupations.

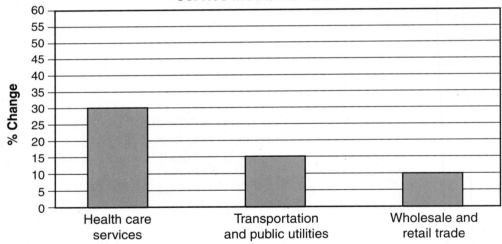

Estimated Change in Employment in Some Service Industries 1996–2006

Source: *Occupational Outlook Handbook* from Bureau of Labor Statistics, January 1998, Bulletin 2500, Chart 4

Reading a Bar Graph   A **bar graph** is often used to make comparisons. The title tells what information is presented in the graph. The labels along the side and bottom of the graph tell the key categories of information. Look at the bar graph above. Each bar shows the estimated percent of change from 1996 to 2006. What types of jobs show the highest estimated percent of change for 2006?

    a.   transportation and public utilities

    b.   health care services

    c.   wholesale and retail trade

Check your answer on page 249.

Choosing a Career

To determine which career is for you, consider your interests and abilities. You can identify these by recalling past successes. You can ask for observations and suggestions from friends, family, and teachers. They may see you differently than you see yourself. School guidance departments and career development centers offer skills and interest inventories or lists of questions that reveal your strong points. These can help you narrow down the many possibilities for your future work.

Once you have decided what you want to do, you must prepare for the career of your choice. Preparing for a rewarding career may include technical courses, on-the-job training, or a four-year college degree. Some programs combine work and learning. In school-to-work programs, for example, students study in a classroom for part of the day and then work on a job for another part of the day. These programs give students the basic academic and workplace skills to succeed at work and in advanced education. Career exploration may also include internships, job shadowing, or mentoring.

Drawing Conclusions   You draw a **conclusion** by reading for the main idea. You also read for details that lead to a conclusion. These details are called supporting statements. Reread the paragraphs under "Choosing a Career."

1 Which conclusion is supported by details in the first paragraph?
   a.   I should choose my career based on how much schooling it requires.
   b.   My career should be in a field that I find interesting.

2 Which conclusion is supported by details in the second paragraph?
   a.   I can prepare for a career in one or more of a variety of ways.
   b.   Going to college for four years is the only pathway to a career.

Temporary assignments at a job or company that interests you are called **internships.** These assignments can last for a few months or a year. Often an internship can lead to a permanent job.

Spending time with someone who has a job in which you are interested is called **job shadowing.** The person you are shadowing introduces you to the people, the equipment, and the skills that it takes to do the job. You see what spending time working in the actual job setting is like. Job shadowing may last several hours or a full day.

Teaching what is important in a job or career by example or discussion is called **mentoring.** The teacher is called a mentor. Mentors allow you to observe. They give advice on how to go about achieving the career goals you have set. A mentor can also provide references to people who make hiring decisions.

Internships, job shadowing, mentoring, or school-to-work programs reinforce what is taught in classes and offer you a variety of career options. All these things increase your chances of being valued and hired by employers.

Thinking About the Article

Practice Vocabulary

The terms below are in the passage in bold type . Study the way each term is used. Then complete each sentence by writing the correct term in the blank.

work ethic	service industries	bachelor's degree
apprenticeship	internships	job shadowing	mentoring

1 A person can earn a(n) _____ at a college or university.

2 A(n) _____ is a temporary work assignment.

3 A(n) _____ consists of on-the-job training and classroom work.

4 _____ employ people who meet the needs of other people.

5 Employers appreciate workers who have a strong

_____ .

6 _____ helps you learn from a professional's experience.

7 _____ may take several hours or a full day.

Understand the Article

Write the answer to each question.

8 What kinds of service jobs are projected to grow fastest in the next decade?

_____

9 What kinds of skills do most jobs today require?

_____

10 How can workers best prepare for today's higher-paying careers?

_____

_____

11 What is job rotation?

_____

_____

Check your answers on page 249.

Apply Your Skills

Circle the number of the best answer for each question.

12 Based on the article, what conclusion can you draw about the way to find a good job?
(1) Get education or training in a field that interests you.
(2) Get a job where you know someone.
(3) Look at the newspaper's classified ads to find a career.
(4) Ask your relatives for a job.
(5) Check to see what the hourly wage is before you consider any job.

13 Look again at the bar graph on page 200. Which statement does the information in the graph support?
(1) Jobs in health services will grow more than jobs in transportation and public utilities between 1996 and 2006.
(2) Jobs in wholesale and retail trade will grow more than jobs in public utilities and transportation between 1996 and 2006.
(3) Jobs in transportation and public utilities will grow more than jobs in health services between 1996 and 2006.
(4) Ten million wholesale and retail trade jobs will be available in 2006.
(5) Wholesale and retail trade jobs will double between 1996 and 2006.

14 Which detail supports the conclusion that technological literacy is more important than manual ability in high-paying jobs?
(1) In the early 1900s, many Americans worked at unskilled jobs in farming and manufacturing.
(2) Workers of the future must be able to follow directions.
(3) Many jobs in the United States today use technologies that process information.
(4) Workers learn different jobs so that they can step in to help other workers.
(5) Groups of employees monitor the quality of a product or service they produce or perform.

Connect with the Article

Write your answers to each question.

15 Why do you think a good work ethic is important to employers?

_____

16 What three subjects or skills would you include if you put together your own school-to-work program for achieving your career goals?

_____

_____

26 The Global Economy

Setting the Stage

    Nations have traded with one another since ancient times. Yet in the past, each nation was mostly self-sufficient. In other words, the nation could produce enough goods and services for its own people. When nations did trade with one another, they tended to trade only with their allies. Trading was often a friendly gesture made when two countries began working together on other governmental policies. Today the world has changed. Most countries have opened their markets to goods and services from many other countries. So consumers from all over the world contribute to the supply and demand for these goods and services. As a result, trade among countries has increased dramatically.

PREVIEW THE ARTICLE

    Read the first two paragraphs on page 205. What are two things you can expect to learn from the article?

_____

_____

RELATE TO THE TOPIC

    This section is about the global economy and how it affects the American economy. What are some products you have recently purchased that were made in another country?

_____

_____

VOCABULARY

interdependent	**free trade**	**protectionist**	**tariff**
quota	**trade deficit**	**currency**	

Check your answers on page 250.

The World's Interdependent Economy

Borders, distance, and different languages were once barriers to trade. But because of telecommunications technology, companies on opposite sides of the globe can work together. Nations' economies have become linked to one another because companies in many countries do so much business together. Nations today are **interdependent.** This means they depend on one another to be successful. The marketplace created by the many business transactions among nations is called the global economy. Because nations are interdependent, what happens in one country's economy affects economies in many other countries.

International Trade

Huge amounts of goods and services are traded among nations every day. Companies that need a natural resource, such as iron or phosphate, may **import** that resource from another country. The companies then make their products and **export** them to the world. For example, American plastics companies import oil from the Middle East. They make computer parts, which they then export for sale to the rest of the world. By importing raw materials, a nation with limited natural resources can produce more than it otherwise could.

The United States imports such resources as oil, aluminum, rubber, tin, and graphite from other countries. It also imports energy resources used to build and run machines. And many consumer goods—from cocoa to cars—come from other countries.

Imported products are important because they give consumers a wider variety of goods at lower prices. These products also affect American producers. American businesses are forced to keep their costs down and to raise the quality of goods to stay competitive in the American market.

International trade also increases the number of places a country can sell its goods. If one country cannot or will not buy a particular product, another one may. As a result, wealth and goods are spread over a larger part of the globe than ever before. Producers in each country, however, must sell enough of their goods to earn enough money to buy the products they need.

International trade increases the demand for goods, which leads to greater production and more use of raw materials and labor. If more people want to buy American products, for example, American companies will need to make more. Consequently, more Americans will have jobs at these companies.

Competition from international trade can force a country's businesses to become more efficient. The businesses develop new and better ways of doing things. Competition from international trade also can drive a company out of business if it does not keep up with other companies making similar products.

American companies export many products. Machinery, chemicals, grains, and beef are just a few. Exports generate the money that companies need to succeed. Successful businesses make the American economy strong.

International Trade Policies

Political and economic matters can make trade between nations complex. When problems arise, nations sometimes create a protectionist trade policy. Governments that have a **protectionist** trade policy place limits on imports to ensure the success of their own nation's businesses.

Some of the protectionist trade barriers that nations set up are high **tariffs,** or taxes on imported goods. The tariff is added to the selling price of the imported item. American consumers then compare the cost of the imported product to the cost of an American-made product. Often they choose the less expensive American-made product. Another barrier is setting quotas. A **quota** limits the amount of goods a country can import.

When one country places a trade barrier on products, other countries often get revenge with their own protectionist measure. For example, Japan might set a quota on the number of computers it imports from American companies. The United States might respond with a high tariff on Japanese cars. Over time, protectionist trade policies discourage international trade.

When a country buys more imports than it sells exports, the country has a **trade deficit.** When nations have a trade deficit, they are more eager to protect their own share of the world market.

During the 1800s and 1900s, the United States took many protectionist actions against other countries. In the 1990s, however, former communist nations began to build new economies. Some economies were modeled after the United States economy. More and more American companies were ready to do business in other countries. As a result, many governments abandoned protectionist actions in favor of free trade. **Free trade** means that no legal or political barriers stop a country from importing and exporting goods. To encourage free trade, the United States and other countries formed trade **blocs.**

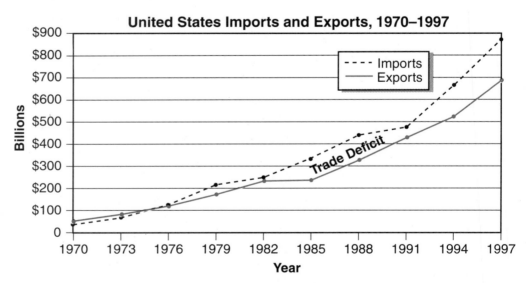

Source: *U.S. International Trade Administration,* U.S. Foreign Trade Highlights No. 1318, "U.S. Exports and General Imports in Goods"

Reading a Line Graph One way to compare information and show change over a period of time is with a line graph. On the graph on page 206, the dotted line represents imports and the solid line represents exports. During the time period shown on the graph, which has risen more?

    a.   exports   b.   imports

Some trade blocs are regional. In North America the United States, Canada, and Mexico have the North American Free Trade Agreement (NAFTA). In Europe, countries have joined to create a regional economic market called the European Union. In 1999 the European Union even created a **currency,** or kind of money, called the Euro. The Euro makes trade among its members easier than ever.

Impact on the United States Economy

From the 1950s to the 1970s, the United States had the strongest economy in the world. But then things began to change. American goods were too expensive for other nations to buy. At the same time, imported goods like cars, cameras, and clothes became cheaper for Americans to buy. In addition, American industries had to buy huge amounts of imported oil and other energy resources. As a result, other countries built strong economies. Their trade with the United States grew rapidly.

These developments were both good and bad for Americans. Increased international trade meant they could choose cheaper goods and services. But the success of imports also put pressure on American companies to lower their prices. Many chose to cut expenses by firing workers. Some businesses even moved to other countries where people worked for very low wages.

In the United States, unions and labor laws force many companies to pay fairly high wages with benefits. In some poorer countries, people work for pennies a day. Some Americans have mixed feelings about this situation. They like the idea of low-priced, imported goods but dislike the fact that the workers are terribly underpaid.

The interdependent global economy has brought many economic benefits to the United States. But it has presented problems for American workers. For example, in the 1990s Japan's economy declined. Most of Asia fell into economic crisis. At first Asia's trouble was good for the United States. Televisions and other electronic goods got cheaper. But because Asia couldn't afford imports, American farmers and manufacturers suffered. Sometimes when factory owners threaten to shut down, workers agree to pay cuts or benefit cuts. When plants *do* close, skilled workers must find jobs elsewhere. They often have to take jobs that pay lower wages.

Supporting Conclusions You draw conclusions by reading for the main idea. You also read for details that support the conclusion. Which statement supports the conclusion: "An interdependent global economy has advantages and disadvantages"?

    a.   Many American businesses moved to where people worked for very low wages.

    b.   From the 1950s to the 1970s, Americans had the world's strongest economy.

Thinking About the Article

Practice Vocabulary

The terms below are in the passages in bold type. Study the way each term is used. Then complete each sentence by writing the correct term in the blank.

interdependent   **free trade**   **protectionist**   **tariff**

quota   **trade deficit**   **currency**

1 _____ means no barriers to trading with other countries.

2 Each nation generally has its own _____, or money.

3 A country with a(n) _____ trade policy limits imports.

4 Nations that are trading partners have a(n) _____ relationship.

5 A tax placed on imports is called a(n)_____.

6 Countries create a(n) _____ by importing more than they export.

7 A country has set a(n) _____ when it allows only a certain number of imports from a particular country.

Understand the Article

Write the answer to each question.

8 Why is a global economy an interdependent economy?

_____

9 How does international trade force businesses to become more efficient?

_____

_____

10 In what two ways does an increase in international trade help a nation's economy?

_____

_____

11 What are two trade barriers that a nation with a protectionist trade policy might build against another country?

_____

Check your answers on page 250.

Apply Your Skills

Circle the number of the best answer for each question.

12 Look at the line graph on page 206. Which of the following best describes the growth of imports and exports in the United States from 1970 to 1997?

(1) sharp increases in imports and decreases in exports

(2) sharper decreases in imports than exports

(3) increases in imports and exports

(4) sharper increases in imports than exports

(5) decreases in exports and increases in imports

13 Look again at the graph on page 206. During which period did imports shoot up while exports remained the same?

(1) 1970–1973

(2) 1973–1976

(3) 1982–1985

(4) 1988–1991

(5) 1994–1997

14 Which statement supports the conclusion that the global economy brings many benefits to the American economy?

(1) The United States may ban trade with Iraq.

(2) Union workers may accept lower wages if owners threaten to shut the factory down.

(3) American consumers can choose from a variety of goods at lower prices.

(4) Imports became less expensive than American-made goods.

(5) Imports help nations with limited natural resources produce more.

Connect with the Article

Write your answer to each question.

15 Protectionist policies discourage international trade and free trade encourages it. Why is this true?

_____

_____

16 Would you choose to buy a Japanese-made automobile with a good safety and repair record at a cost of $8,000 or an American-made automobile (of equivalent size and features) at a cost of $11,000? Explain your answer.

_____

_____

_____

Economics At Work

Horticulture: Flower Shop Manager

Helping customers choose flowers that meet their needs is part of a shop manager's job.

Do you like working with plants and flowers? If you don't mind getting your hands dirty, you may enjoy managing a flower shop. However, being a florist involves more than customer service and arranging flowers. It also requires a good understanding of the economics of running a store.

Flower shop managers are responsible for ordering and maintaining cut flowers and green plants. They must be aware of the best sources for economically priced flowers. They must also know what prices to charge for the flowers so that they can make money while competing with other stores.

Because each type of plant or flower has a specific growing and harvest season, shop managers need to know which plants are in season and which plants are expected in the next season. They must be aware of how a plant's growing season and its availability affect its price during the year.

A major part of each day is spent ordering, caring for, and arranging cut flowers. Managers must be familiar with each type of plant and be able to recommend plant and bouquet selections to their customers.

Look at the Some Careers in Horticulture chart.

- Do any of the careers interest you? If so, which ones?

- What information would you need to know more about those careers? On a separate piece of paper, write some questions that you would like answered. You can find more information about those careers in the *Occupational Outlook Handbook* at your local library.

Use the material below to answer the questions that follow.

Maria is a floral shop manager. She reviewed all the invoices from the past year and recorded the highest and lowest prices she paid for the best-selling flowers. In general, the law of supply and demand dictates that flowers cost more when they are out of season and in scarce supply. Maria made a table of information from the invoices.

Flower	Highest Price Paid	Lowest Price Paid
Calla lily	$2.50 per stem	$1.20 per stem
Carnation	$5.35 per bunch	$1.25 per bunch
Delphinium	$7.95 per bunch	$4.95 per bunch
Hyacinth	$3.95 per bulb	$1.25 per bulb
Poppy	$6.25 per bunch	$2.25 per bunch
Tulip	$2.25 per stem	$0.65 per stem

1 Below is a list of prices Maria paid for each flower. Determine if each flower was purchased in season or out of season. Circle the correct answer.

Calla lily—$1.25 per stem	in season	out of season
Carnation—$5.19 per bunch	in season	out of season
Delphinium—$6.95 per bunch	in season	out of season
Hyacinth—$3.45 per bulb	in season	out of season
Poppy—$2.55 per bunch	in season	out of season
Tulip—$0.72 per stem	in season	out of season

2 Which of the following prices indicates that the plant is out of season?
  (1) Tulip—$0.70 per stem
  (2) Calla lily—$2.25 per stem
  (3) Delphinium—$5.25 per bunch
  (4) Carnation—$1.75 per bunch
  (5) Poppy—$2.75 per bunch

3 For which of the flowers was the highest in-season price paid?
  (1) Calla lily
  (2) Carnation
  (3) Delphinium
  (4) Hyacinth
  (5) Poppy

4 Have you ever noticed how certain items are more expensive during certain times of the year? You may be aware of this when you go grocery shopping or when you buy certain types of clothing. Use a separate piece of paper to describe at least one seasonal pricing difference that you've encountered.

Check your answers on page 250.

Increasing Demand

Producers of goods and services are always looking for ways to increase demand. When consumers want to buy more products and services, producers and sellers are able to make higher profits. One way to increase demand is to find new uses for products. New uses for a product attract new customers. Farm products are a good example. In recent years scientists have found ways to increase the demand for many crops. Take corn, for example.

For years, people bought corn as a food product. Today, however, corn is used to make everything from paint to diapers. In some cases, corn is a good substitute for oil in making paint. It is an ingredient in coatings for wood and metal. Adding a small amount of cornstarch to plastic can help protect the environment. Ordinarily plastic does not decompose or break down. It lasts forever—unless a small amount of cornstarch is added during the plastic-making process. Then the plastic will decompose. As a result, cornstarch is an additive to such products as disposable diapers and plastic bags.

No one is sure how many other products could be improved with a little corn. But scientists continually research the possibilities. As the demand grows, farmers have more reasons to grow corn.

Circle the number of the best answer for each question.

1 According to the article, which of the following would be most likely to encourage the new uses of corn?
(1) people who like to eat corn
(2) people who use corn as animal feed
(3) gasoline producers
(4) wheat farmers
(5) people concerned about the environment

2 Which of the following is the best conclusion that can be drawn from the passage?
(1) Demand for corn is likely to increase.
(2) Demand for corn is likely to decrease.
(3) The supply of corn is likely to stay the same.
(4) The supply of corn is likely to decrease.
(5) Supply and demand will stay the same.

Check your answers on pages 250–251.

The Federal Budget

The Federal Government Dollar
(Fiscal Year 2000 Estimate)

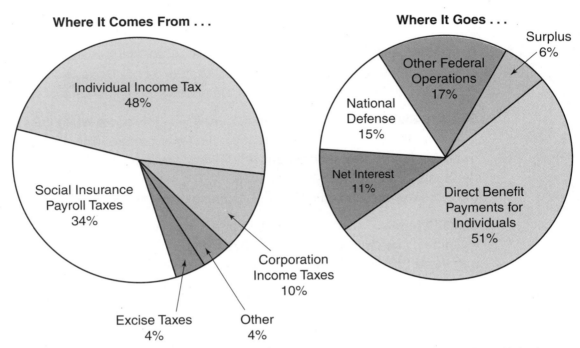

Where It Comes From . . .

Individual Income Tax
48%

Social Insurance
Payroll Taxes
34%

Corporation
Income Taxes
10%

Excise Taxes
4%

Other
4%

Where It Goes . . .

Surplus
6%

Other Federal
Operations
17%

National
Defense
15%

Net Interest
11%

Direct Benefit
Payments for
Individuals
51%

Source: Office of Management and Budget, Executive Office of the President of the United States, 1999, *Citizens Guide to Federal Budget USGPO,* "The Federal Government Dollar Fiscal Year 2000, Estimate October 1, 1999–September 30, 2000"

Write the answer to each question.

3 What makes up the largest percentage of the government's income?

_____

4 On what expense does the government spend more than one-half its income?

_____

Circle the number of the best answer for the question.

5 Which of the following is best supported by the graph with the title Where It Comes From . . .?
- (1) More than four-fifths of the government's income comes from individual income tax and Social Security taxes.
- (2) Corporations pay more taxes than individuals.
- (3) The government does not have to borrow to pay its bills.
- (4) Contributions to Social Security make up more than half the government's income.
- (5) Excise taxes make a large contribution to the government's income.

Deceptive Selling

Almost everyone has been the victim of deceptive selling methods. Perhaps you paid too much for an item. Maybe the product you bought was not worth as much as you thought it was. Smart shoppers learn to be cautious. They watch for one or more of the following selling practices.

Special Pricing.   A seller offers a product at a "special low price." The seller tells the customer to buy now because the price will go up soon. However in many cases, the "special" price is actually higher than the price of the same item at other stores.

Bait and Switch.   An ad offers an item at a very low price. When customers go to buy that item, they are told that the item is an inferior product. The seller then suggests switching to a more expensive model of the same item. The seller may also tell buyers that the advertised item is "out of stock." The seller then urges the customer to buy the more expensive model that just happens to be "in stock."

Chain Referrals.   Customers are told that if they buy a product and then refer other customers, they will receive a gift or a reduced price. Often the price of the product, even with the gift or discount, is higher than the price of the same item at other stores.

Write the answer to each question.

6   An ad offers a deal on a TV. When the customer goes to buy the item, the seller says it is out of stock. The seller notes that a more expensive model is in stock. Which sales method is the seller using?

_____

7   A seller tells the buyer that the price of a compact disc player will go up next month. There will never be a better time to buy than now. Which sales method is the seller using?

_____

Circle the number of the best answer for the question.

8   Which of the following statements is supported by the article?
   (1)   All sellers are dishonest.
   (2)   Let the buyer beware.
   (3)   If a deal sounds good, buy the item.
   (4)   Never check prices in other stores.
   (5)   Don't buy an item if you don't need it.

Check your answers on page 251.

Opportunities in the Work Force

Top 20 Fastest-Growing Occupations, 1996–2006
(Numbers in thousands of jobs)

Occupation	Number of expected jobs in 2006	Expected % change 1996–2006	Most significant source of training
• Database administrators, computer support specialists, and all other computer scientists	249	118%	Bachelor's degree
• Computer engineers	235	109%	Bachelor's degree
• Systems analysts	520	103%	Bachelor's degree
• Personal and home care aids	171	85%	Short-term on-the-job training
• Physical and corrective therapy assistants and aides	66	79%	Moderate-term on-the-job training
• Home health aides	378	76%	Short-term on-the-job training
• Medical assistants	166	74%	Moderate-term on-the-job training
• Desktop publishing specialists	22	74%	Long-term on-the-job training
• Physical therapists	81	71%	Bachelor's degree
• Occupational therapy assistants and aides	11	69%	Moderate-term on-the-job training
• Paralegals	76	68%	Associate's degree
• Occupational therapists	38	66%	Bachelor's degree
• Teachers (special education)	241	59%	Bachelor's degree
• Human services workers	98	55%	Moderate-term on-the-job training
• Data processing equipment repairers	42	52%	Postsecondary vocational training
• Medical records technicians	44	51%	Associate's degree
• Speech/language pathologists and audiologists	44	51%	Master's degree
• Dental hygienists	68	48%	Associate's degree
• Amusement and recreation attendants	138	48%	Short-term on-the-job training
• Physician assistants	30	47%	Bachelor's degree

Source: *1998–99 Occupational Outlook Handbook,* U.S. Department of Labor, Bureau of Labor Statistics, "Top 20 Fastest-Growing Occupations from 1996–2006"

Write the answer to each question.

9 Which occupational group is expected to have the greatest growth by 2006?

_____

10 How much education do medical assistants need?

_____

Circle the number of the best answer.

11 Which of the following *cannot* be determined from the table?
 (1) amount of education each occupation requires
 (2) percent of increase of each occupation
 (3) occupations that are declining most rapidly
 (4) occupations that are increasing most rapidly
 (5) number of jobs expected for each occupation by 2006

Social Studies Extension

Look at the circle graph on page 187 to review the spending of the average American family. Over the next two weeks, write down all that you and your family spend in each of these categories. Then calculate the percentage of your total spending that fell in each category. How similar are your results to those shown on page 187?

Social Studies Connection: Economics and Math

Managed Health Care and the Cost of Caring

For decades medical insurance was out of reach for millions of Americans. The cost of insurance was too great for many businesses to bear and for many individuals to cover on their own. For many people, affordable health care coverage was simply out of the question.

In the 1990s, the attention of the federal government turned toward health care reform. Through public awareness efforts and legislative action, less expensive health care plans, called managed care plans, became more popular. The two most common options were the health maintenance organization (HMO) and the preferred provider organization (PPO).

Managed care plans used economic tools to attract and keep their members. Initially they offered attractive, lower-cost coverage to employers, employees, and individual customers. For many years, managed care plans deliberately kept costs low.

Once they had attracted many members, HMOs and PPOs modified coverage in the plans, required doctors to see more patients within a specific timeframe, excluded certain segments of the population, and restricted coverage of certain medical procedures previously covered by the plans. By enacting these rules, organizations were able to maintain their low costs and still attract new members.

Late in the 1990s, managed care organizations found it increasingly difficult to keep costs flat. They began raising their rates, limiting access to certain services, and eliminating coverage for certain types of members. Many people began criticizing managed health care plans because of these issues.

Math: Comparing Costs on a Graph

The graph on page 217 compares the costs of health care that are covered by managed care organizations (HMOs and PPOs) and indemnity plans (traditional health care). The numbers on the graph represent the average cost per person for each type of insurance provider.

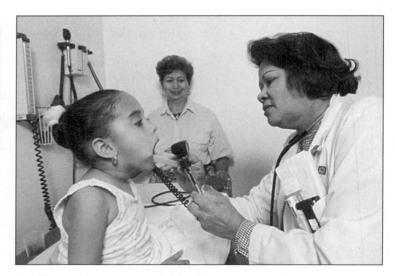

Families take advantage of the lower costs of managed care.

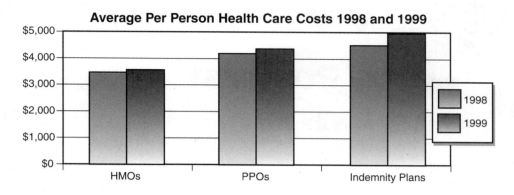

Average Per Person Health Care Costs 1998 and 1999

Use the graph and the information on the previous page to answer the questions below.

1 One result of managed care organizations keeping their coverage costs low was
   (1) they put traditional insurance plans out of business.
   (2) they provided preventative health care services.
   (3) they gained a large share of the health care market.
   (4) the government passed more health care legislation.
   (5) the government began focusing on health care reform.

2 All of the following are true of managed health care plans EXCEPT
   (1) they initially kept their costs low to attract customers.
   (2) their rates began to rise in the late 1990s.
   (3) their coverage and services changed over time.
   (4) many people criticized the plans once they began changing.
   (5) they include HMOs, PPOs, and traditional insurance plans.

3 Which of the following had an average cost of almost $5,000 per person?
   (1) HMOs in 1998
   (2) HMOs in 1999
   (3) PPOs in 1998
   (4) PPOs in 1999
   (5) Indemnity plans in 1999

4 What was the average per-person cost of PPOs in 1998?
   (1) $3,470
   (2) $3,532
   (3) $4,142
   (4) $4,312
   (5) $4,504

5 Using a separate piece of paper, write a paragraph about one reason that you think health care costs are so high. You might talk about the costs of research, medical education, drugs and medical equipment, government programs, or another key factor. Give reasons to support your ideas.

Posttest

The Nile River

The Nile is the longest river in the world. It is more than 4,145 miles long. The river begins in the mountains of central Africa and flows north through Egypt to the Mediterranean Sea. This is different from most rivers, which flow south. The Nile flows between the Libyan and Arabian deserts.

Each spring heavy rains fall in the highlands of central Africa. The rainwater swells the river. At one time the swollen river would flood Egypt by late summer. The water would spread across the river valley until it reached the desert just beyond the river.

In early times Egyptian farmers learned how to live beside a river that flooded each year. They dug channels to carry the floodwaters to their fields. The farmers let the water stand in the fields for weeks until it soaked the ground. Then the water drained, leaving behind fresh, rich, black soil on the land. Because of this natural process, the farmers could use the fields every year without wearing out the soil. But since the Nile River flooded only once a year, the farmers could plant only one crop a year. The rest of the year the land was too dry for farming.

In 1970 the Egyptians completed one of the world's biggest building projects. It was a huge dam at Aswan in southern Egypt. The dam stopped the flooding and trapped the water in a manmade lake 300 miles long. Farmers use this lake for **irrigation,** or carrying water through pipes or canals to crops. As a result, they can grow more than one crop per year. However, since the Nile River no longer floods, Egypt's soil is not as rich as it used to be.

Write the answers to each question.

❶ Why did the Nile River flood each year?

_____

❷ What was one advantage and one disadvantage in building Aswan High Dam?

_____

_____

Circle the number of the best answer.

❸ Since ancient times people have said that Egypt is a gift of the Nile. Based on facts from the passage, what is the best explanation of that saying?
   (1) Without the river the whole country would be a desert.
   (2) The river took away soil that was no longer fertile.
   (3) The river flooded each year.
   (4) The river trapped water in a huge lake.
   (5) Without the river the country would not be united.

Go on to the next page.

World Climates

World Climates

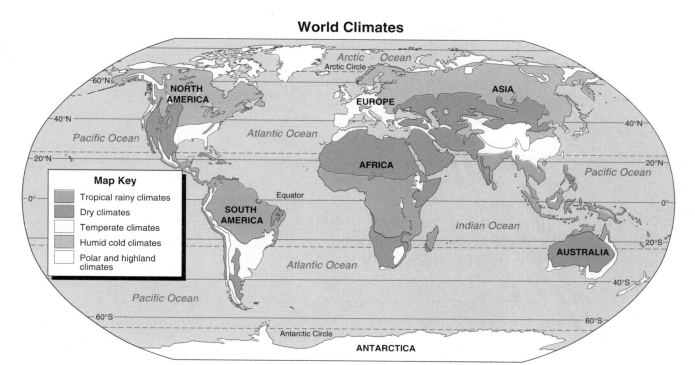

Write the answer to the question.

4 What kind of climate does central Australia have?

_____

Circle the number of the best answer to each question.

5 Near what line are most of the world's tropical rainy climates located?
(1) the Arctic Circle
(2) 40° N
(3) the Equator
(4) 40° S
(5) the Antarctic Circle

6 What kind of climate does most of northern Asia have?
(1) a tropical rainy climate
(2) a dry climate
(3) a temperate climate
(4) a humid cold climate
(5) a polar and highland climate

The World Gains a New Nation

Eritrea (pronounced *ehr uh TREE ah*) is a narrow strip of mountainous land in northeastern Africa. It is one of the world's hottest places and has a coastal plain along the Red Sea. The country lies between the sea and landlocked Ethiopia.

Eritrea was once part of an ancient kingdom linked with Ethiopia, which had a Christian ruler. Muslims from Arabia took over the kingdom's coastline, including Eritrea, in the 600s. They stopped the kingdom's trade with other nations. Today half of the Eritreans are Christian, and half are Muslims.

During the late 1800s, tens of thousands of Italians traveled south across the Mediterranean Sea and colonized Eritrea. They set up cotton and tobacco plantations there and taught Eritreans industrial skills. Eritrea remained an Italian colony through the 1930s. Italy invaded Ethiopia from Eritrea during World War II and even drafted Eritreans into its army. Britain defeated the Italians in 1941, and in time Eritrea became a part of Ethiopia again.

Yet the nine ethnic groups who live in Eritrea grew unhappy again with Ethiopian rule. Muslims faced job discrimination from Christians. Ethiopia outlawed the Muslims' Arabic language in schools. In the early 1960s, Eritrean rebels organized an independence movement. Many rebel leaders left the country. They created a small guerrilla force that returned to Eritrea to attack Ethiopian officials there. By the late 1960s, some disgruntled Christian Eritreans joined the mostly Muslim rebels.

During the late 1970s and 1980s, the Soviet Union gave military aid to Ethiopia. When the Soviets' communist government fell in 1989, the Ethiopian government could no longer defend itself from rebel attacks. After nearly 30 years of fighting and the deaths of 40,000 Eritreans, the civil war ended in 1991.

In 1993 the people of Eritrea voted on a long-awaited issue. More than 99 percent of voters chose independence from Ethiopia. The new nation of 3.2 million people became one of the last to form in the twentieth century. The Eritreans' decades-long struggle to be free was over.

Write the answer to the question.

7 Why do you think Ethiopia did not want to lose control of Eritrea?

_____

Circle the number of the best answer.

8 Which is a <u>result</u> of the civil war between Eritreans and Ethiopians?
   (1) Christian Ethiopians discriminated against Muslim Eritreans.
   (2) Eritreans overwhelmingly voted for separation from Ethiopia.
   (3) Eritreans preferred Italian rule more than being under Ethiopia.
   (4) The Arabic language was banned in Eritrean schools.
   (5) The former Soviet Union no longer sent military aid.

Monitoring World Peace

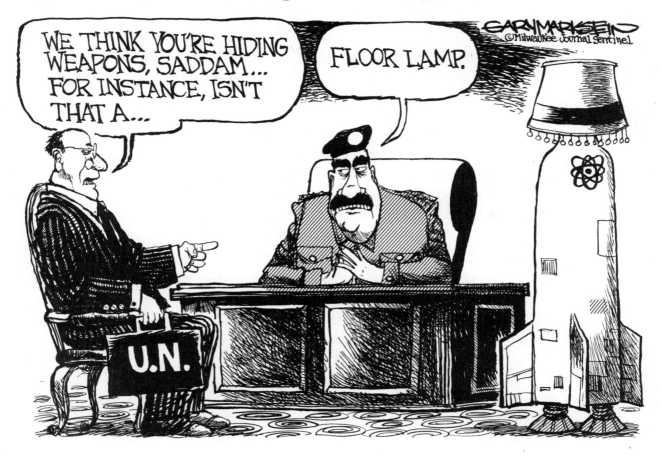

Write the answer to the question.

9 The cartoon is set in Iraq in 1997. The man behind the desk is Saddam Hussein, the leader of Iraq. Whom does the man in the front chair represent? What is the "floor lamp" actually?

_____

_____

Circle the number of the best answer.

10 Which term sums up how the cartoonist portrays Saddam Hussein?
   (1) cooperative
   (2) peace loving
   (3) dishonest
   (4) straightforward
   (5) truthful

Women in Combat

Throughout American history few women have served the armed forces in battle. Perhaps the most famous was Mary Ludwig Hays McCauley, better known as Molly Pitcher. During the American Revolution, she carried water to the gunners during the battle of Monmouth, New Jersey, in 1778. When her husband died in battle, she took his place.

Deborah Sampson also fought in the Revolution. However, she disguised herself as a man and joined a Massachusetts regiment. Sampson fought in several battles and was seriously wounded. When a doctor discovered her secret, he told her commander, who then told General George Washington. Washington ordered that Sampson be honorably discharged. After Sampson's death, her husband received the pension normally paid to the wife of a wounded veteran.

The first American woman to lead soldiers was Harriet Tubman. Tubman, an African American, worked as a spy for the Union army during the Civil War. She also led raids. A Boston newspaper described one of her raids:

> Colonel Montgomery and his gallant band of 300 black soldiers, under the guidance of a black woman, dashed into the enemy's country . . . brought off near 800 slaves and thousands of dollars' worth of property, without losing a man or receiving a scratch.

During the 1980s women in the military challenged the reasons why Americans did not approve of women fighting in battle. In the 1991 Gulf War, women flew transport planes and helped refuel tankers. Others trained combat pilots. Yet women were still not allowed in combat jobs. Between 1992 and 1994, the United States Navy, Air Force, and Army changed their policies. Women joined combat crews on aircraft carriers, ground units, and flight missions. Military leaders have yet to approve women fighting as foot soldiers.

Write the answers to each question.

11 What do Molly Pitcher, Sampson, and Tubman have in common?

_____

12 Of the three women mentioned in the passage, who would appear last on a timeline?

_____

Circle the number of the best answer.

13 Which conclusion is supported by information in the article?
(1) Women never wanted to take part in battle.
(2) Some women have proven themselves in combat.
(3) Women should not be allowed to take part in war.
(4) Some women have fought in every war in American history.
(5) Women are now allowed in all combat jobs.

Go on to the next page.

Labor Reform

Men in front of a labor agency in New York City, 1910.

Write the answer to the question.

14 Why were so many men and boys gathered around the building?

_____

_____

_____

_____

Circle the number of the best answer to each question.

15 The photograph was taken in New York City. What inference can be made from the photograph?
   (1) Few New Yorkers were willing to work.
   (2) No jobs were available in New York City.
   (3) Many people needed work.
   (4) Most jobs paid hundreds of dollars a week.
   (5) Many companies were hiring only women.

16 Who might be <u>most</u> attracted to the kinds of jobs advertised?
   (1) 10-year-old girls
   (2) 10-year-old boys
   (3) young men
   (4) men in their early sixties
   (5) women with young children

Guaranteeing Equal Opportunity

About 54 million Americans have disabilities. Many of them face discrimination every day. Many jobs are closed to them. Of the 26 million people who report having a severe disability, only 26.1 percent have a job.

During the 1970s and 1980s, Americans with disabilities protested that life in the United States had too many barriers for them. The barriers prevented them from participating fully in society. They emphasized that this participation was an important part of the freedom and opportunity the United States guarantees all its citizens. They said that guaranteeing this participation was a part of the civil rights protected by the United States Constitution.

In July 1990 Congress passed the Americans with Disabilities Act (ADA). It defined disability as a physical or mental condition that "substantially limits" a major life activity, such as walking or seeing. The law also covers people with AIDS, alcoholics, and drug users who are in treatment programs. The law includes many rules for businesses, including:

1. Employers, including state and local governments, may not discriminate against an individual with a disability in hiring or promotion if the person is qualified to do the job without endangering himself or others.

2. Trains and buses must be accessible to people with disabilities.

3. Restaurants, hotels, and retail stores must remove any physical barriers to access and provide help for those who cannot hear or see.

4. Companies that provide telephone service must make available special equipment for those who cannot hear.

Write the answer to the question.

17 Why did Americans with disabilities feel that full participation in American society was one of their civil rights?

_____

_____

Circle the number of the best answer.

18 Which situation is considered discriminatory under the ADA?
(1) An alcoholic is fired for drinking on the job.
(2) A deaf woman is turned down for a job because she lacks job skills.
(3) A man in a wheelchair cannot get to work because stairs in the subway keep him from reaching the train.
(4) A blind woman is fired for missing too many days of work.
(5) A company refuses to hire a man who has seizures because he could endanger himself or others with the equipment he must use on the job.

Go on to the next page.

How Two City Governments Spend Their Money

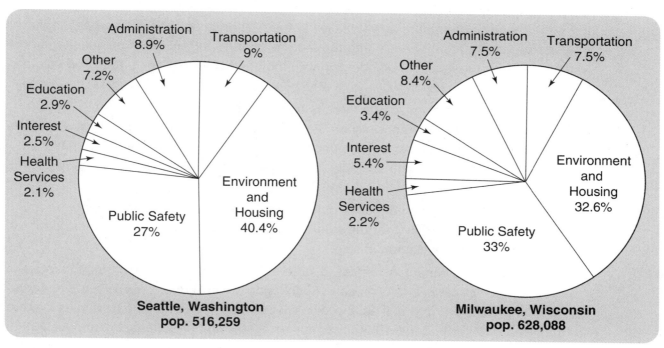

Administration 8.9%
Transportation 9%
Other 7.2%
Education 2.9%
Interest 2.5%
Health Services 2.1%
Public Safety 27%
Environment and Housing 40.4%

**Seattle, Washington
pop. 516,259**

Administration 7.5%
Transportation 7.5%
Other 8.4%
Education 3.4%
Interest 5.4%
Health Services 2.2%
Environment and Housing 32.6%
Public Safety 33%

**Milwaukee, Wisconsin
pop. 628,088**

Source: Bureau of the Census

Write the answer to the question.

19 The populations of Seattle and Milwaukee are similar, even though they are in two different parts of the United States. Compare the graphs. On what category of expenses do the two city governments spend almost the same percentage of their budget?

_____

Circle the number of the best answer to each question.

20 How much more of Milwaukee's budget is spent on interest than on education?
(1) 0.5%   (4) 3.4%
(2) 2%   (5) 5.4%
(3) 2.5%

21 Based on the graphs, which expense is more of a priority for Seattle's city government than Milwaukee's?
(1) health services
(2) environment and housing
(3) public safety
(4) social services
(5) education

The Language of Sales

Sale advertising has a language all its own. For example, an item *on sale* is different from a *clearance sale* item. There are also *promotional sale* items.

The price of an item on sale is lower than the price before the sale began. The store hopes to attract people into the store by putting certain items on sale. When the sale is over, the item is marked again with the original, higher price. Items on sale are available at these lower prices for a short time.

During a *clearance sale,* a store is trying to sell all of a certain item. It greatly reduces prices for different reasons. Perhaps the item has not been selling well at the higher price. The item may only be useful to customers during a particular season, which has now passed. For example, clearance sales on winter coats are common in March.

A *promotional sale* item does not come from the store's regular stock. It is brought into the store just for the sale. Often promotional sale items cost more than the same items at a clearance sale.

In a highly competitive market, a store may do enough business that it can take a loss on certain items it puts on sale. Such items are called *loss leaders.* A grocery store, for example, may sell as a weekly special the Italian breads baked in its in-store bakery for 50 cents a loaf. This price may be 25 percent of its regular price but 10 percent less than the store's cost to make each loaf. The manager is willing to take the loss in order to attract more customers. The store will have most of its items at their regular prices and will make up the money lost on bread sales in the increased total of items it sells that week.

Consumer experts say that the best way to make sure of an item's best price is to check several stores before buying. A good sale offers discounts of about 40 to 50 percent off the original price. Comparing the weekly advertisements of grocery stores side by side also reveals when food manufacturers offer all stores special discounts.

Write the answer to the question.

22 Which type of sale reduces the price of goods to sell out the remaining stock?

_____

Circle the number of the best answer.

23 Which is an example of a promotional sale?
   (1) A store lowers the price of shoes to attract new customers.
   (2) A store brings in a new brand of shoes and sells them at a low price.
   (3) In the spring a store lowers the price of winter boots.
   (4) A store marks shoes at the original price.
   (5) The store reduces the price of shoes by 50 percent.

Average Hourly Earnings

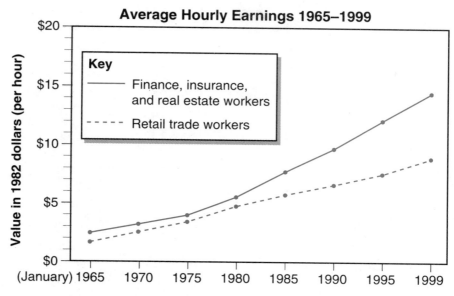

Average Hourly Earnings 1965–1999

Value in 1982 dollars (per hour)

Key

—— Finance, insurance, and real estate workers

- - - - Retail trade workers

(January) 1965 1970 1975 1980 1985 1990 1995 1999

Source: Bureau of Labor Statistics Data, 1999

Write the answer to each question.

24 How is the trend in earnings of retail trade workers similar to that of earnings of finance, insurance, and real estate workers from 1965 to 1999?

_____

25 The graph indicates that wages are in 1982 dollars. In which year on the graph was the average value of wages of finance, insurance, and real estate workers about $5.50 per hour in 1982 dollars?

_____

Circle the number of the best answer.

26 What conclusion is supported by the information in the graph?
On the average:
(1) Insurance agents make less money per hour than store clerks.
(2) Real estate agents make more than insurance agents.
(3) Grocery cashiers will never make over $10 per hour.
(4) Wages in finance, insurance, and real estate have gained more value than wages in retail.
(5) More jobs are available in retail trade than in finance, insurance, and real estate.

Posttest Correlation Chart

The chart below will help you determine your strengths and weaknesses in the five content areas of social studies.

Content Areas	Items	Total Correct	Practice Pages
Geography (Pages 12–45)	1, 2, 3, 4, 5, 6	_____ out of 6	Pages 14–19 Pages 20–25
World History (Pages 46–85)	7, 8, 9, 10	_____ out of 4	Pages 60–65 Pages 72–77
American History (Pages 86–137)	11, 12, 13, 14, 15, 16	_____ out of 6	Pages 94–105 Pages 106–111
Government and Civics (Pages 138–171)	17, 18, 19, 20, 21	_____ out of 5	Pages 152–157 Pages 140–145
Economics (Pages 172–217)	22, 23, 24, 25, 26	_____ out of 5	Pages 192–197 Pages 198–203

TOTAL CORRECT FOR POSTTEST _____ **out of 26**

Directions

Circle the number of each item that you answered correctly on the Posttest. Count the number of items you answered correctly in each row. Write the amount in the Total Correct space in each row. (For example, in the Geography row, write the number correct in the blank before *out of 6*.) Complete this process for the remaining rows. Then add the 5 totals to get your Total Correct for the whole 26-item Posttest.

If you answered fewer than 23 items correctly, determine in which areas you need further practice. Go back and review the content in those areas. Page numbers for specific instruction in those areas of social studies appear in the right-hand column above.

Answers and Explanations

INVENTORY

PAGE 1
1. below 1,000 feet
2. the Great Plains

PAGE 2
3. Possible answers are that all deserts are dry and few plants grow there.
4. Some deserts are hot. Others are cold.
5. **(2) Living things have developed ways to survive in difficult environments.** According to the article, animals can live in all deserts so option 1 is incorrect. Options 3 and 4 are just details stated in the article. The article does not discuss Option 5.

PAGE 3
6. to honor Zeus
7. **(4) way of life** The sentence immediately following *culture* explains its meaning. The other options are definitions of *culture* but not the one intended in the passage.

PAGE 4
8. North Korea invaded South Korea.
9. China joined North Korea. The United States and the United Nations joined South Korea.
10. **(1) North Korea gained control of South Korea's capital.** According to the timeline, option 3 took place a year and option 2 almost two years after China entered the war. Options 4 and 5 took place before China entered the war.
11. **(5) Neither side gained territory from the war.** Nothing on the timeline supports option 1. Options 3 and 4 refer to parts of the timeline, but they do not reflect the outcome of the entire war. Option 2 is false.

PAGE 5
12. American Patriots wanted to gain freedom from Britain. Loyalists wanted to remain under British rule.
13. Slave owners feared the African Americans would use their guns to try to end slavery.
14. Many enslaved African Americans joined the British army. Patriot leaders allowed African Americans to join their army.

15. **(3) the loss of so many soldiers at Valley Forge** Options 1, 4, and 5 had no bearing on the feelings of Patriot leaders about African Americans. Option 2 resulted in Patriot leaders allowing free African Americans to join, but not slaves.

PAGE 6
16. Idaho, Wyoming, Colorado, and Utah
17. **(1) In 1900 men influenced American government more than women did.** No information is given in the map about options 2, 3, and 5. Option 4 is false.

PAGE 7
18. Answers will vary. A sample answer is that *segregated* means "African Americans and white Americans did things separately."
19. to demand that Congress pass a civil rights bill
20. **(2) live up to the nation's values and beliefs.** In his speech King reminds Americans of the values and beliefs that built the United States. He was not asking Americans to change their values or to follow Kennedy, so options 1 and 5 are incorrect. Americans were already marching in Washington, D.C., so option 3 is incorrect. Option 4 was the goal of the march but not the main point of King's words.

PAGE 8
21. from state primaries and state caucuses and conventions
22. **(3) electors of the Electoral College** According to the diagram, the voters elect the electors. The electors, in turn, choose the president and vice president from the national candidates. So option 1 is incorrect. The diagram does not support options 2, 4, and 5.

PAGE 9
23. People pay a benefit tax in proportion to the goods and services they use. An ability-to-pay tax is a tax on income, and those who make more income pay at a higher rate.
24. The person who makes $25,000 would pay more taxes under a flat tax.

25. **(4) fairness** According to the article, option 2 has been an issue in the debate for a flat-rate tax but has not been approved. Options 3 and 5 are not supported in the article, and option 1 is not related to taxes.

PAGE 10

26. the United States economy
27. The U.S. has saved itself by holding on to the branch with one hand and holding up the Asian economy with the other.
28. **(3) Global economies succeed or fail together.** The United States is holding up Asia, so option 1 is false. Option 2 is a literal interpretation of the cartoon and not the message the cartoonist is trying to communicate. Option 4 is unlikely in light of what is happening to the U.S. and Asian economies. Option 5 contradicts the message of the cartoon.

UNIT 1: GEOGRAPHY

SECTION 1

PAGE 14
Preview the Article
Answers may include the following: About the Arctic, the vegetation and climate of the Arctic, who the Inuit are, their history, and what life is like for them today in Canada

Relate to the Topic
Answer should reflect the location of your home. You should mention features that make your neighborhood different from others nearby.

PAGE 16
a

PAGE 17
a

PAGES 18–19
1. tundra
2. climate
3. Vegetation
4. tree line
5. region
6. The climate includes long, cold winters and short summers. The vegetation includes algae on the rocks near the Arctic Ocean and tundra—small plants and shrubs (no trees) growing in the thin layer of soil above the frozen ground underneath.

7. They fished, hunted caribou, whales, and seals, and gathered berries. They wore clothes made of seal skins and caribou hides. They traveled on foot during the short summer and by boat or dog team during the rest of the year.
8. They organized an annual Inuit conference, which gave them political power to help hold on to their way of life. Canada's Inuit began demanding control of their hunting grounds in the Northwest Territories. Canada's Inuit worked with Canada's government to establish the state of Nunavit. Canada's Inuit insisted the schools teach native languages and customs to Inuit students.
9. **(5) Most of Greenland is covered in ice.** The map contradicts options 1, 2, and 4. The map and map key do not give enough information on which to base option 3.
10. **(1) The Inuit met their needs by fishing and hunting.** The statements described in options 2, 3, 4, and 5 are details mentioned in the paragraph but none summarizes the main idea.
11. Possible answers are land and mineral rights, political power, and the chance to hold on to their way of life. Some people may feel that the land and mineral rights are most valuable since these are tangible assets. Others may think that the more abstract gains of political power and keeping their way of life are most valuable because they give people self respect.
12. Many answers are possible but may include that the children might use words, dress, and other practices common in the other country, and that they may lose a sense of connection to their family and old way of life.

SECTION 2

PAGE 20
Preview the Article
Answers might include factors determining climate, the relationship between the equator (or latitude) and climate, how water and wind affect climate, how mountains affect climate.

Relate to the Topic
Answers should describe the climate of a place where you would like to live.

PAGE 21

b

PAGE 23

1. a
2. c

PAGES 24–25

1. equator
2. current
3. Precipitation
4. latitude
5. elevation
6. longitude
7. Your answer should indicate three of the following factors: a place's latitude, nearby mountains, nearby bodies of water, ocean currents, and winds.
8. Places in the tropics are warm year-round.
9. In summer, ocean water stays cold long after the land has grown warm. So the summer winds blowing off the oceans bring cooling breezes to the land. Large bodies of water also hold the summer's heat as the land cools in fall. So winter winds blowing off the oceans bring warm air over the land.
10. **(5) The tropics receive almost direct rays from the sun.** According to the article, direct rays from the sun produce warm temperatures in the tropics. Options 1 and 3 are false. Option 2 explains why a place in the tropics that is near the ocean might get more rainfall. Option 4 helps to explain why southern Alaska has a mild climate.
11. **(4) 10° N latitude** According to the article, the area between the equator and the Tropic of Cancer is part of the tropics. Option 1 is the South Pole. Options 2, 3, and 5 lie in the middle-latitude areas.
12. **(2) South America and Africa** The map shows that North America, Europe, and continental Asia lie north of the equator, and Australia lies south of it.
13. western Montana Sample explanation: When winds reach the Rocky Mountains, the winds rise and cool. Cold air cannot hold as much moisture as warm air. So clouds form and rain falls on the western side of the mountains. When the winds reach the eastern side of the mountains, the air is dry.

14. Your description should include such climate words as temperature, precipitation, and wind.

SECTION 3

PAGE 26

Preview the Article
Answer may mention the following topics: oil spill, Prince William Sound and its environment, how the oil spill was cleaned up.

Relate to the Topic
Answer should describe specific actions, such as organizing friends to pick up trash or writing local officials about cleaning up the park.

PAGE 27

You may have circled many words. Here are the words in bold type you should have circled: sound, environment, glaciers, crude oil, iceberg, conclusion. The definitions you have written will depend on the other words you have circled.

PAGE 29

Answers may include that the oil spill was the largest any group had ever cleaned up; several groups helped but they had no leader; oil spread quickly within the sound and along the coastline; oil itself was a difficult substance to remove from water or the gravel beaches.

PAGES 30–31

1. sound
2. environment
3. glacier
4. crude oil
5. iceberg
6. In 1989 an oil tanker hit a reef in the bottom of the sound and started leaking oil into the sound.
7. Answers should include at least one of the following causes: wind, movement of water, the storm, or ocean currents.
8. Fish, animals, and birds died; the fishing and tourist industries suffered; the water in the sound was polluted.
9. **(3) A long inlet of the ocean that runs along the coast.** Options 1, 4, and 5 are definitions for totally different uses of sound. Option 2 cannot be correct because the map does not show the sound connecting two large bodies of water.

10. **(5) The cleanup helped some living things in the environment.** The article contradicts options 1, 3, and 4. No information in the article supports option 2.

11. Answers may include that tourists probably stayed away from refuges and beaches spoiled by oil. As a result, hotels in the area probably fell on hard times and laid off workers.

12. Your answer should address whether or not the cost of the tax for the oil-spill cleanup fund is likely to be passed along to gasoline customers through higher gas prices.

SECTION 4

PAGE 32
Preview the Article
Possible answer: the Middle East and its oil and water resources

Relate to the Topic
Many answers are possible. Most people agree that water and oil are very important to daily life.

PAGE 34
1. Saudi Arabia
2. Iran

PAGE 35
1. b
2. a

PAGES 36–37
1. desalination
2. irrigation
3. resource
4. oasis
5. nonrenewable resource
6. desert
7. Until automobiles were invented, few people had any use for oil.
8. The Middle East has a dry climate with some desert. Temperatures are hot, and rainfall is scarce.
9. Possible answers: the peace pipeline for carrying water and cooperating to manage river resources
10. **(4) Most oil fields are located near bodies of water.** The map contradicts options 1, 2, and 3. The map and map key do not give enough information on which to base option 5.

11. **(5) traps water, whenever they need it** The phrases described in options 1, 2, and 4 refer to the river. Option 3 refers to the effect of the dam on the fish.

12. Many answers are possible but should include that the Middle East has about 65 percent of the world's known oil reserves, and since oil is so much in demand, Middle Eastern countries can sell it for high prices.

13. Many answers are possible but may include scarcer supplies of gas, long lines waiting for gas, higher prices per gallon, quotas of certain amounts per family or business per month, etc.

GEOGRAPHY AT WORK

PAGE 39
Agent: 3 trains; numbers 18, 126 and 150.
Agent: 12:29 P.M.; 9:44 A.M.
Agent: Baltimore

UNIT 1 REVIEW

PAGE 40
1. **(3) Peary and his group were the first people to reach the North Pole.** Option 1 is not true. Options 2, 4, and 5 are true, but are details, not the main idea.
2. **(5) Peary followed a northerly route along the 70° W line of longitude.** Options 1 and 3 are not true. Information on the map contradicts option 2. No facts presented in the map would lead you to option 4.

PAGE 41
3. Peary's final trip began at Cape Columbia on Ellesmere Island in Canada.
4. 85° N
5. 87° N
6. **(2) figuring the latitude of his current location** If Peary could figure out the latitude of his location, he would always know where he was and how far he had to go to reach 90° N, the North Pole. The other options may have been important to Peary but not in terms of his location and goal.

PAGE 42

7. **(4) to get water for their crops and animals.** According to the article, irrigation is used to create a water supply, so options 1, 2, and 3 are incorrect. Nothing in the article supports option 5.

8. **(4) Texas is large with varied landforms.** The other options are true, but option 4 provides the most complete reason.

PAGE 43

9. an oil derrick

10. a steer

11. **(3) how much oil is produced in the top oil-producing states** The map does not show the quantities of oil produced. The map does show the number and location of top cattle-raising and oil-producing states, so the other options are incorrect.

SOCIAL STUDIES CONNECTION: GEOGRAPHY AND EARTH SCIENCE

PAGE 45

1. **(3) Honduras**

2. **(5) Catastrophic**

3. **(2) Cool, dry air above the Caribbean Sea**

4. Alex, **tropical storm, TS**
   Georges, **hurricane, 3**
   Ivan, **hurricane, 1**
   Nicole, **hurricane, 1**

UNIT 2: WORLD HISTORY

SECTION 5

PAGE 48

Preview the Article

Why the Great Wall began, how the Mongols ruled China, and what the Ming dynasty was like

Relate to the Topic

Answers will vary. Possible answers are that large kingdoms and companies offer more power, more profit, and less competition than smaller companies do.

PAGE 50

a. s

b. d

PAGE 51

a and b

PAGES 52–53

1. barbarian

2. peasants

3. dynasty

4. civilization

5. empire

6. Shi Huangdi had the wall built to mark China's northern border and to keep out invaders.

7. They built up the army instead of the wall.

8. The Mongols put themselves and foreigners into high positions. The Chinese also resented the way their Mongol rulers accepted religious groups who did not follow traditional Chinese ways.

9. The builders during the Ming dynasty used more durable materials than the earlier builders had used.

10. **(5) The Chinese valued learning over physical strength.** Option 1 cannot be determined from the text. Options 2 and 3 list similarities, not differences, and option 4 is false.

11. **(2) Sui and Ming** Option 1 cannot be correct because the Yuan were Mongols and the Ming were Chinese. Options 3 and 4 are not correct because although they were all Chinese, one built the wall and the other built the army. Option 5 is not correct because the Mongols and the Yuan are the same.

12. **(3) Tang** The rulers in options 1, 2, and 5 relied on the wall rather than an expanded army and weapons for defense. The Mongols in option 4 attacked rather than counterattacked.

13. Answers should point out that aircraft can go over the wall to deliver invaders and bombs.

14. Answers will vary. Possible answers include the Sears Tower, Mount Rushmore, and the Hoover Dam, which are awe-inspiring because of their large sizes and because of the imagination and effort that went into their making.

SECTION 6

PAGE 54

Preview the Article

Musical inventions, clocks, and disease preventatives

Relate to the Topic

Answers will vary. Possible answers are that music would be less varied, the pace of life would be less hurried, and life might be shorter.

PAGE 56

b, d, e, c, a

PAGE 57

Answers will vary, but they should be similar to the following sentences:

a. Dr. Edward Jenner observed that **milkmaids who had had cowpox did not catch smallpox.**

b. He experimented by **injecting a boy with cowpox and later injecting him with smallpox.**

c. The results of the experiment were **that the boy was protected from smallpox, vaccination was invented, and eventually, smallpox was eliminated.**

PAGES 58–59

1. smallpox
2. orchestra
3. vaccination
4. chronometer
5. century
6. immune
7. The harpsichord makes sounds by plucking strings, and the piano makes sounds by hitting strings.
8. The pendulum could not swing regularly on a rolling ship.
9. Timepieces with pendulums would not be very portable and people's movements would make them inaccurate. Harrison's timepiece was small and worked by springs.
10. He got the idea from observing that milkmaids who had cowpox never got smallpox. He then injected a healthy boy with cowpox, which prevented him from getting smallpox.
11. **(2) steam engine and steamboat** Options 1 and 3 appear totally unconnected. In option 4, the spinning machine may have created a greater demand for cotton, but the cotton gin was mechanically unrelated to the spinning machine. In option 5, the steamboat and hot-air balloon both used gases for powering travel, but the machinery of the two inventions was unconnected.
12. **(4) one hundred years** All other options are false.
13. **(4) To win a prize, John Harrison spent 34 years inventing a seagoing chronometer.** Options 1 and 2 refer to important details in the paragraph but are not the best summaries. Options 3 and 5 are false.
14. Both, because the hammers inside the piano hit the strings and the strings make the sound.
15. Answers will vary. Possible answers include AIDS, leprosy, cancer, and the common cold. Reasons you might choose the diseases you did include how deadly the diseases are, how painful they are, or how common they are.

SECTION 7

PAGE 60

Preview the Article

Mexico's outdated economy and society, changes under Díaz, and hardships suffered by Mexicans

Relate to the Topic

Answer should reveal your feelings about authority taking control.

PAGE 61

a

PAGE 63

b

PAGES 64–65

1. capital
2. liberals
3. Duties
4. conservatives
5. diplomat
6. democracy
7. Díaz put local bosses in power in villages. He also sent troops throughout the country and gave them permission to shoot suspected criminals and to stop protests.

8. He wanted to show the diplomats that Mexico had a strong leader and hoped that their countries would invest there.

9. Widespread homelessness led to illness and death.

10. **(4) All foreign diplomats to Mexico approved of its government.** The word *all* signals a hasty generalization. It was unlikely that all foreign diplomats approved of the government under Díaz. So this is a hasty generalization. All the other choices simply state facts.

11. **(2) Manufacturing doubled while Díaz was in office.** The facts contradict options 1, 3, 4, and 5.

12. **(1) Americans invested more money than the combined investment from Europeans.** The facts in the graph contradict options 2, 3, 4, and 5.

13. A possible answer is that the people ate because the economy was better, but the police used violence to enforce Díaz's laws.

14. Answers will vary. One possible answer is that no amount of money or job security could compensate for the loss of any of my rights and freedoms.

SECTION 8

PAGE 66
Preview the Article
Land, race, and democracy

Relate to the Topic
Answers will vary. You should defend your position with a statement of your values or beliefs.

PAGE 67
1. they wanted to start farms.
2. b

PAGE 69
b

PAGES 70–71
1. parliament
2. apartheid
3. civil rights
4. Racist
5. republic
6. sanction
7. suffrage
8. They considered the land of southern Africa their own and wanted to remain in control.

9. Three possible answers are: (1) They no longer had freedom to move where they wished. (2) They could not qualify for certain jobs. (3) Their privacy was violated because they had to carry passbooks with personal information.

10. The African National Congress tried to set up private schools, encouraged protest among black Africans, and prepared to fight.

11. **(5) They tried to open nongovernment schools for black children.** Option 1 indicates the ANC valued self-defense. Option 2 indicates that it valued human rights. Option 3 indicates it valued cooperation. Information in option 4 was not indicated in the article.

12. **(2) They are proud.** The cartoonist's exaggerated expression of snobbery with the men's heads tilted back and noses in the air suggests this emotion. Nothing the artist shows suggests the emotions in the other options.

13. **(3) the water** The buckets in option 1 stand for solutions to the problems. The boat in option 2 stands for racial harmony. The white clothing in option 4 indicates the white population of South Africa. The black clothing in option 5 indicates the black population of South Africa.

14. Many explanations are possible but should indicate that South Africa's economy would suffer if nations refused to buy their resources such as high-cost diamonds and gold.

15. Answers will vary. A possible response is that you would end all apartheid laws still in force.

SECTION 9

PAGE 72
Preview the Article
Countries in the Middle East and Africa, including Rwanda and Somalia

Relate to the Topic
Answers will vary but should recap a recent world news story involving conflict in a foreign country.

PAGE 74
a

PAGES 76–77

1. mediator
2. neutral
3. charter
4. deadlocked
5. provinces, cease-fire
6. civilians
7. Observers are unarmed and few in number. Peacekeeping forces are lightly armed and can number in the thousands.
8. Many British people had money in the company that ran the canal, and Great Britain probably needed access to the canal to carry on trade.
9. Fighting drove the farmers from their fields, which were producing very little anyway because of a three-year drought.
10. **(2) More than half the refugees were women and children.** The photo contradicts options 1, 4, and 5. The photo does not offer enough information to support option 3.
11. **(3) fighting between people of the same country** All other options are false.
12. **(2) countries that help each other** Options 1 and 3 refer to alternate meanings for *allies*. Option 4 defines *alloys*, and option 5 defines *alleys*.
13. Answers will vary. A possible answer is that the UN troops were successful in that they protected civilians.
14. Answers will vary. Sample answer: If I took the side of one friend, the other friend would be less willing to let me help find a solution to the dispute.

HISTORY AT WORK

PAGES 78–79

1. **(2) statue.**
2. **(3) France**
3. Answers may vary. Sample answers: The Statue of Liberty's face is 14 feet long. "Liberty Enlightening the World" is the original name for the Statue of Liberty. The Statue of Liberty was a gift from the people of France to the people of the U.S. The Statue of Liberty is covered in copper.

UNIT 2 REVIEW

PAGE 80

1. **(2) Russians have had little experience with democracy.** Options 1 and 3 are not true. Option 4 is true, but the article does not give details on this fact. The article does not provide enough information on option 5 to determine this.

PAGE 81

2. Russia; the Russian leaders' version of democracy
3. Answers may vary. A possible answer is that Russia is not following the recipe for democracy.
4. The way Russia is "cooking up" democracy is not successful.
5. **(5) freedom, open-mindedness, give and take** Options 1 and 2 can be positive, but even authoritarian societies can value respect, honesty, courage in battle, citizenship, loyalty, and uniformity of beliefs. Options 3 and 4 reflect government systems with unequal levels of power.

PAGE 83

6. **(4) fleet of ships** The other options are false.
7. **(2) He named an inexperienced nobleman as fleet commander.** Option 5 is false. The other options are true, but only option 2 showed poor judgment.
8. Answers will vary but should indicate that, when preparing for battle, a ruler must consider the strengths of his forces and the strengths of his opponents'. Because England is an island, its navy would have been its strongest defense. King Philip II was too confident in his nation's strength. Spain required an experienced seaman to plan the attack.
9. Spain used ships to carry riches from the distant parts of its empire back to Spain. So Spanish rulers established settlements on coasts where the riches could be loaded on to the ships.

WORLD HISTORY AND LIFE SCIENCES

PAGE 85

1. **(2) during World War I**

2. **(4) England needed to focus on the war effort.**
3. Answers may vary. Some examples follow.
   a. Some antibiotics interfere with the bacterial cells' ability to divide and reproduce.
   b. Some antibiotics prevent bacteria from making the proteins they need to reproduce
   c. Some antibiotics don't let protective cell walls form on new cells.
4. **(1) cell wall.**
5. 4–World War II begins
   1–World War I begins
   2–Fleming discovers penicillin
   3–Florey and Chain invent the process of mass-producing penicillin
   5–Mass production of penicillin moves to U.S.

UNIT 3: AMERICAN HISTORY

SECTION 10

PAGE 88
Preview the Article
Possible answers are who came to the Americas, where they came from, and where they settled.

Relate to the Topic
Answers should indicate your ethnic background and your feelings about how it has affected you as an American.

PAGE 90
   a

PAGE 91
   4
   2
   1
   3

PAGES 92–93
   1. conquistadors
   2. indentured servants
   3. migrated
   4. missions
   5. pueblos
   6. Immigrants
   7. The first people from Asia were following wild game.
   8. The Spanish explorers sought adventure and wealth. French fur trappers sought profit. The British settlers wanted land, a better life, and freedom of religion.
9. disease, starvation, lack of supplies, and attacks by Native Americans
10. The founders of Rhode Island and New Hampshire wanted more religious freedom than they had in Massachusetts.
11. **(2) Early English settlements lay north of Spanish settlements.** Option 1 cannot be determined from the map. Options 3, 4, and 5 are false.
12. **(4) The English settled at Jamestown, Virginia.** The other options, in chronological order, are (3), (1), (5), and (2).
13. **(3) Pennsylvania** The other options, in chronological order, are (2), (1), (4), and (5).
14. Answers will vary but may indicate that later settlers were eager to profit from the land and did not seek help from the Native Americans. Instead the settlers stole the Native Americans' land.
15. Answers will vary but should indicate that most came to make a better living or to escape persecution in their homeland.

SECTION 11

PAGE 94
Preview the Article
Possible answers are disagreements between the British and the colonists, the Boston Tea Party, and the fighting at Lexington and Concord.

Relate to the Topic
You may point out that parents often see their teens' behavior as rebellion against house rules. The children resist the decisions of authority because they want to make decisions for themselves.

PAGE 95
   a

PAGE 97
   1. 1765
   2. 1770
   3. after

PAGES 98–99
   1. exports
   2. repealed
   3. legislature
   4. Minutemen
   5. imports
   6. boycotted

7. Angry colonists forced tax collectors out of town, protested the tax, and refused to buy British goods.
8. Parliament would not repeal the tea tax.
9. The Declaration of Independence explains to the world why the colonists were fighting to be free of British rule.
10. They hid behind fences, barns, and farmhouses along the road.
11. **(2) the Declaration of Independence** According to the article, the Declaration of Independence was approved *after* the war began. Options 1, 3, 4, and 5 were all *causes* of the American Revolution.
12. **(5) The American Revolution began.** According to the article, all the other options were *causes*, leading up to the battles.
13. **(4) 12** The war with France ended in 1763 and the Revolution began in 1775. The other options are incorrect.
14. Many answers are possible. A sample answer is that many colonists in Spanish colonies may have wondered if they would be better off without their colonial rulers.
15. Many answers are possible. A sample answer is that people might protest or rebel when laws are unfairly enforced.

SECTION 12
PAGE 100
Preview the Article
Possible answers could include differences between the North and South, slavery, and war.

Relate to the Topic
There are many possible answers. You should briefly describe the situation and how it was resolved.

PAGE 102
My paramount object in this struggle is to save the Union, and is not either to save or destroy slavery.
   a

PAGE 103
   a

PAGES 104–105
   1. Confederacy
   2. Emancipation Proclamation
   3. Abolitionists
   4. discrimination

5. regiment
6. Union
7. cash crop
8. Plantation owners feared financial ruin if slavery was abolished.
9. Lincoln feared that allowing African Americans to join the army would upset the border states, causing them to side with the Confederacy.
10. The answer should include two of the following: as camp cooks, barbers, gravediggers, messengers, nurses, scouts, and spies.
11. The answer should include two of the following: African Americans were not allowed to be officers. They were paid only half as much as white soldiers. They were not allowed to fight beside white soldiers.
12. **(1) African-American soldiers fought bravely for the Union.** According to the article, option 2 is true, but it is not an idea expressed in the painting. Option 3 is false because the African-American Union soldiers, not the Confederates, are attacking. Options 4 and 5 are details that support the main idea.
13. **(4) a plantation owner** Options 1, 2, 3, and 5 would have applauded Smalls' heroics.
14. **(5) Freeing slaves in the Confederacy was a Union goal.** Options 1, 3, and 4 are false. Option 2 is true but not the main idea of the Emancipation Proclamation.
15. Many answers are possible including the following: The North had more people than the South. The North had textile mills and other factories, while Southerners farmed and owned plantations. Many enslaved African Americans lived in the South, but most African Americans in the North were free.
16. Many answers are possible. One possible answer is that minorities who move into the community feel uncomfortable. A possible plan is 1. Welcome minorities who move into your community. 2. Introduce them to civic and religious organizations in the neighborhood. 3. Defend the minority neighbor's rights when other neighbors make racial or religious slurs.

SECTION 13

PAGE 106
Preview the Article
Possible answers are children who work, how young people learned a trade, apprentices, and masters.

Relate to the Topic
Answers will vary with the individual.

PAGE 107
b

PAGE 109
b

PAGE 110
1. Child labor
2. reformers
3. master
4. literate
5. apprentice
6. Franklin's master supplied clothing, food, and a place to live.
7. Some parents did not earn enough money to pay for their family's expenses so they needed their children's income to make ends meet.
8. The owners claimed that children could do some jobs better than adults and they paid children less than they paid adults.
9. Factory owners did not want Hine to take photographs of the conditions in which children were working, nor did they want the state or Congress to pass child labor laws.
10. **(1) Work in garment factories as well as in coal mines posed health hazards for children.** Options 2, 3, and 4 do not say how the two persons or groups in each statement are alike. Option 5 is a contrast, not a comparison.
11. **(2) crowded workplace** The photo shows windows so option 1 may not be true. Option 5 is not detectable from the photograph. Options 3 and 4 are not supported by the photograph.
12. **(4) An apprentice learned more valuable skills than a factory worker.** Option 1 is true but is a comparison, not a contrast. Options 2, 3, and 5 are false.
13. Many answers are possible. One possible answer is that the picture shows more clearly than any written description why factories are unsuitable for children.
14. Your answer should indicate two separate ideas about teenage labor. Possible answers are that teenage workers should stop work by 9 P.M. on school nights and that when a teenager works more than five hours, he or she should get a half-hour break.

SECTION 14

PAGE 112
Preview the Article
Possible answers are that American industry searched for new workers, doors opened for new workers, new workers were called soldiers without guns, the labor force changed during the war, and women were in the labor force during and after the war.

Relate to the Topic
Answers will vary but should refer to the team's common goal and to team members' efforts to accomplish the goal.

PAGE 113
a

PAGE 115
a

PAGE 116
1. defense contracts
2. defense industry
3. labor force
4. stock market
5. Allies
6. labor unions
7. Many Americans had been without work during the Great Depression and welcomed being employed.
8. There are many possible answers. Sample answers are that the government was backing the campaign and that experts from New York and Hollywood worked on the ads.
9. Many women left their jobs or were let go.
10. They had enjoyed the benefits of a good job with good wages.

11. **(5) It ended discrimination in companies with national defense contracts.** According to the article, option 1 is incorrect because the order did not end all discrimination. Option 2 is incorrect because the order applied only to companies in the defense industry. The article does not discuss option 3. The article does state that women and African Americans earned more than they had before the war. However, it does not say this was an effect of the presidential order. Therefore, option 4 is incorrect.

12. **(1) Many women were unwilling to return to the way life was before the war.** Options 2 and 4 are true but unrelated to changes on the graph. Option 3 is related to one change but does not best summarize the changes on the graph. Option 5 is false.

13. **(4) women working in the defense industry** According to the article, Rosie the Riveter symbolized women in the entire defense industry. Therefore, options 1 and 3 are incorrect. Rosie the Riveter appeared in the movies and on the cover of a magazine but as a symbol of women in the defense industry, not as an actress or a model. So options 2 and 5 are incorrect.

14. There are many possible answers. A sample answer is yes, because World War II helped employ millions of Americans.

15. Many answers are possible. Sample answers are that you would have joined the armed forces or worked in the defense industry.

SECTION 15

PAGE 118
Preview the Article
Possible answers are that there was competition for world power, a Cold War, United States involvement in the Vietnam War, and disagreements about the war.

Relate to the Topic
You should describe one fact about the Vietnam War and write a question about the war. A sample answer is that the war took place in the 1960s and early 1970s. A sample question is "Why did the war last so long?"

PAGE 121
b
a

PAGES 122–123
1. Cold War
2. containment
3. draft
4. deferment
5. communism
6. guerrilla
7. One reason is that the Soviet Union wanted to gain back lands in eastern Europe that had once been theirs.
8. The United States wanted to stop the spread of communism to Southeast Asia.
9. Several answers are possible. Sample answers are that the war cost the government too much money and that young Americans were dying halfway around the world.
10. through demonstrations and educational programs
11. **(4) Guerrilla tactics made the job of American soldiers difficult.** Options 1 and 2 are opinions that cannot be substantiated with facts from the article. No facts in the article address options 3 and 5.
12. **(3) the 17th parallel** The other options are features on the map but none was the boundary between North Vietnam and South Vietnam.
13. **(5) South Vietnam's capital is a far distance from North Vietnam.** North Vietnam's success in capturing South Vietnam would depend on its gaining control of South Vietnam's political center, its capital. Options 1, 2, and 3 are facts about Vietnam's geography. Option 4 deals with China, not North Vietnam.
14. The Soviets suffered hardships because of the destruction in World War II and wanted to punish the Germans. Americans had not suffered the same kind of hardships but wanted to avoid another war. They felt the best way to do this was to return German life to normalcy.
15. Many answers are possible. Your recommendation should describe what conditions are present in the other nation, what are the motives of the attacking nation, and what goal the United States has in sending such assistance.

SECTION 16

PAGE 124
Preview the Article
Possible answers are changes experienced as the result of technology, changes in the way information is spread, and how computers were developed.

Relate to the Topic
Answers might include telephone, television, radio, computer, fax machine, and photocopy machine.

PAGE 126
a

PAGE 127
b

PAGE 128
1. World Wide Web
2. technology
3. Transistors
4. Internet
5. telecommunications
6. laser
7. communicate
8. It allowed them to communicate quickly and easily over long distances.
9. Possible answers are individualized computer lessons, computer labs, research capability on the Internet, and teaching by television.
10. Many people work at home and send their work electronically to their office.
11. Answers may include breaking down the communication roadblocks of distance and high costs and encouraging discussions among people from all cultures.
12. **(2) the number of computers in each country** The other options are false.
13. **(3) In the first 10 years, the number of computers in the United States went up 400 percent.** Options 1 and 2 cannot be determined from the graph. Options 4 and 5 are false.
14. **(2) voice broadcasts** The other options are false.
15. Many answers are possible. They include that new communications technology helped scientists share information more quickly so applications came more quickly.
16. Your answer should reflect your experience.

HISTORY AT WORK

PAGE 130
1. **(3) hot coals**
2. **(1) Colonial irons are one-third larger than modern irons.**
3. **(4) all of the above**
4. Many answers are possible. A sample answer follows: I took a walk through my apartment. As I entered a dark room, I flicked on the light switch. Finally, it hit me. We take the electricity we use today for granted. We think nothing of turning on the light at any hour of the day or night. Back in the colonial era, people did not have electricity. They used candles for light. It took dozens of candles to get the same amount of light we now get from a single light bulb. People had to carry the candles with them when they moved from room to room in order to light the way.

UNIT 3 REVIEW

PAGE 132
1. **(1) to protect Spain's claim to La Florida** According to the article, the king claimed all of La Florida. Option 2 is incorrect because the king wanted to rid La Florida of the French colonists. Option 4 is incorrect because Spain reached the Americas long before England or France even tried. There is no evidence in the article to support Options 3 or 5.
2. **(4) to remove the French colonists** According to the article, Ponce de León searched for the Fountain of Youth, so option 1 is incorrect. The guarding of the Spanish ships occurred after the French were driven out so option 2 is incorrect. Menéndez de Avilés founded St. Augustine so option 3 is incorrect. There is no evidence in the article to support option 5.

PAGE 133
3. South Carolina
4. Tennessee
5. 11

6. **(4) They separated the Union and the Confederacy.** According to the map, none of the border states lies along the northern or southern borders, so options 1 and 2 are incorrect. They did not all separate the states from the territories so option 3 is incorrect. Option 5 is incorrect because Delaware and Missouri do not lie along the Ohio River.

PAGE 134

7. **(3) The government feared that Japanese Americans might be spies for Japan.** According to the article, options 1 and 4 were not causes of the internment. There is no evidence to support options 2 and 5.

8. **(2) The internment of Japanese Americans was an injustice.** According to the article, the U.S. government apologized many years later and paid survivors money for damages, thus admitting the injustice. Option 4 is true, but it is not a conclusion supported by the article. Options 1 and 3 are incorrect because the opposites were true. There is no evidence in the article to support option 5.

PAGE 135

9. 1945
10. Union membership steadily decreased to present.
11. World War II because war production increased when more workers, including women and African Americans, joined the labor force. So more workers joined unions. Production increased even more after the United States entered the war in 1941. The war ended in 1945.
12. **(1) Union membership was greater in 1995 than in 1930.** According to the graph, union membership was about 15 percent in 1995 and only about 11 percent in 1930. The graph does not support the information contained in the other options.

SOCIAL STUDIES CONNECTION

PAGE 136

1. (5) New York
2. (2) an inspection
3. (4) excited to be reunited with his father
4. (1) compassion for those who did not pass the inspection

5. Sample answer: Dear Leif: I am writing this goodbye letter as I prepare to leave for America. You are my younger brother and I am so sad to be leaving you. I will work hard to send money home to help make your lives better. I will also work hard to save enough money to bring you, Mother and Father to America. Many have told me of this new land. They say the streets are paved with gold. Many call it the Land of Opportunity. I choose to be positive about the opportunities America may hold for me. I believe I will not be disappointed.

UNIT 4: GOVERNMENT AND CIVICS

SECTION 17

PAGE 140
Preview the Article
Answers include how state and local governments take care of everyday needs, how they handle trash, whose responsibility trash disposal is, and how some states get rid of their trash.

Relate to the Topic
Your answer should include your explanation of why you do or do not recycle certain items. A sample explanation is that you recycle aluminum cans at work but have no storage space at home to recycle other items.

PAGE 142
b

PAGE 143
a

PAGES 144–145
1. landfill
2. ordinances
3. recycling
4. groundwater
5. Constitution
6. Hazardous wastes
7. In the U.S., different levels of government, including federal, state, and local governments, all share the power to tax.
8. They burn, bury, compost, or recycle trash.
9. Some are full, and old landfills have been leaking poisons into the groundwater.
10. Recycling is reusing some trash for the same or new purposes. Composting is letting plants and food waste decay on its own.

11. **(1) Americans are too lazy to recycle.**
Option 2 does not take into account the
symbols within a political cartoon. Option
3 may be true but is not the cartoon's focus.
The cartoonist is likely to agree with
options 4 and 5, but the character's words
center on the cartoonist's main idea.

12. **(5) Local governments have set up
different ways to get people to recycle.** The
subjects of options 3 and 4 are mentioned,
but they act as details supporting the main
idea. The article does not support option 1.
Option 2 is a conclusion one might reach
from reading the entire article, not just the
one paragraph.

13. **(3) People care about trash when it hits
their pocketbooks.** This statement
summarizes that people produce less trash
when they have to pay according to how
much trash they produce. Options 1, 2, 4,
and 5 do not relate to the success of these
programs.

14. Many answers are possible. A sample answer
is that in most states, more trash is placed in
landfills than is burned or recycled.

15. Many answers are possible. A possible
answer is that you recycle newspapers and
magazines and that you could collect
aluminum cans that litter parks and streets.

SECTION 18

PAGE 146
Preview the Article
Possible answers are about the executive,
legislative, and judicial branches of government
and the difference between separation of powers
and checks and balances.

Relate to the Topic
Your answer should describe what the action
was, which branch was responsible for it, and
how you felt about the action.

PAGE 148
  c

PAGE 149
  a

PAGE 150
1. judicial branch
2. bill
3. executive branch

4. separation of powers
5. legislative branch
6. checks and balances
7. The President can veto bills.
8. The Supreme Court can rule any of the
President's actions or orders unconstitutional.
9. The President and some members of
Congress thought that the line-item veto
would help control wasteful spending and
thus lower the federal deficit.
10. The Constitution states that a President can
veto only an entire law, not just parts of it,
so the Supreme Court considered the line-
item veto, which allows the President to
veto part of a spending bill, to be
unconstitutional.
11. **(2) Each branch of government checks the
power of the other branches.** Options 1
and 3 are opinions, not facts. Nothing in
the diagram is related to options 4 and 5.
12. **(5) The line-item veto was a powerful tool
to protect taxpayers.** Options 1 and 4 are
facts, not opinions. Option 2 is an opinion,
but it is unlikely to be true. Option 3 is also
an opinion but not one that relates to the
line-item veto.
13. **(4) It gave too much power of Congress
to the executive branch.** As stated in
option 1, governors do have the line-item
veto power, but this does not disrupt the
balance of power among the branches of
the federal government. Options 2 and 3
are incorrect. Option 5 is an opinion that
may have been true, but it is not the reason
the law disrupted the balance of power.
14. Separation of powers divides the
government's power into three equal
branches. Each has a specific job that it
shares with no other branch. The checks
and balances system gives each branch
powers to check the other two branches.
These checks help the three branches
balance the power.
15. Many answers are possible. A sample
answer would be that you would like the
President to have a line-item veto, because
it would allow the President to veto
spending on items that seem to be a waste
of the taxpayers' money.

SECTION 19

PAGE 152
Preview the Article
Possible answers are rights and guarantees of
freedom and justice, the Gideon case, and how
cases get to the United States Supreme Court.

Relate to the Topic
Answers will vary. Possible answers are that you
may not understand the legal definition of
shoplifting, that you will not have help in
investigating the evidence the government has
against you, that you will have to take time off
work to prepare for the case, and that your lack
of familiarity with courtroom proceedings might
work against you.

PAGE 154
Applying an Idea to a New Context
b
Making Inferences from a Diagram
a

PAGES 156–157
1. warrant
2. amendment
3. due process
4. landmark
5. Bill of Rights
6. probable cause
7. The First Amendment guarantees basic
   freedoms.
8. The Fourth through Eighth Amendments
   guarantee justice to a person accused of a
   crime.
9. Due process is the set of steps that officials
   who work in law enforcement and in the
   courts must follow to protect the rights of
   the accused.
10. Many answers are possible. A sample
    answer is that providing lawyers to all poor
    persons accused would have cost too much
    money. Florida's government officials may
    have thought that cases involving the death
    penalty put the accused person's life at risk
    and so were worth the cost to the state.
11. **(3) Sixth Amendment** According to the
    article, the Sixth Amendment allows
    persons accused of a crime to question
    anyone who testifies against him or her. The
    other options are incorrect.
12. **(4) At least two courts must hear any case
    before it moves to the Supreme Court.** In
    the diagram, at least two courts appear in
    each of the three routes to the Supreme
    Court. Therefore, option 1 is incorrect.
    Cases can start in any one of four courts so
    option 2 is incorrect. The diagram does not
    indicate that the Supreme Court must hear
    all cases from any court, so option 3 is
    incorrect. There is nothing in the diagram
    about option 5.
13. **(1) Know your rights under the law.** The
    other options list rights that the Bill of
    Rights protects but that are unrelated to
    Gideon's case.
14. There are many possible answers. A sample
    answer is that Virginians wanted all
    Americans to have the same protections and
    that future states might not guarantee basic
    rights to their citizens.
15. Many answers are possible. One possible
    answer is that yes, you would have
    confidence in a court-appointed lawyer
    because you are innocent; another possible
    answer is that you would not have
    confidence in a court-appointed lawyer
    because you cannot be sure that the lawyer is
    competent and is focusing on your interests.

SECTION 20

PAGE 158
Preview the Article
Possible answers are the groups of Americans
who have not been able to vote through
American history and what qualifies a person to
vote in the United States.

Relate to the Topic
Answers should describe the issue or the
candidate and what your opinion was. If you can
vote, it should include whether you did or didn't
vote and your reason for voting or not voting. If
you cannot vote, it should include your
assessment of whether you think voting would
or would not have been a good outlet for your
feelings.

PAGE 159
b

PAGE 161
a

1. campaign
2. media
3. political action committee
4. politics
5. primary election
6. political party
7. general election
8. A voter must be at least 18 years old, a citizen, and a resident of the state where he or she votes.
9. He or she may be running in a primary, which is in the spring, and also in the general election in November.
10. Many answers are possible. Candidates for president today have to spend a lot of money campaigning for office, and the media plays a much greater role in campaigns.
11. **(4) A magazine includes information about only one candidate for senator.** Options 1, 2, 3, and 5 are ways that the media try to present a balanced picture of a campaign.
12. **(4) Ann will not be the only assembly member deciding whether or not to repeal the law.** Options 1 and 2 are true statements but do not point out the faulty logic in making Ann responsible for motorcycle deaths. Option 3 may be true but also does not show faulty logic. Option 5 is a false statement that relates to the issue, but it is not connected to the election situation.
13. **(2) to support a candidate who shares the group's views** According to the article, the special interest groups want to elect people who have the same or similar views. So options 1 and 5 are incorrect. There is no evidence to support options 3 and 4.
14. Many answers are possible. A sample answer is that yes, television ads are a wise use of funds because people pay more attention to television than to any of the other media.
15. Many answers are possible. Sample answers are that you would negotiate a deal with the major television stations to get a better rate for political campaign ads and you would limit the number of weeks during which candidates can campaign.

SECTION 21
PAGE 164
Preview the Article
A possible answer includes the arguments for and against gun control.

Relate to the Topic
Many answers are possible. One possible answer is that citizens should not be allowed to buy assault weapons and other military-style guns; another possible answer is that no gun should be banned for law-abiding citizens.

PAGE 165
   a

PAGE 167
   b

PAGE 168
1. self-defense
2. gun control
3. militia
4. permit
5. federal law
6. The Second Amendment first affirms the need for a well regulated militia and then says that citizens have the right to keep and bear arms; people disagree about whether the word *citizens* refers to everybody or just to members of the militia.
7. The Second Amendment speaks about a well regulated militia, and a militia would not have used a sawed-off shotgun.
8. The groups do not agree that gun-control laws will stop violence and that the Constitution guarantees the right to have a gun.
9. The groups agree that violence is a problem in the United States.
10. **(1) An honest citizen should not be deprived of a firearm for sport.** The other options are facts, not opinions.
11. **(4) Owning a gun is a sacred right that cannot be taken away.** Options 1 and 5 are false. Option 2 is unrelated to the cartoon. Option 3 is likely but is not the focus of the cartoon.

12. **(5) A gun kept for protection is more likely to kill someone the gun owner knows than an attacker.** Options 1 and 4 are opinions related to gun control, but not those expressed in the cartoon. The cartoon is not about the criminal use of guns, so option 2 is not a good answer. The cartoon is not about the use of guns for protection, so option 3 is not a good answer.

13. Answers will vary. A sample answer is that people who plan to kill someone in the heat of anger will have time to cool off.

14. Answers will vary. One sample answer is that you support gun control because it could help prevent some people from using violence when they are having difficulties or help prevent some people from engaging in violent crimes; another sample answer is that you oppose gun control because having a gun helps you protect your family from criminals.

CIVICS AT WORK
PAGE 171
1. **(3) distribute election flyers at Stone Elementary School.**
2. **(1) the right to be on the school district's property**
3. **(3) the local law specified she must be that distance from the entrance.**

UNIT 4 REVIEW
PAGE 172
1. Your answer should include two of the following: they both involve rape, the police questioned both men before discussing their rights with them, and neither man had a lawyer present during questioning.
2. **(2) When suspects threaten public safety, their rights are not fully protected.** According to the article, option 1 is true but is not the best conclusion. There is nothing in the article to support options 3, 4, and 5.

PAGE 173
3. **(3) The council chooses the mayor in the weak-mayor plan.** Option 1 is false because the voters go to the polls in both plans. There is no information in the diagram about option 2. Option 4 is false because voters elect the mayor in the strong-mayor plan. Option 5 is false because the mayor, not the council, selects department heads in the weak-mayor plan.
4. **(1) The power of voters is greatest in the strong-mayor plan.** Options 2, 3, and 4 are not covered in the diagram. Option 5 is not covered in the diagram and is also incorrect because the opposite is true.

PAGE 174
5. public library and auto registration office
6. A person must be at least 18 years of age to vote.
7. **(5) Votes can make a difference in all kinds of elections.** According to the article, the outcome of past elections might have been different if more people voted. Option 1 is incorrect because paying taxes is not one of the requirements for being eligible to vote. Registration is a way of checking if a person is eligible to vote. It is not a way of helping people vote, so option 2 is incorrect. Option 3 is incorrect because the opposite is true. There is no evidence in the article to support option 4.

PAGE 175
8. The man with the beard is Uncle Sam and represents the United States.
9. Bill Gates represents big business and the computer industry.
10. **(2) Protecting the right to privacy is challenging because computers make information easily available.** The cartoon suggests that the federal government, businesses, and the computer industry use paper files and computers to collect key information about Americans. Option 4 is what the characters shown in the three panels say, but the cartoonist implies that Americans should not trust these people. Option 5 is true but is not supported by the cartoon. No evidence supports options 1 and 3.

GOVERNMENT AND CIVICS EXTENSION

A possible list at a city council meeting might include introducing new traffic signals at cross streets, repairing pot holes on main streets, and extending the 20-mile-per-hour speed limit near schools for an extra hour in the morning. The council may immediately approve the extension of the time the 20-mile-per-hour speed limit is in force. So you would circle that on your list.

SOCIAL STUDIES CONNECTION

PAGE 177
1. **(4) 10 years.**
2. **(5) the old method yielded errors and high costs.**
3. **(5) 253,000,000 persons**
4. **(3) Black**

UNIT 5: ECONOMICS

SECTION 22

PAGE 180
Preview the Article
Possible answers are the free enterprise system and farming, how competition leads to efficiency, and how competition helps farmers and consumers.

Relate to the Topic
Many answers are possible. Sample answers are Cheerios® brand breakfast cereal and Legos® brand blocks. Cheerios® brand breakfast cereal has lasted because the manufacturer has created other flavors besides the basic recipe. Legos® brand blocks are durable, promote creativity and fine motor skills, and have universal appeal to children.

PAGE 181
a

PAGE 183
b

PAGES 184–85
1. free enterprise system
2. consumer
3. market
4. demand
5. cooperative
6. corporation
7. efficiency

8. New methods of farming allow farmers to increase the amount of crops produced, so they can make more money on their crop without increasing the price.
9. Two possible answers are that consumers gain low prices and many choices as results of competition.
10. A **market** could be a place where producers sell their products to sellers, a place where people who buy products from producers sell to consumers, or all the potential customers for a particular product or service.
11. **(1) Farmers earn more when they produce goods that are in demand.** Options 2, 3, 4, and 5 are details stated directly in the paragraph.
12. **(1) Farms will be fewer but about the same size as in 1997.** The two graphs do not suggest option 3. Options 2, 4, and 5 cannot be determined from facts on the graphs.
13. **(2) If there was less competition among farmers, food prices would be higher.** Options 1, 3, and 4 are directly stated in the paragraph. Option 5 is not addressed.
14. Many answers are possible. A sample answer is that a high demand can result in a product not being readily available and create competition among buyers. This will raise the price. If demand for a product is low, however, the price will be low, too, even if the product is not easy to find.
15. Many answers are possible. Sample answer: Competition makes long-distance services lower their prices. I choose the service with low prices. If less competition existed prices for long-distance calls might be higher, and my phone bill would probably go up.

SECTION 23

PAGE 186
Preview the Article
Answers should include how to use money wisely and how to set up a budget.

Relate to the Topic
Many answers are possible. A sample answer is that family members are spenders. They often buy things on credit when they cannot pay their existing bills.

PAGE 188

b

PAGE 189

b

PAGES 190–91

1. opportunity cost
2. net income
3. interest
4. annual percentage rate
5. fixed expense
6. budget
7. flexible expense
8. Answers should include two of the following: Sticking to a budget helps people know how much money they have to spend. It helps them know what they are spending their money on each month. It helps them know what the opportunity cost of a purchase will be. It helps them identify where money can be saved.
9. The person should consider the opportunity cost and the cost of borrowing the money.
10. Four possible rules include: Create and follow a spending plan. Consider all the costs involved in a purchase before deciding. Do not borrow money often. Read and understand the terms of a loan.
11. **(3) They had less money to put into savings.** Option 1 is incorrect. The expenses in option 2 are fixed expenses, so they remained the same. Option 4 is not related to the situation. No evidence in the chart supports option 5.
12. **(3) They could switch to less expensive insurance.** Option 1 would increase, not reduce, the Riveras' fixed expenses. Options 2, 3, and 5 would affect their flexible expenses, not their fixed expenses.
13. **(5) It spends less on electricity, gas, telephone, and other utilities than it does on credit card debt.** The graph contradicts the other options.
14. Many answers are possible. A sample answer is that lenders make money when a person takes out a loan for many years because interest is charged every month. When the loan is paid off early, the lender will charge a penalty to gain back some of the interest money it will lose.

15. Many answers are possible. A sample answer is that after buying a TV on the spur of the moment, you did not have enough money to pay for repairs on your car.

SECTION 24

PAGE 192

Preview the Article

Possible answers include supply and demand, the changing market for baseball cards, and how scarcity and price are connected.

Relate to the Topic

Many answers are possible. Sample answers are that you bought several boxes of cookies when they were on sale *and* cookies are a want *and* that you refused to buy a gold chain because of the price *and* a chain is a want.

PAGE 194

a

PAGE 195

a

PAGES 196–197

1. inelastic supply
2. profit
3. elastic supply
4. scarce
5. inelastic demand
6. elastic demand
7. supply
8. The price usually goes down.
9. Many answers are possible. A sample answer is that elastic stretches. So when a supply or demand is elastic, it moves either up or down in reaction to a price change.
10. Milk and dish soap are necessities that people always need and buy. This means that the demand is inelastic.
11. **(4) The new owner of the Ryan card will make a profit.** Option 1 is a fact, not a prediction. The paragraphs do not support a prediction of either option 3 or 5. Option 2 is wrong because the opposite is likely to happen.

12. **(5) Clemens' Fleer card is in shorter supply than his Donruss card.** According to the article, there is no evidence to support options 1 and 4. Option 2 is true but does not explain the difference in values. Option 3 might have happened but is not the best reason for buying the card.

13. **(5) Kerry Wood** Options 1, 2, and 4 are older players. The older the player, the more limited the supply and usually the greater the value. Option 3, although not a particularly old player, is a player whose card has increased in value because of his record-breaking playing.

14. If demand is high, this will make supplies more scarce. So companies will enter the market to sell products, hoping to make profit by meeting the demand. If supplies are high, demand will be low. So companies will leave the market if they cannot sell enough of the product to make a profit.

15. Many answers are possible. A sample answer is that you would advise against investing in baseball cards. Many companies make baseball cards, and the value of the cards may fail to rise in the future.

SECTION 25

PAGE 198

Preview the Article

Possible answers are work in the twenty-first century, how the nature of work has changed, how getting an education can help me, and how to choose my career.

Relate to the Topic

Answers will vary based on what kind of work you want to do. Answers might include finishing the GED, learning to use a computer, and enrolling in a community or four-year college.

PAGE 200

b

PAGE 201

1. b
2. a

PAGES 202–203

1. bachelor's degree
2. internship

3. apprenticeship
4. Service industries
5. work ethic
6. Mentoring
7. Job shadowing
8. health-care jobs, jobs in transportation and public utilities, and jobs in wholesale and retail trade
9. Most jobs today require some kind of technical skill with machines or computers as well as the abilities to follow directions, to work on a team, to be punctual, to act responsibly, and to use common sense.
10. by pursuing more education and training, especially in modern technologies
11. Workers learn to do different jobs so that they can help other workers when needed.
12. **(1) Get an education or training in a field that interests you.** Options 2 through 5 are not discussed in the article.
13. **(1) Jobs in health services will grow more than jobs in transportation and public utilities between 1996 and 2006.** Based on the graph, options 2, 3, and 5 are false. Option 4 cannot be determined from the graph.
14. **(3) Many jobs in the United States today use technologies that process information.** Option 1 is true but has nothing to do with high-paying jobs today. Option 2 is true but is only indirectly related to technological literacy. Options 4 and 5 refer to needed personal skills, not technological literacy.
15. Many answers are possible. Sample answers are that a business runs better when employees come in on time and when employees act responsibly; employers want workers to complete tasks dependably, and employers want employees that can use their common sense to figure out what to do.
16. Answers should describe the subjects you would study from books and the skills you would learn on the job. Examples are studying computers and technical drawing and having on-the-job experience with reading blueprints to reach your goal of becoming a draftsperson.

SECTION 26
PAGE 204
Preview the Article

Possible answers are about the world's interdependent economy and about how international trade and trade policies have an impact on the U.S. economy.

Relate to the Topic

Many answers are possible. Sample answers are shoes, clothing, televisions, electronic equipment, and automobiles.

PAGE 207
Reading a Line Graph

b

Supporting Conclusions

b

PAGES 208–209
1. Free trade
2. currency
3. protectionist
4. interdependent
5. tariff
6. trade deficit
7. quota
8. Many nations depend on one another for raw materials and finished goods.
9. International trade creates competition among the companies of many countries instead of just among the companies of one country. When the competition is great, a company must make products more efficiently to make money.
10. An increase in international trade offers a nation a larger market for its goods and a greater supply of raw materials to make its products.
11. Your answer should include tariffs and quotas.
12. **(4) sharper increases in imports than exports** Options 1, 2, and 5 are incorrect interpretations. Option 3 is true but it is not the best and most complete interpretation of the graph.
13. **(3) 1982–1985** During the period in option 1, exports outstripped imports. During the periods in options 2, 4, and 5, both exports and imports increased.
14. **(3) American consumers can choose from a variety of goods at lower prices.** Options 2 and 4 are negative results of the global economy. Option 1 deals with a political or protectionist policy. Option 5 does not describe the United States, full of natural resources.
15. Protectionist policies use different kinds of barriers to block trade, whereas free trade encourages many nations and companies to conduct business with one another.
16. Many opinions may be offered. A sample opinion is that because cost is more important to you than the country where it was made, you would buy the car made in Japan.

ECONOMICS AT WORK
PAGE 211
1.
Calla Lily	In Season
Carnations	Out of Season
Delphinium	Out of Season
Hyacinth	Out of Season
Poppies	In Season
Tulips	In Season

2. **(2) Calla Lily—$2.25 per stem**
3. **(3) Delphinium**
4. Sample answer: I have noticed how the price of grapefruits fluctuates in the grocery store. I live in the north. Around October, the price of grapefruits begins to fall. It seems grapefruits get really cheap in December and January. As spring approaches, the price of grapefruits begins to climb again. This makes me think that grapefruits are in season in fall and winter and out of season in spring and summer.

UNIT 5 REVIEW
PAGE 212
1. **(5) people concerned about the environment** According to the article, cornstarch helps plastic decompose, which helps the environment. Corn has always been considered a food so options 1 and 2 are incorrect. Options 3 and 4 are incorrect because these groups could possibly be hurt by the new uses of corn.

2. **(1) Demand for corn is likely to increase.** According to the article, the new products will increase the demand for corn so options 2 and 5 are incorrect. The supply is likely to increase also, so options 3 and 4 are incorrect.

PAGE 213
3. The largest percent of income comes from individual income tax.
4. The largest percent of the government's income is spent on direct benefit payments for individuals.
5. **(1) More than four-fifths of the government's income comes from individual income tax and Social Security taxes.** According to the graph, corporations pay less tax than individuals so option 2 is incorrect. Social security is 34 percent of the income so option 4 is incorrect. Excise tax makes up 4 percent of the government's income, so option 5 is incorrect.

PAGE 214
6. The seller is using bait-and-switch advertising.
7. The seller is using the special-pricing method.
8. **(2) Let the buyer beware.** According to the article, buyers should be wary of selling methods used by some sellers. The article does not state that all sellers are dishonest so option 1 is incorrect. Option 3 is incorrect, because although it may sometimes be true, it is not supported by the article. Option 4 is incorrect because the article implies customers should check prices. Option 5 may be true but it is not supported by the article.

PAGE 215
9. Database administrators, computer support specialists and all other computer scientists
10. moderate-term on-the-job training
11. **(3) occupations that are declining most rapidly** The table shows occupations that are growing and the number of jobs in each occupation. The other options are supported by the table, so they are incorrect.

ECONOMICS EXTENSION ACTIVITY
A possible budget may resemble the average American family's spending habits. However, it should reflect your family's needs and wants. For example, your family may want to take a long summer vacation, and so you allow a larger percentage of your budget for savings and a smaller percentage for entertainment.

SOCIAL STUDIES CONNECTION
PAGE 217
1. **(3) they gained a large share of the health care market.**
2. **(5) they include HMOs, PPOs, and traditional insurance plans.**
3. **(5) Indemnity plans in 1999**
4. **(3) $4,142**
5. Sample answer: I think that one reason for the rising cost of health care is that the cost of prescription drugs is not regulated. My cousin who has lived in Europe told me that a medicine that costs me $70 to have filled cost her the equivalent of just a few dollars. I have heard that the government in some other countries regulates what drug companies can charge.

POSTTEST
PAGE 218
1. Heavy rains in the highlands of central Africa caused the Nile to swell.
2. There are several possible answers. Answers may include that one advantage of the dam is more water for irrigation, and one disadvantage is that soil is less rich now.
3. **(1) Without the river, the whole country would be a desert.** The river divides two deserts. Options 2 and 4 are incorrect. Option 3 is true, but doesn't explain the saying. There is no evidence in the article to support option 5.

PAGE 219
4. a dry climate
5. **(3) the Equator** Most areas with tropical rainy climates are within 20 degrees of the Equator. The lines of latitude of all other options are 20 degrees from the tropical rainy areas.

6. **(4) a humid cold climate** Only a narrow strip of northern Asia has the polar and highland climate, so option 5 is incorrect. The climates mentioned in options 1, 2, and 3 are all found in Asia, but none are the main climate in northern Asia.

PAGE 220

7. Answers may vary. A likely reason is that Eritrea offers Ethiopia an outlet to the sea for trade.
8. **(2) Eritreans overwhelmingly voted for separation from Ethiopia.** Options 1, 3, and 5 are true but are not effects of the civil war. No information in the article supports option 3.

PAGE 221

9. the United Nations; a nuclear weapon—a missile
10. **(3) dishonest** Options 1, 4, and 5 are false, since the cartoon shows Saddam is trying to convince the U.N. that the missile is a floor lamp. Saddam's military dress and the hidden missile contradict option 2.

PAGE 222

11. All three are women who fought in wars.
12. Harriet Tubman
13. **(2) Some women have proven themselves in combat.** Option 1 is incorrect. Some people will agree with option 3, but it is not a conclusion that can be drawn from the article. The article has insufficient facts to support option 4. Option 5 is incorrect.

PAGE 223

14. They were looking at the job postings at the labor agency.
15. **(3) Many people needed work.** Option 1 is incorrect or the agency would not have been crowded. There is no information in the photograph to support or refute option 2. Option 4 is incorrect because the wages advertised are from $2 to $3 per day, which would amount to far less than hundreds per week. Option 5 is incorrect because at least one sign specifies men, not women.
16. **(3) young men** The physical nature of the jobs suggests that options 1, 2, and 4 are incorrect. The absence of women in the picture suggests option 5 is incorrect.

PAGE 224

17. A sample answer is that the Constitution guarantees them the right to full participation in society.
18. **(3) A man in a wheelchair cannot get to work because stairs in the subway keep him from reaching the train.** According to the article, trains must be accessible to people with disabilities. Option 1 is not discriminatory. The woman in option 2 was turned down because she did not have the skills needed to do the job. In option 4 the reason the woman was dismissed had nothing to do with her disability. Option 5 is not discriminatory.

PAGE 225

19. health services
20. **(2) 2%** To find the answer, subtract the percentage of its budget Milwaukee pays for interest (3.4%) from the percentage the city pays for education (5.4%). Option 1 is too low. Options 3, 4, and 5 are too high.
21. **(2) environment and housing** Seattle spends more than 7 percent more in this area than Milwaukee does. Milwaukee spends more than Seattle for options 1, 3, and 5. Option 4 is not even on the graphs.

PAGE 226

22. clearance
23. **(2) A store brings in a new brand of shoes and sells them at a low price.** According to the article, bringing in new items and selling them at a low price is a promotional sale. Option 1 is true of any kind of sale. Option 3 is an example of a clearance sale. Option 4 is not a sale. Option 5 is a sale price, but the purpose of the sale is not stated.

PAGE 227

24. Earnings for both kinds of workers steadily rose from 1965 to 1999.
25. 1980
26. **(4) Wages in finance, insurance, and real estate have gained more value than wages in retail.** Options 1 and 3 are incorrect. Not enough information is given in the graph to determine whether option 2 is correct. The graph does not give information about option 5.

Glossary

abolitionist a person who is against slavery

alien a person living in the United States who is not an American citizen

allies countries that help each other

Allies all the nations, including Great Britain, Russia, France, and the United States, who fought Germany and its supporters in World Wars I and II

amendment an addition or change

annual percentage rate (APR) the percent of interest a lender charges each year for every $100 borrowed

apartheid a policy in South Africa that separated black Africans from white society

appeal to bring a court decision from a lower court to be reexamined in a higher court

apprentice someone who learns a trade from an expert called a master

apprenticeship a period of training that includes on-the-job training

aquifer an underground layer of rock or earth that holds water

bachelor's degree a degree earned after a four-year college education

bail money paid for the temporary release of an accused person before trial

bar graph a graph often used to make comparisons

barbarian a person that others consider inferior and ignorant

bill a proposed law

Bill of Rights the first ten amendments to the United States Constitution; these amendments list the rights of individuals

bloc a group of nations that acts together for military, political, or economic purposes

boycott to protest by refusing to use a service or to buy a certain item

broadcast the sending of a radio or TV program by radio waves

budget a detailed plan showing the earnings and expenses of a person or group over a period of time

campaign a series of events designed to get people to vote a certain way

candidate a person who runs for public office

capital 1) money, assets, or property used for investment 2) a town or city that is the center of government for a province, state, or country

cash crop a crop grown for sale rather than for personal use

cause why something happens

cease-fire a pause in fighting

census a counting of all the people in a country

century a period of 100 years

charter a plan that sets up an organization and defines its purpose

checks and balances the idea that each branch of a government has powers that limit the other branches' powers

child labor the practice of using children as workers

chronometer a very accurate clock

circle graph graph used to show parts of a whole; also known as a pie chart

civilian a person not in military or government service

civilization the society and culture of a particular group, place, or period

civil rights freedoms guaranteed to citizens, including the right to be treated equally

civil war a war between people who live in the same country

climate the general weather of a region over a long time

Cold War the struggle for world power between the United States and the Soviet Union fought mainly with words and money

colony a settlement or group of settlements far from the home country

communicate to exchange information

communism a political and economic system that does away with private property and places production under government control

compare to tell how people, events, or things are alike

composer a person who writes music

composting producing rich organic matter by letting plants and food waste decay

computer an electronic machine for processing, storing, and recalling information

conclusion a logical judgment based on facts

Confederacy the southern states during the American Civil War

conquistador Spanish word meaning "conqueror"

conservative a person who opposes changing traditional and established values and practices

Constitution the plan for the United States government, proposed in 1787

consumer a person who buys and uses goods and services

containment a policy to prevent the spread of communism to other nations

context 1) the rest of the words in a sentence 2) one particular situation

contrast to tell how people, events, and things are different

cooperative people who join together to ensure the best price for their products

corporation a business owned by stockholders

crude oil untreated oil

culture customs or way of life

currency a kind of money

current part of any body of water that flows in a definite direction

deadlocked unable to agree; a tie vote

defense contract agreements that government makes with private companies to produce weapons and supplies needed by the military

defense industry companies that produce military supplies

deferment a temporary postponement of military service

demand the amount of goods or services consumers are willing to buy at a certain price at a given time

democracy a system of government in which the power to make choices belongs to the people

desalination a process that removes salt from salt water

desert a region that gets less than 10 inches of rainfall in a year and has little vegetation

details small pieces of information

diagram a drawing that shows steps in a process or how something is organized

diplomat a person who handles relations between nations

discrimination the unequal and unfair treatment of a person or group

draft a system of required military service

due process steps in the legal process that protect the rights of an accused person

duty a tax collected on goods brought into a country and sometimes on goods sent out of a country

dynasty a family of rulers whose generations govern one after another over a long time

e-mail a message a writer sends electronically from his or her computer to the computers of people that he or she wants to receive it

economics the study of how people use their resources to meet their needs

effect what happens as the result of a cause

efficiency the state of being productive without wasting time, money, or energy

Eighth Amendment the part of the Bill of Rights that outlaws cruel and unusual punishment

elastic demand a willingness to buy that increases or decreases as the price of a good or service changes

elastic supply an amount of a good or service that increases or decreases as the price changes

elevation the height of the land above sea level

Emancipation Proclamation the statement made by President Abraham Lincoln declaring freedom for slaves in states fighting against the Union during the American Civil War

empire a group of widespread territories or nations under a single ruler or government

environment all of the living and nonliving things that make up a place

equator an imaginary circle exactly halfway between the North and South poles

estimate to guess an amount based on past experience

executive branch the branch of government that carries out the laws

export 1) to send and sell a nation's goods to other nations 2) a good produced in one country and sent to another country for sale

fact a statement of something that can be proved

federal deficit the amount of money the national government spends in excess of its income

federal government the government with authority over the entire United States

federal law a law that applies to the whole country

Fifth Amendment the part of the Bill of Rights that states that someone cannot be brought to trial unless a formal charge has been made and that a person may choose not to speak at the trial

fixed expenses costs that stay the same each month

flexible expenses costs that vary from month to month

Fourth Amendment the part of the Bill of Rights that guarantees a person the right to be safe and secure

free enterprise system an economic system in which buyers affect which goods and services are produced

free trade importing and exporting without political barriers, such as tariffs or taxes

general election a regularly scheduled election for state, local, or federal officials

glacier a huge mass of ice that moves slowly over land

glossary an alphabetical listing of important words and their definitions located at the end of a text

graph a drawing that is used to compare numerical information

gross national product (GNP) the money value of all goods, services, and products of a nation's industries

groundwater an underground source of water, such as a spring, well, pond, or aquifer

guerrilla a fighter or style of fighting that uses irregular and independent tactics

gun control legal limits on the sale of guns to the public

hasty generalization a broad statement based on little or no evidence

hazardous waste something thrown away that is harmful to the environment

iceberg a huge block of floating ice that has broken off from a glacier

immigrant a person who moves from his or her homeland to another country

immune protected against a disease

import 1) to bring in or purchase goods from another country 2) a good brought into a country from another country

incentive a reason for action

indentured servant a person who works for a period of time in exchange for something of value, such as fare to another country

indicted to be formally charged with a crime

inelastic demand a willingness to buy that is not affected when the price of a good or service changes

inelastic supply an amount of a good or service that cannot change

inference an idea a person figures out based on details in given material and on what the person already knows

interdependent several parts, such as nations, relying on one another to be successful

interest the fee paid for borrowing money

interned to be forced to live in a camp away from home

Internet a network of computers connected by telephone lines

internship a temporary job assignment

irrigation a system of canals or pipes for bringing water to crops

job rotation a system that trains workers in many tasks so they can step in to help other workers when the need arises

job shadowing following a worker on a typical day to observe his or her job responsibilities

judicial branch the branch of government that interprets laws

judicial review the federal courts' power to determine whether a law or an executive order follows the Constitution

justice a judge who serves on the Supreme Court

labor force all the people capable of working

labor union a group of workers organized to improve working conditions and to protect the interests of its members

landfill a place where trash is buried

landmark an event so important that it changes the future

laser a narrow beam of intense light

latitude distance north or south of the Equator

legislative branch the branch of government that makes laws

legislature a group of persons that makes the laws of a nation or state

liberal a person who supports political change

line graph a graph using lines to show how something increases or decreases over time

literate able to read and write

logic a systematic method of thinking that is based on reasoning correctly

longitude distance east or west on Earth, measured from the Prime Meridian in Greenwich, England; also called meridians

main idea the topic of a paragraph, passage, or diagram

map key part of a map that explains what the map symbols mean

market 1) a place where buyers and sellers meet 2) potential customers for a product or service

master an experienced tradesperson

media agencies of communication, such as television, radio, newspapers, and magazines

mediator a person who settles differences between persons or groups

mentoring teaching a less experienced person about a job through example and discussion

meridians the lines on a map or globe that are used to measure distances east and west on Earth; lines of longitude

microchip a tiny electrical circuit

migrate to move from one place to another

militia a citizen army that provides protection during emergencies

minutemen American colonists who were ready to fight at a minute's notice

mission a settlement centered around a church and established for the purpose of winning over people to a religion

navigator a person who charts the position and course of a ship during a voyage

net income money left after taxes are paid

neutral to refuse to be on one side or the other

nominate to choose a candidate to run for an elected office

nonrenewable resource a metal, mineral, or other resource that cannot be replaced once it is used up

oasis a place in the desert with an underground spring

opinion a statement that expresses what a person or group thinks or believes

opportunity cost the cost of choosing one thing over another

orchestra a large group of people who play a variety of musical instruments together

ordinance a law or regulation

override to cancel the executive branch's veto or rejection of a proposed law

parallels the lines on a map or globe that are used to measure distances from the equator; lines of latitude

parliament a lawmaking body

peasant a poor person who owns or rents a small piece of land that he or she farms, especially in poorer countries

pendulum a suspended weight, usually in a clock, that swings back and forth at regular intervals

permit written permission for a particular action

point of view how someone feels or thinks

political action committee (PAC) a group that gives money to candidates who have interests similar to its own

political cartoon a drawing that expresses an opinion about an issue

political map a map that focuses on showing boundaries, such as those between countries or states

political party a group of people who have similar ideas about public issues

politics ideas and actions of government

precipitation moisture that falls to Earth as rain, snow, or some other form

predicting outcomes trying to figure out what will happen next

primary election an election to choose delegates to a political party's nominating convention at which they decide on candidates to run for office in the general election

prime minister the head of a parliament

probable cause good reason to link a suspect with a crime and to make an arrest

profit to make money by selling something at a higher price than the original cost

protectionist supporting tariffs on imports to protect a nation's own market of goods and services

province a political region in some countries that is similar to a state in the United States

pueblo building made of sandy clay

quality circles workers who check the quality of products and services they produce

quota a set limit of something such as imports

racist favoring one race of people over another

recycling reusing solid and non-solid waste for the same or new purposes

reformers people who work to change things for the better

regiment a large military group

region an area that differs in one or more ways from the places around it

register to complete a form with such things as name, address, and date of birth in order to vote

reparations money paid to make up for damages, such as suffering during wartime

repeal to take back or do away with something, such as a law

republic 1) a self-governing territory usually headed by a president 2) a government in which the power is given to elected officials who represent the people

resource any part of an environment that people can use to meet their needs

resource map a map that uses symbols to show the resources of a region

sanction an economic or military measure that several nations use to force another nation to stop violating some international law or human right

scarce describes a limited supply of something that is in demand

self-defense to defend oneself or one's property

separation of powers a system that divides the functions of government among independent branches so that no one branch becomes too powerful

sequence a series of events that follow one another in a particular order

service industry business that employs people who meet the needs of other people

Seventh Amendment the part of the Bill of Rights that gives those accused of a crime the right to a trial by jury

Sixth Amendment the part of the Bill of Rights that gives those accused of a crime the right to a speedy trial

smallpox a deadly disease which has been eliminated through vaccination

sound an inlet of the sea

stock market place where shares in companies are bought and sold

strike to stop work in protest

suffrage the right to vote

summarize to reduce a large amount of information into a few sentences

supply the amount of goods and services sellers are willing to offer at certain prices at a given time

switchboard a device for controlling, connecting, and disconnecting many telephone lines within one building or location

table a type of list that organizes information in columns and rows

tariff a tax on imports

tax money a government collects from people and uses to provide public services

technology the tools and methods used to increase production

telecommunications ways to send messages over long distances

timeline an illustration that shows when a series of events took place and the order in which they occurred

topic sentence the specific sentence in a paragraph that contains its main idea

trade deficit the value of the nation's imports that exceeds the value of the nation's exports

transistor a small device that controls the flow of the electricity in electronic devices

tree line the beginning of an area where temperatures are too cold for trees to grow

tundra a treeless region with a thin layer of soil over permanently frozen earth

Union the northern states during the American Civil War

union *see* labor union

vaccination an injection that protects a person from a disease

values ideas or qualities that people feel are important, right, and good

vegetation the plants that grow naturally in an area

veto to refuse to sign a bill into law

warrant a document that permits a police search in connection with a crime

work ethic the belief in the value of work, demonstrated through commitment to job responsibilities

World Wide Web all the stored information available through an Internet connection

Index